Exploring Nottinghamshire Writers

*This book is for my husband,
Rob Edlin-White, with love.*

Exploring Nottinghamshire Writers
Rowena Edlin-White

Five Leaves Publications

Exploring Nottinghamshire Writers
Rowena Edlin-White

Published in 2017 by Five Leaves Publications
14a Long Row, Nottingham NG1 2DH
www.fiveleaves.co.uk
www.fiveleavesbookshop.co.uk

ISBN paperback: 978-1-910170-35-9
ISBN hardback: 978-1-910170-36-6

Collection copyright © Rowena Edlin-White, 2017
Essays copyright © individual writers
Front cover image copyright © Gillian Elias

Printed in Great Britain

Contents

Preface	xi
Introduction	1

Writers

Ruth Adam	4
Launcelot Andrewes	6
Mary Bailey	8
Philip James Bailey	10
Thomas Bailey	12
Matthew Henry Barker	14
Andy Barrett	16
James M. Barrie	18
John Beckett	20
David Belbin	22
Stephen Booth	24
William Booth	26
Ebenezer Cobham Brewer	28
Thomas Brown	30
Ruth Bryan	32
Wayne Burrows	34
Samuel Butler	36
Mary Butler	37
Derrick Buttress	38
Lord Byron	40
Philip Callow	42
Graham Caveney	44
John Stuart Clark	46
Stephan Collishaw	48
Samuel Cox	50
Thomas Cranmer	52
Helen Cresswell	54
John Cullen	56

Mary Ann Cursham	58
Cecil Day Lewis	60
Caroline Dexter	62
Robert Dodsley	64
John Drinkwater	66
Sue Dymoke	68
Joan Adeney Easdale	70
Michael Eaton	72
Rowena Edlin-White	74
Jonathan Emmett	76
Rose Fyleman	78
Winifred Marshall Gales	80
Rosie Garner	82
Abigail Gawthern	84
Ann Gilbert	86
Anne Gilbert	88
Josiah Gilbert	90
Sidney Giles	92
Elizabeth Glaister	94
Elizabeth Sarah Villa-Real Gooch	96
Catherine Grace Frances Gore	98
Ray Gosling	100
Gwen Grant	102
Graham Greene	104
Spencer Timothy Hall	106
William Hallam	108
John Harvey	110
Elain Harwood	112
Paul Augustus Herring	114
Anthony Hervey	116
George Hickling	118
Walter Hilton	120

Edward Hind	122
Muriel Hine	124
Henry Hogg	126
Charles Hooton	128
Margaret Anastasia Howitt	130
Mary Howitt	132
Richard Howitt	134
William Howitt	136
Lucy Hutchinson	138
William Ivory	140
Sarah Jackson	142
Jane Jerram	144
Lucy Joynes	146
Fred Kitchen	148
D.H. Lawrence	150
William Lee	152
Hilda (Winifred) Lewis	154
David Love	156
Stephen Lowe	158
John Lucas	160
Annie Matheson	162
Pat McGrath	164
Arthur Mee	166
Stanley Middleton	168
Thomas Miller	170
Robert Millhouse	172
Nicola Monaghan	174
Mary Wortley Montagu	176
Elinor Mordaunt	178
Katharine Morris	180
Peter Mortimer	182
Tanya Myers	184

Julie Myerson 186
Henry Normal 188
Eliza Sarah Oldham 190
John Oldham 192
Geoffrey Palmer 194
Helena Pielichaty 196
Samuel Plumb 198
Charles Plumbe 200
James Prior 202
Paula Rawsthorne 204
Laura Ridding 206
Cecil Roberts 208
Gertrude Savile 210
Miranda Seymour 212
Alan Sillitoe 214
Kim Slater 216
John Collis Snaith 218
Michael Standen 220
Henry Septimus Sutton 222
Jenny Swann 224
Charles Bell Taylor 226
Christopher Thomson 228
J.R.R. Tolkein 230
Geoffrey Trease 232
Sarah Agnes Turk 234
Anna Mary Howitt Watts 236
Matthew Welton 238
Dorothy Whipple 240
Henry Kirke White 242
Amanda Whittington 244
Sarah Johanna Williams 246
Leslie Williamson 248

- Nick Wood 250
- Gregory Woods 252

Essays
- The Sherwood Forest Group 257
- Old Nottinghamshire Libraries 261
- Charles Dickens in Nottingham 268
- Graham Greene in Nottingham 271
- Comic Creators of Nottingham, Arise! 278
- A Working-Class Hero is Something to Be 282

Publisher's Note 290
Bibliography 294
Acknowledgments 298
List of Subscribers 300
Index 301

Preface

Sandeep Mahal
Director, Nottingham UNESCO City of Literature

In December 2015, Nottingham was awarded the UNESCO designation as a City of Literature on account of the city's and county's literary heritage, its international outlook, its burgeoning and varied writing community, and its commitment to improving literacy across the city. Winning the UNESCO designation took a lot of hard work; work demonstrating that Nottingham and Nottinghamshire is full of diverse voices and talent.

It is therefore a great pleasure to write the foreword to this new guide book. As the directory testifies, Nottingham has made a remarkable contribution to literature and learning over many centuries of writing, publishing, reading and celebration of the written word. Many writers have been influenced by Nottinghamshire, and many have, in turn, left their mark.

From the literary heritage of Byron, Lawrence and Sillitoe to the proliferation of today's writing scene, Rowena Edlin-White invites you to explore Nottingham, a city built on writers, and the county of Nottinghamshire. I was fascinated to discover the many voices that, throughout history, have been silenced or undervalued. This directory puts them under the spotlight they have always deserved and takes you on a journey through a county brought alive in and by its writers; a quality and diversity that represent perfectly the vitality of Nottingham literature.

I would like to express my gratitude for the work of each and every collaborating individual who, through their dedication and professionalism, have made it possible to put this window on our city's writers into print.

And thanks to you, the readers, for buying this book. You will get to know the city in depth through its pages: travelling through time, and learning about the lives of those who have constructed the spirit of this city.

Nottingham, as a UNESCO City of Literature, is a city that loves words, and our mission is to "Build a Better World with Words". If Nottinghamshire is your home, find out how it has shaped some of the most significant literary works of our time. If you are a visitor, take this book home and discover an important part of our literary culture.

Sandeep Mahal
October 2017

NOTTINGHAM
UNESCO City of Literature

Introduction

This book has been a long time in the making – it must be ten years since Ross Bradshaw of Five Leaves and I agreed that a historical directory of Nottingham writers was well overdue, and five since I got down to it in earnest. Even then I didn't realise how long it would take or just how many authors Nottingham has to her credit. I rummaged, read, dug, delved and traipsed through graveyards until I'd assembled nearly a hundred Nottinghamshire writers, beginning way back in the fourteenth century with Walter Hilton of Thurgarton, author of *The Ladder of Perfection*, the spiritual handbook of choice for the solitary religious.

This is a guide book – Alan Sillitoe loved guide books, and sad we are that he is not here to bless it – a guide to writers and places. Literature springs up from the landscape and, in turn, leaves its indelible mark upon it, affecting how we feel about our surroundings. Can you imagine Eastwood without D.H. Lawrence or Lord Byron without Newstead and Annesley? There – I've named the Big Three already – but Nottinghamshire's literary heritage is so much more. Never heard of Muriel Hine, J.C. Snaith, the Howitt family or Katharine Morris? You will in this book. The Sherwood Forest Group, anyone? Prepare yourself to meet a unique collection of early nineteenth-century ruralists who loved and celebrated this county in all its mucky, beautiful, gritty glory. Want to know who is writing now and carrying on the great tradition? Sprinkled amongst the women and men of the past you will find a representative collection of today's authors, bearing witness to what it means for them to be 'Nottinghamshire Writers'.

As Nottingham receives the well-deserved accolade of UNESCO City of Literature, I think this book proves we are more than worthy of it. Some writers have inevitably slipped through the net, but if you tell us about them, we'll try to include them in a future edition. Some more recent authors we just couldn't contact in time, though we tried very hard – I'd specially like to mention two of my favourites: the playwright and novelist Jenny McLeod and Worksop-born fantasy writer Susanna Clarke (*Jonathan Strange and Mr Norrell*). And Pat McGrath – if you're out there somewhere, do please make contact! One or two didn't feel they wanted to be in the book, and that's up to them.

Personally, I feel enormously privileged to have been able to spend the past few years exploring our literary landscape and to have discovered such treasure. I hope you will too.

Rowena Edlin-White, 2017

Nottinghamshire Writers

Ruth Adam 1907-1977

Ruth Augusta King, feminist, author and teacher, was born in Arnold, the second daughter of the Rev. Rupert Wearing King and his wife Annie. Educated at St Elphin's School for daughters of the clergy, near Matlock, she left at eighteen and without any further training began work as an elementary teacher.

King taught for several years in deprived mining communities of Nottingham and her 1938 novel, *I'm Not Complaining*, is based on those experiences during the Depression in an area she calls 'Bronton'. The narrator, Madge Brigson, observes the daily mess of humanity in Upper and Lower Bronton with an affectionate but unsentimental eye. Staffroom tensions erupt as worn-out teachers struggle to hide their own domestic woes whilst attempting to support chaotic families suffering poverty and unemployment. But there is humour, too, and a frank insight into the lives of women teachers in the 'twenties and 'thirties.

> **My childhood was spent in draughty Vicarages, where ends never quite met...**
> (*A House in the Country*)

In 1935 King married local boy Kenneth Adam who was to become Controller of the Light Programme and later Director of Television for the BBC. Towards the end of the war, they became obsessed with the idea of living in a country house with a group of friends: *A House in the Country* (1957) is the story of eight years spent in a dilapidated thirty-three room house in Harpenden which finally beat the inhabitants into submission. Funny, poignant and wise-after-the-event, the book is evidence of a changing social climate in Middle England after World War Two and an experiment in communal living which was a few years ahead of its time.

Adam's writing includes ten novels, essays, radio plays and a biography of Beatrice Webb, co-authored with Kitty Muggeridge in 1967. She is perhaps best remembered for *A Woman's Place: 1910-1975*, a perceptive overview of the modern women's movement, which was republished by Persephone Books in 2000.

Places to visit

St Mary's Church, Arnold: The draughty vicarage that was Ruth's childhood home was replaced long ago by a modern house, but pay homage anyway at the fine medieval church of St Mary's in Arnold, where her father was vicar for more than twenty years.

Bronton: Several ex-mining districts in Nottinghamshire might contend for the original of 'Bronton' – read the book and speculate!

Launcelot Andrewes 1555–1626

Andrewes was born in London, the eldest of twelve children of a wealthy mariner. He was destined for a glittering career in the church, eventually rising to be Bishop of Chichester, Ely and Winchester and dean of the Chapel Royal, though it is his literary expertise which interests us here. In his early career, 1589–1609, he held the prebendary of North Muskham, though whether he actually spent much time at Southwell is unknown.

Andrewes was able to speak sixteen modern and five ancient languages and was an able preacher and liturgist, but his greatest contribution to the church and to the English language was in connection with the King James Bible, published in 1611. James I, alarmed by Calvinism and other dissenting parties in the Church of England, sought a potent symbol to unite all shades of religious and political opinion, and so commissioned a new translation of the Bible in English which would be the 'official' version and bear his name.

> **Inestimable treasure which exceedeth all the riches of the earth.**
> (preface to *King James Bible*)

It was not an easy task: six groups of eight scholars were appointed to translate different portions of the text; it was tightly controlled and much cross-referencing and negotiation took place. Launcelot Andrewes was appointed to head up the entire project which took seven years in all. Arguably, Andrewes and his team produced a masterpiece which is still the translation of choice in many Anglican churches, alongside Cranmer's *Book of Common Prayer*.

Places to visit

Southwell Minster: there is a portrait of Andrewes in the Great Hall.

Southwell Minster

Mary Bailey Early nineteenth century

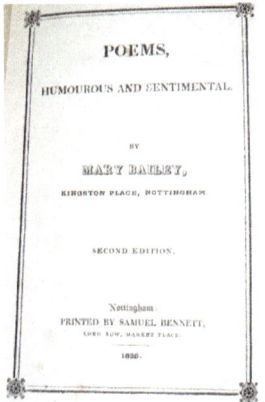

We have no dates for Mary Bailey; all that we know is that she was a poor woman with several children who lived in Kingston Place, Sneinton and eked out a living selling old clothes. She may also have been a lace runner, embellishing lace from the factories, on a piecework basis.

In 1826 she published *Poems, Humourous (sic) and Sentimental* – a mere twenty-six pages and thirteen poems in all. The first edition was printed and sold by C. N. Wright, Chapel Bar and must have sold well, because a second edition appeared the same year printed by Samuel Bennett of Long Row. It was published by subscription – quite common in that period, and revealing: Bailey's patrons included Lady Parkyns of Ruddington, a Mrs Boothby of Standard Hill, a Mrs Gilbert and a Mr Howitt.

> **They'd only set their wit against a Woman!**
> ("To the Critics")

In her Preface she confesses she is "conscious that [the poems] are very deficient; but as some Ladies have been pleased to express a favourable opinion of them, she has been encouraged to commit them to the press."

In 'Petition To the British Fair' she addresses the fine ladies who adorn themselves with Nottingham lace, little thinking of the hard-working, ill-paid workers:

> You Ladies of Britain, we most humbly address,
> And hope you will take it in hand,

And at once condescend on poor RUNNERS to think,
When dress'd at your glasses you stand.

How little you think of that lily-white veil
That shields you from gazers and sun;
How hard have we work'd, and our eyes how we've strained,
When those beautiful flowers we run.

Mary Bailey's poems are witty, political and literate, and one wonders where she acquired her education, given her circumstances. In the poem 'Lines' she refers to Virgil, Milton, Byron and Kirke White. Only two copies are extant, but the editions may have been printed in quite small quantities. Perhaps some of her subscribers were ladies whose cast-off clothes she sold on? We may never know, but this enterprising, feisty, working-class poet deserves to be put on the record.

Places to visit

Kingston Place was in Newington Street, off Manvers Street in Sneinton. Newington Street was still there in the 1920s.

Nottingham Local History Library has copies of *Poems, Humourous and Sentimental*, which may be seen on request.

Nottingham lace-runners

Philip James Bailey 1816–1902

Contrary to the plaque on the corner of Middle and Low Pavements, Bailey insisted he was born on 22nd April 1816 in Portland-place, a cut-through between Cur-lane and Coal-pit Lane. His father was the journalist Thomas Bailey (see page 12) and it was at his home, Basford House, that his *magnum opus*, the epic poem *Festus*, was conceived and written – though "...unfortunately, for fifty years [he] expanded the book into 800 pages and 40,000 lines... largely unreadable." (Mellors, 1924). It passed through eleven editions in England and, apparently, no less than thirty in America.

The young Bailey was well-educated and entered Glasgow University at the age of sixteen. He was subsequently called to the bar, but never practised, returning to his father's house in Basford where he assisted in editing *The Mercury* until its demise in 1857.

Death is another life
(Festus)

Festus may not have been to everybody's taste but its author was admired as a literary giant locally. He also wrote *The Angel World* (1850).

Bailey died 6th September 1902 at home at 54, The Ropewalk, aged eighty-seven, and was buried with his second wife, Anna Sophia *née* Carey in the Church Cemetery. According to the *Nottingham Evening Post*, he had a very grand funeral at St Andrew's Church. He was buried in the red robes of Glasgow University, his coffin was lined with laurel leaves and many local luminaries followed the coffin. The inscription on the headstone is a quotation from *Festus*:

> Death is another life. We bow our heads
> At going out, we think, and enter straight
> Another golden chamber of the King's
> Larger than this we leave, and lovelier.

Places to visit

Church Cemetery: Bailey's grave is in Section C in the Church Cemetery among the Careys – look for a very plain pink marble headstone from which the gold lettering has faded. It is on the left behind a headless angel and the first name on it is that of Anna Sophia.

54, The Ropewalk

54, The Ropewalk: During his life Bailey also lived at 16 & 18, Denman Street and 449, Alfreton Road but these areas have changed greatly. 54, The Ropewalk in the Park is still to be admired.

Bromley House Library: A handsome portrait by Sylvanus Redgate and the Bailey Collection can be seen at Bromley House Library, of which he was a member.

Thomas Bailey 1785–1856

Reform Act memorial

Thomas Bailey was born in Coal-pit Lane, son of a stocking-maker who later became the town jailer. He became a wine and hop merchant in Low Pavement and proprietor of *The Mercury*, retiring in the 1830s to Basford House to become a full-time poet and journalist.

The Annals of Nottinghamshire in four volumes (1852–55) is considered his most important work, and he also wrote guide books to Nottingham Castle and Newstead Abbey. He was also no mean poet, his works including *Ireton*, *St Ann's Well* and *Lays of Ancient Nottingham*. His tribute to St Ann's Well is worth quoting:

> **But blithely flow St Ann's! ... Sweet well!**
> *(St Ann's Well)*

> But blithely flow St Ann's! This little stream,
> Though temples fall, and sink the wise and brave;
> And still, as splendid glows yon orb's bright beam,
> Whether its rays fall on a monarch's grave
> Or rustic's sleeping child: and thou dost teem,
> Sweet well! As much with healing, and dost lave
> The lip as coolly now, and fresh, as when
> Sherwood's famed hero roused the deer in this deep glen.

He was buried in the old cemetery opposite Basford House, though few memorials remain and his has vanished. However, a column which he raised in his garden to commemorate the passing of the Reform Act in 1832 was removed to the cemetery after his death as a memorial to his friend Mr R. B. Spencer and may still be seen.

Places to visit

Basford House (circa 1730) is the handsome brick house at 61, Church Street, Basford, now flats.

Bailey's burial site: The cemetery is up the jitty opposite Basford House and the Reform Act column is near the top of the hill.

Basford House

'Captain' Matthew Henry Barker 1790–1846

Barker was born in Deptford, the son of a dissenting minister. He went to sea and served in the Royal Navy. He wrote many sea-stories under the name of 'The Old Sailor' and at one time edited a newspaper in the West Indies. Somehow he washed up in Nottingham in 1827 and remained until 1838, where he became a popular figure amongst the writers who met at Howitt's pharmacy (see page 134).

"Author of many 'tough yarns'... who sent jokes about him as quick and thick as shot... and whose merry tide of laughter I can yet hear," wrote Wylie (1853).

Barker's *Walks Round Nottingham* (1835) was published under the pseudonym, 'A Wanderer'. In it, he explores the region, commenting on its topography and history, and collecting anecdotes from elderly inhabitants. As one might expect, Barker tells a good yarn and his account of Joan Phillips, executed at Gallows-hill, Mansfield Road in 1685 for highway robbery, is worth reading.

> **The wide fields are free to the wanderer's feet.**
> (*Walks Round Nottingham*)

Two stories are appended to that volume: *St Ann's Well: a legendary tale* and *The Fair Maid of Clifton*, as well as an account of the Nottingham riots. *St Ann's Well* suggests that Richard the Lionheart slept beside the Holy Well the night before he seized back power from wicked King John. Throw in a wronged maiden, some monks, and a bloody encounter at Nottingham Castle; it's all over in three short chapters!

Although the author of many books, it appears Barker never received the remuneration he was due, and he died in poverty in London on 29th June 1846.

Places to visit

St Ann's Well was a popular meeting place from the thirteenth
century, in the days when Sherwood Forest was still very
close. It was associated with Robin Hood and many legends
persist. The well's location was rediscovered in the 1980s in
the car park of the Gardner's Pub (now a housing
development). It's a historic area, changing all the time and
worth a look.

St Ann's Well

Andy Barrett 1966–

photo © Andrew Hallsworth, Marlow Photographic

"I'm a playwright and theatre maker who's been living in the city since 1991, and over that time I've written around fifty stage and radio plays, many of which have dug deep into the history, culture and stories of the city, county and region. My first real success was a Sony Award-winning series based on the life of a fictional Nottingham centenarian for BBC Radio Nottingham, and my first afternoon play for Radio Four was about the women of Upton during the Civil War.

"I'm lucky to have had a great relationship with Nottingham Playhouse and New Perspectives, for whom I've written around a dozen main stage and touring shows. *The Day That Kevin Came* resulted from a three-month tour of ex-pit villages; *The Allotment* from spending time with Bosnian refugee gardeners; and *The Second Minute* from being given access to letters sent to and from men of the Sherwood Foresters during World War I.

"My plays have come in all shapes and sizes, from short monologues through to a five-hour show on Bosworth Field for the Leicester Haymarket. *The Story Traders of Sichuan* was a dual language script performed by a cast of British and Chinese performers; *Dolly* was a cloning-meets-country-and-western musical; *Skybus* literally took place on a bus (and in an airport); and recently I adapted B.S. Johnson's Nottingham-based novel, *The Unfortunates*, for a performance that took place across twenty-five venues in the city.

"I also run a theatre company called Excavate that

has created shows with thousands of people, exploring the histories and lives of communities across the East Midlands, many of which have been performed in locations that are central to these stories (we once took over the tannoy at Nottingham train station, to much consternation). In many ways this is the work that I'm most committed to. And I write about writing community theatre as well.

"Having adapted *Robinson Crusoe* for Radio Four, and Ibsen's *The League of Youth* for the Nottingham Playhouse, as well as recently bringing Tony Benn's diaries onto the stage (*Tony's Last Tape*) I realise how much more liberated I feel when the story is taken care of and I can just get down to finding the best way to tell it. But gathering stories is still something I relish, having been invited into hundreds of houses to talk to people about their lives. In the end it's these conversations, and the endless surprises they contain, that fuel just about everything I do."

James M. Barrie 1860–1937

The Scottish author and playwright J.M. Barrie was born in Kirriemuir, one of ten children of a linen weaver. After graduating from Edinburgh University he came to Nottingham in 1883 to work as a leader-writer on the *Nottingham Journal* for £3.3s a week.

His 1888 novel, *When a Man's Single*, was based on his early experiences. Nottingham is 'Silchester' in the book. Young Rob Angus comes down from Thrums (the fictional name Barrie gave his birthplace) to work on the *Mirror* and falls in love with romantic novelist Mary Abinger, daughter of the impoverished owner of Dome Castle. Sent to cover the Colonel's Christmas Eve dinner, in his emotional state he forgets to submit his copy, only to discover the speech gets reported anyway, the editorial team having made it up themselves. Similar journalistic practises are described with good humour. Although the novel begins as gloomy vernacular, it soon turns into a comedy of the literary world:

Most men are hero and villain several times in a day...
(*When a Man's Single*)

> The editor's room had a carpet, and was chiefly furnished with books sent in for review. It was more comfortable, but more gloomy-looking than the reporters' room, which had a long desk running along one side of it, and a bunk for holding coals and old newspapers on the other side. The floor was so littered with papers, many of them still in their wrappers, that, on his way between seat and the door, the reporter

generally kicked one or more into the bunk. It was in this way, unless an apprentice happened to be otherwise disengaged, that the floor was swept. (*When a Man's Single*, page 31)

Angus soon leaves for London and the interest shifts. Barrie did likewise when made redundant in 1884, one of several 'birds of passage' who would later become famous authors.

Places to visit

Birkland Avenue: Barrie lodged at 5, Birkland Avenue off Annesley Grove, North Sherwood Street. There is a green plaque on wall in tribute to the author of *Peter Pan*.

30, Pelham St: (now Tanners, Chartered Surveyors) where an inscription at first floor level reads "In Honour of James Matthew Barrie BART OM 1860–1937 who in 1883 & 1884 worked in this building on the staff of the Journal."

5, Birkland Avenue, Nottingham

John Beckett 1950–

"I was born in London but moved to Nottingham in 1957 when my father took up the position of Vicar of St Stephen's, Hyson Green, the W.D. Caroe church on Bobbers Mill Road now best known for The Vine community centre. I had all my secondary schooling in Nottingham which I came to regard as my home town. In 1968 I departed for Lancaster University, and after ten years away enjoying life as a student and then making ends meet with a series of short-term university posts, I ended up back in Nottingham, as a History lecturer at the University.

"Although my day job involved the usual round of lectures, seminars, marking, and administration, I came to enjoy working with adults. Undergraduate students were intelligent, but the people I met at adult education classes, and then through the MA in Local and Regional History at the University (1983–2006) were enthusiastic. They hoovered up knowledge, to coin a phrase. And, in doing so, they encouraged me to research and write books on the locality, including *The East Midlands from AD1000* (1988), *Laxton: England's Last Open Field Village* (1989), and several books on Nottingham. Of the latter, *A Centenary History of Nottingham*, which I edited (and contributed to) was published in conjunction with the centenary of the City Charter in 1997. The first copy was given to Queen Elizabeth II on her visit to Nottingham.

"I have continued to write about Nottingham and its past. Between 2013 and 2016 I headed up a University and local community project on the city's Green Spaces, and in 2016 I produced a history of the University of Nottingham. Researching that book enabled me to see how the first University College had been a community initiative and that this had led to the building of the original premises on Shakespeare Street, before the modern university moved in 1928 to the current campus at Highfields.

"Working with communities is a privilege and also a responsibility. They expect me to know what I am doing and to put them right when they go wrong. That is a challenge on both counts! But wherever I have worked, and that includes a five year stint in London (2005–10), I have done my best to work with local communities, volunteers, and enthusiastic MA students and to encourage them in their research and writing. I hope they have found my books helpful as a way of providing knowledge and stimulating ideas about how to write, and the subjects on which to put fingers to keyboards."

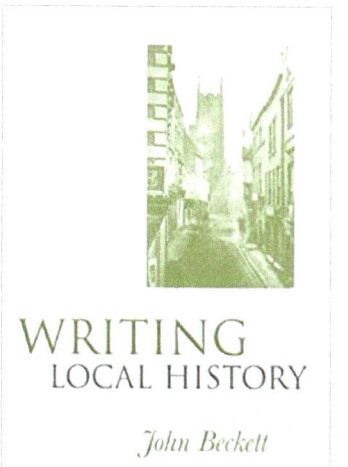

David Belbin 1958–

"I was born in Sheffield in 1958, but my family moved when I was two, and kept moving, so Nottingham is the one place I call 'home'. I came to study and never left. My partner Sue Dymoke and I live in Sherwood, a varied community close to the city centre, with many friends nearby. Novelist Stanley Middleton was a near neighbour. I've become embedded in the city: writing gig reviews for the *Nottingham Post*, being a trustee at Nottingham Playhouse, teaching at Nottingham Trent University, where I ran the Creative Writing MA for many years.

"When I was first published in 1989, I knew all of the city's active writers. You could count them on the fingers of one hand. These days, it's hard to keep up. That's one reason why Nottingham's 2015 bid to become a UNESCO City of Literature was successful. I led the bid and chair the company that runs our UNESCO organisation. It's early days, but we've hired a great director and are very ambitious to do good for the city. It's exciting, interesting work.

"Whether I'm writing for teenagers or adults, I keep returning to the theme of social justice. Nottingham has a rich, varied topography that makes it easy to portray extremes of the social scale. *Secret Gardens* is about an asylum seeker and a trafficked girl hiding out in Hungerhill Gardens, St Ann's, where Sue and I used to share an allotment. *The Beat* (1995–2000) follows a group of young police officers through their probationary period. The mysteries weave in real events of the 1990s, from racists attacking Mushroom Bookshop to the laying of the tram-lines. My most popular novel, *Love Lessons* (1998), features Rock City, Henry Mellish School, where I once taught, and houses we rented in Radford and Mapperley Park. *Student* is largely inspired by my undergraduate years at the University of Nottingham.

"My sequence about Nottingham crime and politics, *Bone and Cane* (2011), takes protagonists Sarah Bone and Nick Cane through the New Labour era. She's the MP for the marginal constituency of Nottingham West, and lives in The Park. He's her edgy ex-boyfriend, an ex-con with a flat opposite the Arboretum. They still have feelings for each other, but his past and her position mean they can't get back together. *Bone and Cane*'s instigating scene was inspired by friends showing me the cannabis plants they'd found in a cave beneath their new flat in The Park. *What You Don't Know* (2012) is an imaginary aftermath to the real Crack Action Team scandal of the late 1990s. Nottingham's biggest drug rehabilitation project turned out to be run by the city's biggest drug dealer. You couldn't make it up, but I put the story to good use. *The Great Deception* (2015) is about an undercover police operation, among other things, and was partly inspired by local events.

"Not all of my work is in the crime genre. Shoestring Press publish my New & Collected Short Stories, *Provenance*, which shows the full range of my fiction, written over thirty years."

Stephen Booth 1952–

"I was born and raised in Lancashire, and worked in local newspapers for many years. Three decades ago I landed in Nottinghamshire, when I became News Editor and later Deputy Editor of the *Worksop Guardian* series. As a journalist, it was always important to me to know my patch thoroughly, so I became more knowledgeable about North Nottinghamshire than most people born in the county. I was fascinated by Nottinghamshire's diversity and the sometimes hidden history of its towns and villages.

"When I arrived in 1986, the Miners' Strike was very recent, and I saw the consequences of it all around me. Some years later I wrote a novel called *Top Hard*, set in Nottinghamshire's pit villages in the late 1990s, when the mines were closing. I thought it was a significant time and place to write about. The result was a rather political novel which also managed to be funny – a sort of Robin Hood story. Unfortunately, London publishers weren't interested. Pit villages had become deeply unfashionable by then.

"I subsequently became best known for my *Cooper and Fry* crime novels, set in the Peak District and featuring two police detectives from neighbouring Derbyshire, Ben Cooper and Diane Fry. The *Cooper and Fry* series has brought me unexpected worldwide success, which encouraged me to release *Top Hard* under my own imprint, so that my Nottinghamshire story could reach readers too.

"One of my crime writing heroes was John Harvey, whose Nottingham-set Charlie Resnick novels I'd been reading for years. In fact, the city already had a thriving crime fiction scene then, including fellow journalist Frank Palmer and retired detective inspector Raymond Flynn.

"Although I gave up the day job sixteen years ago, I've settled in Nottinghamshire and I'm not planning to leave. I've been a Reading Champion for Nottinghamshire Libraries, and I'm a trustee of Writing East Midlands as well as a member of the Newstead Abbey Byron Society. My home is in the historic farming village of Laxton, deep in the rural heartland of the county. I'm lucky to be near both Newark and Nottingham, a city which is endlessly inspiring for a writer.

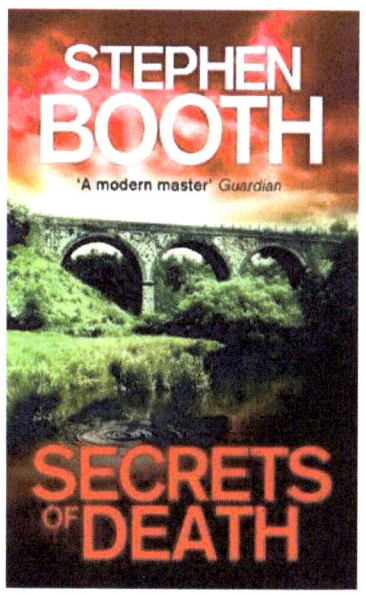

"One of my series characters, Detective Sergeant Diane Fry, is very much a city girl. Recently, she's transferred to the East Midlands Major Crime Unit, so she's based at St Ann's police station and has moved from the Peak District to live in Wilford. As a result, my latest novel *Secrets of Death* is substantially set in Nottingham. The city must have an irresistible attraction!"

William Booth 1829–1912

The founder of The Salvation Army was born in Sneinton in 1829. His father had made and lost a fortune before his birth and sent his son to a good school; however the family descended into poverty and William was apprenticed to a pawnbroker in Goose Gate. In 1844 he converted to Methodism at Broad Street Chapel and began preaching on the streets of Nottingham. He and his wife Catherine moved to London where William became a Methodist minister, but he longed to take his ministry back to the streets, to the poor and disadvantaged, so he resigned and in 1865 formed the Christian Mission. In 1878 this became The Salvation Army.

In 1890 William Booth wrote a remarkable account of life among the poor in London and further afield, *In Darkest England and The Way Out*. It likens post-Industrial England to an unenlightened, primitive country. Unemployment, lack of education and social degradation were commonplace, and Booth had a vision for salvation, not only for souls but for the bodies and minds of "the sinking classes" as he calls them. On a colourful fold-out picture headed 'Salvation Army Social Campaign' he shows the poor sinking into a sea of drunkenness, beggary and starvation; but a lighthouse sends out life-boats to save them, and through the agency of rescue homes, food depots and useful employments,

> **The poor Stockingers of my native town... toiling like galley slaves.**
> (*In Darkest England*)

Notintone Place

conveys them to a Utopian future, a promised land of full employment and plenty. Radical stuff! No wonder some of Booth's contemporary social reformers thought him dangerous.

Booth gave lectures and sermons on the book for the rest of his life and other organisations like The City Mission and reformers like Charles Booth (no relation) took up the batten – his *Life and Labour of the People in London* was published in 1903, the year William Booth received the Freedom of the City of Nottingham. He died in 1912.

Places to visit

Notintone Place, Sneinton: Booth's birthplace can't be missed for the imposing statue of the General outside.
The Broadway Cinema, Broad Street: the building where Booth was converted – there is a plaque.

Rev. Dr Ebenezer Cobham Brewer 1810–1897

Born into a Baptist family in Norwich, Brewer attended Trinity College Cambridge and was ordained on graduation, whereupon he returned to Norwich to teach in his father's school. He moved to Edwinstowe in 1884 with his daughter Ellen and her family, when her husband Henry V. Hayman became vicar. Although he never had a parish of his own, Brewer helped his son-in-law with preaching and weddings.

Brewer was the author of the eponymous *Brewer's Dictionary of Phrase and Fable* (1870) as well as about forty other self-help and information books. At the vicarage in Edwinstowe he worked on his various publications, particularly revisions of his famous dictionary, supported by a meticulous indexing system and random notes which he used to write on the walls of his room as they occurred to him. The Duchess of Portland visited him there. When he died on 6th March 1897, the mourners included Countess Manvers.

He was of a kindly disposition and remarkably cheerful

(J. Rodgers, 1908)

Places to visit

St Mary's Churchyard, Edwinstowe: Brewer is buried under a beech tree a few yards from the west side of the tower.

Brewer's grave at St Mary's Church, Edwinstowe

Thomas Brown 1781–1848

A framework-knitter and poet, Brown was born at South Normanton Toll-bar, Feb 5th 1781. South Normanton is now in Derbyshire, but in Brown's day it was in Nottinghamshire. Spencer T. Hall discusses these changeable boundaries in his *Days in Derbyshire* (1863).

Hall met Brown, who became something of a literary mentor for him, in 1835, and describes him as "a gentle, sedate, ingenious, affectionate, and sociable man" who, "without harshness or vulgarity... sometimes used his pen against petty oppression and injustice." He lived "just beyond the verge of Sherwood... wandering oft, as he loved, among the bowers of Brookhill and other rural scenes. How happily, though pensively, we have strolled down Carnfield-lane, on a summer sabbath-evening, enjoying all the sweet influences of a Derbyshire sunset." (*Sketches* 1873)

> **Without harshness or vulgarity... used his pen against petty oppression...**
> (Hall, *Sketches of Remarkable People*)

Hall quotes from Brown's poem, 'The New Church Clock at Warsop':

> Useless now the crowing cock
> To proclaim the morning near,
> While the well-adjusted clock
> Strikes on every waking ear.
> Hark, a sound, before unknown,
> Issues from the village tower,
> Measuring with solemn tone
> Man's existence by the hour.

And he comments: "The rural poet, even should his fame never extend beyond the bounds of his own parish, appears to me to be an important character. Inspired by the spirit of his time and place, he puts into those forms of language that are best understood by the simple minds around him such genial sentiments as they can comprehend and approve."

Carnfield Lane

Brown contributed poems and articles for over thirty years to *The Nottingham Review* and *The Derby Reporter* as 'T.B.'

He died 25th May 1848 at The Woodhouse, South Normanton.

Warsop Church

Places to visit

Carnfield Lane: The well-loved path taken by Hall and Brown can still be found: leaving S. Normanton on the B6019 Alfreton Road, look out for Woodhouse Lane on your right. Opposite is a lay-by from which a woody footpath (the old Carnfield-lane) leads down the hill, emerging just before Carnfield Hall.

Warsop: The clock was installed in 1844 on the tower of the church of St Peter and St Paul, and may be seen from the A60 – but the clock-face celebrated by Brown has been replaced. The original is now the centre of a flowerbed, on the right when entering Warsop from the direction of Mansfield.

Ruth Bryan 1805–1860

Born in Newgate, London, Ruth came to Nottingham as a small child in 1807 when her father, John Bryan, was appointed minister of Sion (Calvinist) Chapel at Halifax Place. The chapel moved in 1819 to Fletcher Gate and John was buried beside the pulpit when he died in 1823.

Ruth Bryan was a mystic and spiritual writer, forgotten in Nottingham but still celebrated in America. Her diary, which she kept from 1822 until her death, was published as *Handfuls of Purpose*, as were her *Letters*, some of which had appeared during her lifetime. She was well-read theologically and the advice offered to her correspondents found an appreciative audience in *The Gospel Magazine* under the name of 'Ruth the Gleaner. '

> **When it is winter in my feelings, Christ is my spring...**
> *(Handfuls of Purpose)*

The family appear to have owned property in Nottingham and London, and in her diary Ruth worries over the receipt of rents. She was obliged to earn her living as a seamstress, struggling to maintain herself and her mother at their home at 18, High Pavement which she refers to as 'Bethel Cottage'.

Apart from her spiritual journey, which was often an agony to her, Ruth's diary is of interest in that she notes events and places within her immediate radius:

for example, rumours of riots in April 1837, and again in April 1848, and a terrible cholera epidemic for which there was a national day of prayer on 25th September 1849, and for which Lucy Joynes, a few streets away, wrote a hymn. She also mentions the death of Anthony Hervey, the almshouse missionary and author of *The Sherwood Gipsy*, who was attached to Sion Chapel.

Very occasionally her friends persuaded her to go away with them for a rest, and then she recorded her delighted impressions in her diary. At home she lived an austere life of prayer and hard work. Her mother died in 1846 and was buried in the General Cemetery, where Ruth joined her in July 1860 after suffering for a long time with a cancer she refused to have treated. In 1888, when Sion Chapel closed, the body of John Bryan was exhumed and re-buried in the same plot as his wife and daughter.

Places to visit

General Cemetery: The Bryan grave is just on the left of the right-hand path leading from the main gates of the General Cemetery.

18, High Pavement: It is thought Ruth's home was between the National Justice Museum and High Pavement Chapel (now the Pitcher and Piano).

Ruth Bryan's grave, General Cemetery, Nottingham

Wayne Burrows

"I keep it fairly quiet but the truth is that I was born in Derby. I grew up around Heanor before moving to Mid-Wales at the age of ten. It wasn't until financial pressures pushed my parents back to Derbyshire in my teens that Nottingham began to register as anything more than the place we'd go for occasional shopping trips, which always involved waiting for the Rowland Emmett clock in Victoria Centre to strike.

"Returning from mid-Wales had been a shock, especially after all the 'sixties-grade LSD circulating among the hippies and eccentrics who kept the decades there confused well into the 1990s. A second brief stint near Aberystwyth, this time on my own, had been scuppered, like my parents' efforts, by lack of money and available work. When it came to choosing a place to live, at least Nottingham had retail jobs.

"This meant my first proper experience of the city was living in Sneinton, in walking distance of one of Nottingham's periodic culture highs, with the NOW Festivals and *Overall There Is A Smell Of Fried Onions* magazine going strong. Ruth Mackenzie was at the Playhouse and Simon Will, now a key member of the Gob Squad, was programming at The Powerhouse. Lots of weird and wonderful experiences were on offer.

"But no commitment was made and I was soon elsewhere, first Sheffield, then East London. Coming back to Sneinton in 2004, I found the city I'd remembered on life-support. For a year, I thought a terrible mistake had been made. Luckily, new things took shape. *LeftLion* began to appear in the streets, for one.

"A decade later, I've spent months reading through everything I've written since my arrival and I'm surprised myself how much of Nottingham has soaked in.

"Sometimes it's obvious how it got there. A commission to make work about Sneinton Market led to *The Apple Sequence* (2011) which responded to the history of the fruit and vegetable trade on the site and the under-sung allotments of Sneinton and St Ann's. Another commission, *The Disappearances*, became a series of occult histories attached to blameless Nottingham caves.

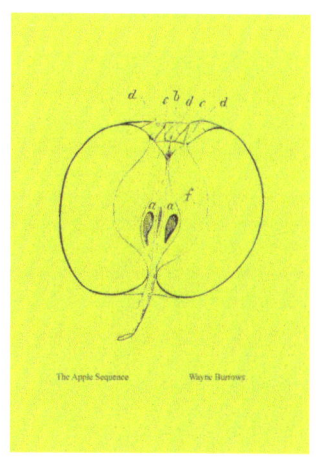

"I assume the city's influence comes because I'm crossing Market Square while the night-time drunken carnage unfurls, or because it happens to be where I am when lines take shape in my head. Then again, I recently wrote a fake prayer to the Hawaiian goddess Laka, to be recited among the illuminated bus-stop adverts on Carlton Road. Perhaps another reason is that the city of Xylophone Man and Owl Man sometimes feels half-way already to being a kind of hallucination."

Samuel Butler 1835–1902

Samuel Butler was born at Langar where his father, Canon Thomas Butler, was rector. He resisted his father's desire that he should be ordained and, after graduating from Cambridge in 1858, emigrated to New Zealand where he became a sheep farmer. He returned to England, financially independent, in 1864 and embarked upon his career as an author and artist.

If Butler's semi-autobiographical novel, *The Way of All Flesh*, is true, life at Langar Rectory was Victorian in the extreme. The Rev. Theobald Pontifex, modelled on Canon Butler, is a harsh father who whips his son Earnest from the age of two and is blind to all but his own narrow beliefs. The mother is hardly better. The whole book was not published until after Samuel's death, when it naturally caused anger and dispute in the family.

> **I am the *enfant terrible* of literature and science.**
> (Notebooks XII)

Throughout his life Butler wrote on a variety of philosophical subjects, but one of his first and most remarkable books was the Utopian novel, *Erewhon*, published anonymously in 1872. The title is an anagram of 'Nowhere' and it describes a self-sufficient country inspired by the New Zealand landscape, but hidden from the world, and where everything is opposite to Victorian England. It was an instant success and his name appeared on the second edition, which caused further division between him and his parents, who made it clear he was not welcome at Langar. Butler remained fascinated by alternative realities and *Erewhon Revisited* was published in 1901.

Although he had intense relationships with both men and women, Butler never married. He died at St John's Wood on 18th June 1902, and his ashes were buried at St Paul's Churchyard.

Mary 'May' Butler 1841–1916

Samuel Butler's younger sister shared his literary and artistic interests and managed to maintain an affectionate relationship with him through all the family upheavals. At Langar she was a typical unmarried daughter of the manse, visiting the poor, teaching in the school; but after their father retired she moved with him to Shrewsbury, where she came into her own. Here she became involved in social work with girls and earned herself a modest reputation as a poet and hymn writer in this connection. She and Samuel corresponded regularly until his death.

Looking upward every day, sunshine on our faces.
(*Methodist Hymn Book*)

Places to visit

Langar Rectory: the impressive home of the Butler family for forty-two years, is now called Langar House and is at the top of Main Street.

St Andrew's Church: described as "vastly over-improved" by Canon Butler, it has a semi-permanent exhibition appertaining to the family, and Samuel Butler in particular.

Derrick Buttress 1932–2016

"I was born in New Basford in 1932. In 1939 the family moved into a council house on the new Broxtowe Estate. I attended the Player Elementary School, leaving at the age of fourteen to work in various clothing factories in Nottingham. The only thing I valued as a result of my short education was a love of reading. There were no books in the house, but I joined the public library and read voraciously. I read anything from Raymond Chandler to essays by Addison and Steele, from Shakespeare's histories to H.G. Wells. Reading is the key to becoming a writer, thinking about style, construction, and the choice of language as you read.

"Reading D.H. Lawrence's early stories, and *Sons and Lovers*, revealed how the lives and language of ordinary folk like Nottinghamshire miners could be presented as 'literature'. I was familiar with the landscape in which the early work was set. The quality of Lawrence's writing gave validity to a place as 'ordinary' as a mining village and the lives of the characters who lived in it.

"Alan Sillitoe's work was even more relevant to me. Both my parents were from Hyson Green, in Radford. I knew Sillitoe's Radford intimately. His characters were almost as familiar to me as members of my own extended family. It was a world similar to the one I tried to present in my poetry collection, *Waiting for the Invasion*, and in my memoir, *Broxtowe Boy*.

"I didn't start to write until I was forty years old. I wrote poems that were published in small circulation magazines. A few poems were read on BBC Radio 4, and this led me to writing radio plays, five of which were broadcast on Radio 4 in the 1970s. Two television plays were transmitted by BBC 2 in the 1980s. By this time I had taken a degree in English at York University and was teaching in the Colonel Frank Seely School in Calverton. Pressure of work there more or less stopped me writing for several years.

"When I began writing again in the late 1990s I was fortunate enough to be published by the indefatigable John Lucas's Shoestring Press, based in Beeston. Poetry collections published by Shoestring are: *Waiting for the Invasion* (2002), *My Life as a Minor Character* (2005), *Destinations* (2009) and *Welcome to the Bike Factory* (2014). Two memoirs about living and working in Nottingham are *Broxtowe Boy* (2004) and *Music While You Work* (2007). A collection of short stories, *Sing to Me*, was published in 2011."

Lord George Gordon Byron 1788–1824

The famous poet arrived from Scotland as a ten-year-old boy in 1798 and lived temporarily with his widowed mother on the south-east corner of Pelham St. where he received medical attention for his lame foot and Latin lessons from a Mr 'Dummer' Rogers at 76, St James Street. Mother and son also lived for a while at the Burgage in Southwell before moving to Newstead Abbey.

Byron's first volume of poetry, *Fugitive Pieces*, was published when he was fourteen and printed in Newark.

Aged twenty-four, on 27th February 1812, Byron made his maiden speech in the House of Lords on behalf of the poor stockingers of Nottingham, when he denounced the Bill which made frame-breaking a capital offence. The starving workers had rioted the previous year, and he spoke out for those who had been "famished into guilt." When the Bill went ahead he wrote his 'Ode to the Framers of the Frame Bill.'

Hills of Annesly (sic), bleak and barren...
(Fragment)

The same year the first two cantos of his epic poem 'Childe Harold' were published and overnight he became a celebrity. Much has been written about his eccentric and unorthodox lifestyle, but there is no doubt he is one of our most colourful poets. He lived for seven years in Italy before joining the war for

Greek independence, dying in Missolonghi from fever at the age of thirty-six.

After his death his body was returned to England and on 15th July 1824 it lay overnight at the Blackamoor's Head, High Street, at the bottom of Pelham Street. William and Mary Howitt went to pay their respects and on July 16th William followed the cortege on foot to Hucknall Torkard and wrote a long poem about Byron on his way home. Many local literary figures would afterwards make the pilgrimage to Hucknall, adding their tributes to the visitor's book.

Newstead House, Nottingham

Places to visit

Burgage Manor at Southwell, a private house occasionally opened to the public.
Newstead Abbey for the full Byronic atmosphere.
Byron's funeral route: Why not follow the route of Byron's funeral cortege to Hucknall Parish Church? It passed down Smithy Row, along Market Place and Chapel Bar, round into Parliament St., proceeding up Milton St. and along the Mansfield Rd. as far as the seventh milestone, where it turned off to Hucknall by way of Papplewick. At 3.30 it entered the churchyard, Rev. Mr Nixon taking the lead. Byron was buried at 4pm. (from Deering's *Date Book*)
Newstead House, 76, St James Street, Nottingham. There is a plaque on the wall commemorating Byron.

Philip Callow 1924–2007

Callow was born in Stechford near Birmingham, and grew up in Coventry. Although he only lived for a short time in Nottingham in 1950, he was deeply influenced by the region and his novels and short stories about the Midlands are a wonderful evocation of working-class life after WW2, though I would argue that Callow isn't *per se* a working-class novelist. He settled in Plymouth and trained as a teacher.

In his book of essays, *In My Own Land* (1965), he wrote:

> Nottingham unites things for me, more than any other place. Unites things inside me. . . I died more than once, had more than one rebirth. I meet a group of anarchists, adrift like myself, and all this time in Nottingham – nine months! – I am living my first book, though I have to go away and wait years to write it. . .
>
> I see *Sum Total* in a bookshop window and think no more of it. But it works away, ferments, and I end up knocking on the author's [Ray Gosling's] door. This writer tells me nothing about the city. He takes me to a pub, I sit listening to scraps of conversation, see him mixing with the locals, hear arguments about the police, a bus strike, and the whole place takes on a new dimension.

> **Nottingham unites things for me, more than any other place.**
> (*In My Own Land*)

The 'first book' was *The Hosanna Man* (1956), first of a trilogy, which famously was pulped after a Nottingham bookseller recognised himself in it and threatened to sue for libel. The publisher also pulped his second novel, *Common People*, for good measure.

The Hosanna Man was finally reprinted by Shoestring Press in 2014.

Callow loved D.H. Lawrence and wrote a three-volume biography of him. Other biographies include Robert Louis Stevenson, Walt Whitman and artists, Cezanne and Van Gogh. He has nearly twenty novels and books of short stories to his credit and was also a fine poet, publishing a dozen collections

Places to visit

Nottingham: Callow used to enjoy walking from the Midland Station, through the passage by St Peter's, to Slab Square to get the number 31 bus. It went round by the Theatre Royal, down Sherwood Street, past the former public library and the fire station, up Mansfield Road and then up the Woodborough Road to Mapperley. The bus route has changed, and the number, but to walk this way at dusk can still evoke the 'Nottingham-ness' of the area – as it always did for Callow.

Graham Caveney 1964–

"I began my writing career – by which I mean being paid to write – by submitting book reviews to the *New Musical Express*. It was the mid-1980s and the term 'music journalist' was one of those elastic terms that covered a wide variety of disciplines, few of them directly connected with traditional journalism (or actual music). It was a world more closely allied with Cultural Studies, and the *NME* had become the natural home for writers with a semiotic swagger. I wrote about subjects as diverse as Coca-Cola and Ivor Cutler, the film critic David Thompson and situation comedy. I reviewed books by new voices from the US: writers like Louise Erdrich, David Leavitt and Armistead Maupin.

"Thatcher's Enterprise Allowance Scheme allowed me to set myself up as a freelance writer. I got a regular gig at *City Limits* writing about music, a monthly books column in *GQ* and began writing features on American fiction for places like *The Face* and *Arena* magazine. In America writers were being packaged like rock stars and I regularly interviewed people like Brett Easton Ellis, Jay McInerney and Michael Chabon. It was the golden age of the Men's Mag. My job was to tell this new breed of New Man what he thought of the books he was much too busy to read himself. Yet it taught me to write to deadlines, to think of writing as craft rather than inspiration.

"I co-wrote my first book with another freelance writer, the critic Elizabeth Young. We were both convinced that there was a new way of writing about

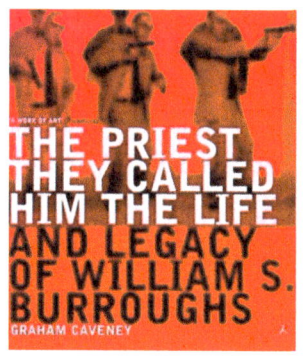

literature, one that could weld scholarship to journalism. The result was *Shopping In Space: Essays on Blank Generation American Fiction*.

"This book did well enough to get me a teaching job at the University of East Anglia and it was there that I wrote my biographies on Burroughs and Ginsberg. Originally these works had been part of a PhD on Beat writing and I re-wrote them as crossover introductions to the two writers, not as definitive biographies. The Burroughs book – *'The Priest' They Called Him* – was well received and went into paperback both here and the US.

"I moved to Nottingham in 2000 on a one-year contract teaching American Literature at the University.

"And then I got ill. The so-called noughties were pretty much a blur. I went into rehab in 2009 and would spend the next few years learning to live sober. In 2014 I got a five-month job at Five Leaves Bookshop and began to think again about books, about writing, about the difference that words could make. The result was my last book, *The Boy With The Perpetual Nervousness*. It remains to be seen where I go next."

John Stuart Clark (aka Brick) 1949–

"I have written short stories, adventure travel articles and books, music and comics criticism, 'graphic novels' and comics pages, and have had one radio play and one film script independently produced. First published in the early 1970s, I have survived on my wits as a writer and cartoonist, largely thanks to the cushion dear ol' Snottingham, the Queen of the Midlands, has provided.

"I settled in Nottingham in the late 'sixties, choosing her over other cities for the number of trees lining her streets and the claim she employed the tallest coppers (and thus had to have clothes shops that catered for men of my footage). I got a Fine Art degree here (useless but educational) and became a scrapman, bouncer, tarmac layer, roadie, taxi driver, steel erecter, milkman, community artist, boxer's minder and film lecturer here, none of which did it for me. Throughout I was writing and drawing essentially subversive satirical material, which did do it for me. The last legitimate job I had was in 1976 and I have Maggie Thatcher to thank (dammit!) for her Enterprise Allowance Scheme propelling me into semi-secure self-employment as a creative. The city has been my refuge, sometimes inspiration, and companion through those years, and a convenient proximity to plug into the mighty London pound.

"Fifty years on I still say 'barth', rather than 'baff', but have come to consider Nottingham as my place of birth, or maybe rebirth. Early involvement in local community and union politics opened creative opportunities for me (without actually being aware I was being creative or at the start of a career), but it was the self-generated cultural life of the townies, specifically the local music scene, that provided the inspiration and wherewithal to keep on going. The literature scene was staid and dominated by old school university types, but the film scene was vibrant, with the Nottingham Film Theatre, Moulin Rouge, Classic and Peachy Street Flick (which I  started with a bloke from Bux independent bookshop) exhibiting a plethora of foreign films that heavily influenced my approach to combining text and image.

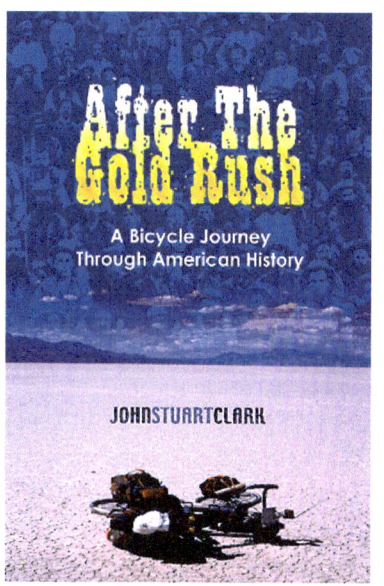

"But possibly the most important benefit the city has provided has been ready access to the hills of the Peak District and South Yorkshire. Without the ability to bogger off into the wilds, the city and my work would have driven me mad. Come to think of it, they did, but maybe you're not earned your stripes as a satirist until you've achieved the obligatory breakdown."

Stephan Collishaw 1968–

"I am a historical novelist, author of a number of novels that explore how ordinary people live through extraordinary times. Three of my novels are set in the Baltic region of Lithuania and Poland where I lived for a year in the 1990s.

"Born in the City Hospital, Nottingham, in 1968, I spent my first twenty years living less than a mile from it. I was educated at a local comprehensive school where I failed to gain more than a single O-level. After retaking the exams the following year and failing again, I worked briefly in an accountancy firm, but was soon fired after being caught sneaking to the toilet with a cup of tea and Jane Austen.

"It was at comprehensive school that my love of reading and writing was born. There I was introduced to the stories of Guy de Maupassant and Nottingham writer, Alan Sillitoe. I began to read voraciously and unselectively, jumping from Virginia Woolf to Sidney Sheldon, from the writing and poetry of Gerard Manley Hopkins to Nevil Shute.

"At the age of twenty, after a brief trip to Africa, where I was arrested on suspicion of being a spy in the tense last days of Kaunda's Zambia, I returned to England to study English and History at Goldsmith's University just as my brother, the artist, Mat Collishaw was graduating with his extraordinary cohort of friends who were in the process of transforming the art world.

"In 1995 I moved to Vilnius, Lithuania. It was a difficult year for the small nation which had been independent for only four years; banks collapsed, almost bringing down the government, violent crime was at its highest recorded rate, there was a diphtheria epidemic and temperatures plummeted. I fell in love with a city that was falling to pieces; with its narrow twisting lanes, church spires and rivers, cafes and snow.

"Before the Second World War, Vilnius had been home to one of the most important Jewish populations in the world,

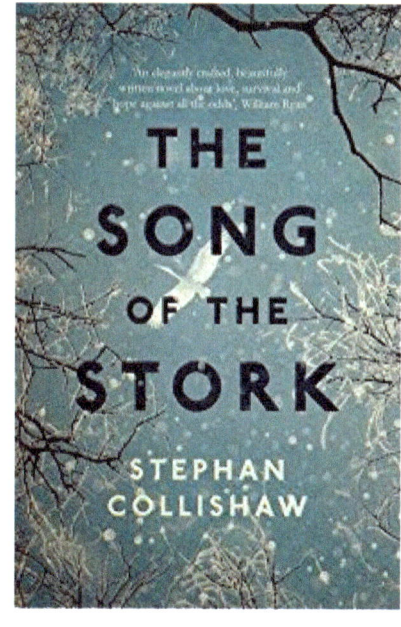

and in an attempt to understand what had happened to this community I wrote my first novel the next year while living in Palma de Mallorca with my Anglo-Lithuanian family.

"In 1998 I returned to Nottingham with my young family and have lived here ever since. In 2016 I established a small press, Noir Press, which focuses on bringing the top Lithuanian writers to an English readership."

Rev. Samuel Cox 1826–1893

Born in 1826 in the vicinity of Stoke Newington where he also went to school, Cox began work aged fourteen in the London Docks with his father and brother. He trained for the Baptist ministry at Stepney College and served in Southsea and the Isle of Wight before coming to Mansfield Road Baptist Church in 1863, where he remained for twenty-five years and wrote most of his books.

His great friends in Nottingham were fellow-ministers James Martin and James Matheson (father of Annie). They went walking most Sundays after they had fulfilled their duties. Cox was a great walker, and enjoyed cricket and music. He wrote many books, the best known of which is *Salvator Mundi* (1877). He was also editor of *The Expositor*.

In 1873 Cox married Eliza Tebbutt. He was a much-loved pastor, possessing a broad, open-minded Catholic theology. In 1888, in failing health, he retired to Hastings where he continued to write, remaining 'Pastor Emeritus' of Mansfield Road Baptist Church. He died on 27th March 1893. At his request his funeral was conducted at his old church and he was buried in the General Cemetery.

> **Love Him who first loved you.**
> *(The Bird's Nest)*

Mansfield Road Baptist Church

Places to visit

General Cemetery: Samuel Cox is buried in plot number 4448 – this author has so far failed to locate it.
Mansfield Road Baptist Church is still standing at the junction of Gregory Boulevard and Sherwood Rise.

Archbishop Thomas Cranmer 1489–1556

Thomas Cranmer was born in the village of Aslockton on 2nd July 1489. At the age of fourteen he went to Jesus College, Cambridge, and became a Fellow of the University. He was ordained in 1520.

A scholar by inclination, Cranmer became embroiled in the domestic difficulties of Henry VIII in 1529. He argued the issue of Henry's divorce in Rome and was appointed Ambassador to the Holy Roman Emperor Charles V. Henry summoned him back to England in 1532 to be Archbishop of Canterbury.

The implications of Henry's divorce and remarriage to Anne Boleyn led to the Reformation in England. Cranmer worked with the King writing new liturgies for church services which supported the now independent Church of England with the Monarch at its head, rather than the Pope. In 1544 the first service in the vernacular (i.e. in English rather than Latin) was published. In 1549, during the reign of Henry's son Edward VI, use of what we know today as the *Book of Common Prayer* was made compulsory.

> **Spare thou them, O God, which confess their faults.**
> (*Book of Common Prayer*)

The BCP, as it is affectionately known, is still used and preferred in parts of the Church of England: it is written in graceful, poetic language and usually used with readings from the King James Bible (see the entry for Launcelot Andrewes on page 6).

When Henry's daughter Mary, a Catholic, succeeded to the throne in 1553, she put Cranmer on trial for heresy. Although he recanted his Protestant faith Mary was determined to get rid of him and he was burnt at the stake 21st March 1556. However, he recanted again before he was burnt and died a Protestant.

Places to visit

Aslockton: Cranmer-associated sites are displayed on a board in front of the church and Thomas Cranmer Centre. A window in the parish church is dedicated to him, though there was no church there in Cranmer's time and the family worshipped at Whatton, where Thomas Cranmer Snr. is buried in the church.

Cranmer Street runs between Mapperley Road and Woodborough Road in Nottingham.

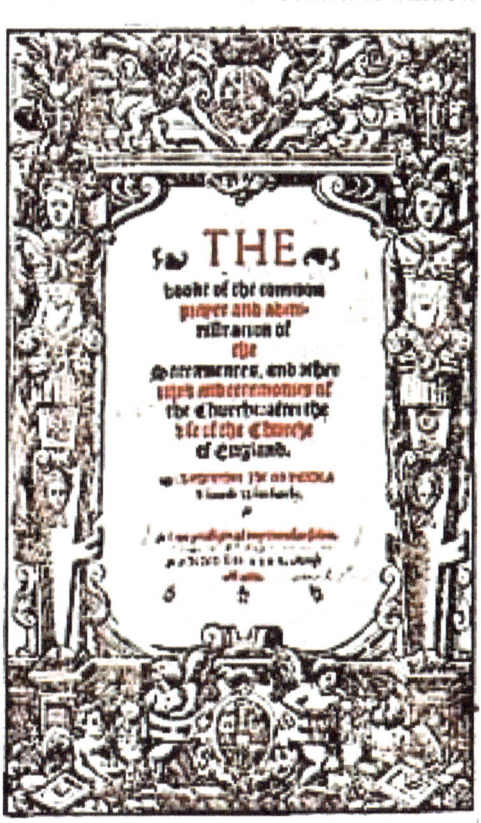

Helen Cresswell 1934–2005

This accomplished children's author was born in Kirkby-in-Ashfield and educated at Nottingham High School for Girls. She graduated from Kings College, London with a degree in English Literature.

Four of her early novels were short-listed for the Carnegie Medal: *The Piemakers* (1967), *The Night-Watchmen* (1964), *Up the Pier* (1971) and *The Bongleweed* (1973).

Helen lived at Eakring in a Georgian farmhouse and found inspiration in local places and traditions for several of her books. *The Secret World of Polly Flint* (1984) begins in Wellow near the famous maypole, and also features the little tunnel in the middle of the lake at Rufford Abbey. *Moondial* (1987) is another delightful time-slip story set in the gardens of Belton House. The five Lizzy Dripping books are set in the village of 'Little Hemlock' and they were filmed for television in Eakring.

> All she saw was the maypole...
> *(The Secret World of Polly Flint)*

Several of Helen's series were televised, including the saga of the Bagthorpes, a distinctly 'different' family, which ran to ten volumes in book form. She also wrote the scripts for adaptations of other authors, including Edith Nesbit's *Five Children and It* and *The Phoenix and the Carpet*. Her sequel to these well-loved stories, *The Return of the Psammead*, became a series in its own right.

Helen died at Eakring in 2005.

Gwen Grant has written, "Helen Cresswell... was one of our very best children's writers who gave enormous pleasure not only to children but to everyone who loved good writing. " (Obituary in *County Lit*, 2005)

Places to visit

Wellow: A small village near Rufford. The famous maypole is a permanent fixture on the village green.

Rufford Abbey Park: It depends on the water-level whether you can see the tunnel. Walk up the left side of the lake from the Abbey, and it is just before Lifebuoy Station 2.

Belton House, Grantham: *Moondial* takes its name from the elaborate sundial in the herb gardens.

'Moondial' at Belton House

picture © Gillian Elias

Rev. John Cullen 1838–1914

Born and educated in Ireland, John Cullen was curate of Knipton in Leicestershire from 1867 to 1869, where he married Leontine Eugenie Dordinger, who was of German origin. They moved to Bottesford in 1869 where John was curate for five years.

Cullen published his first collection of poetry, *Horae Poetica*, soon after his arrival. In 1874 he became vicar of Radcliffe-on-Trent, a post he held until his death. He was a well-loved pastor, campaigning for improved public health in the village. If his poetry is anything to go by, he also held strong views on temperance and women's rights.

Cullen wrote sacred songs and poetry, but also narrative and dramatic verse with a social or political message. *Poems and Idylls*, published in 1904, carries examples of these: 'A Welcome: To Lady Henry Somerset and Miss Willard' was written in 1892, on the occasion of the visit to England of American temperance campaigner Emma Willard, to join forces with Lady Henry Somerset who headed up the British Women's Temperance Society.

> **Of stately Queens with honour crowned.**
> (*Queens Regnant*)

Two long poems, 'Queens Regnant' and 'A Vision of Good Women' were specially written for public recitation at Baltimore Female College in America, in 1886. They are dedicated to women "who advocate and work for Liberty, Temperance, Literature, and Art." Although no names are named, at the time, many could be recognised from the text. He mentions, for example, doctors Elizabeth and Emily Blackwell –

> Physicians skilled are they of your own sex;
> A battle they have fought with might and main
> For women's rights...

– as well as "a mighty army" of writers, musicians, prison reformers, and ministers.

Cullen wrote a number of other books. He died at Radcliffe-on-Trent in 1914 and is buried at Bottesford with his wife and one of their children.

Places to visit

Bottesford: The Cullen grave is a handsome Celtic cross in the

area behind the church.

picture © Gillian Elias

Mary Ann Cursham 1794–1881

Colwick Hall

The fifth of ten children of the Rev. Thomas Cursham and his wife Ann Leeson, Mary Ann was born in Sutton-in-Ashfield, where her father kept an academy for young gentlemen. She appears to have received a good education and was an intelligent writer whose subject matter identifies her with the Sherwood Forest Group (see page 257).

While she was still a baby, her father was presented with the living of Annesley Church by the Chaworth family. Mary Chaworth was nine and the families came to know one another well. Thomas Cursham died in 1805, but Mary Ann's step-father took his place as vicar.

The *very* stone which guards *His* ashes!
(written in the visitor's book at Byron's tomb)

The romantic story of Byron's infatuation with Mary Chaworth is well-known: he adored her but she married the dashing Jack Musters, though she and Byron continued to exchange poems and *billets-doux*. Mary Ann Cursham was also affected by the Byron legend, and would later take Newstead as the setting for her novel *Norman Abbey*, in which fact and fiction became a little too close.

Her first book, a heroic poem entitled *Martin Luther* (1825), mentions Newstead as an example of the devastation caused by the Reformation. She could not resist mentioning Byron, who had died the previous year, and in 1828, with other admirers, she visited his grave at Hucknall and dashed off a few lines of poetry in the visitor's book.

Mary Ann became a close friend of Mary Chaworth-Musters'; they shared a love of literature and Mary Ann read aloud to her from her manuscripts. She also acted as chaperone when Thomas Moore came gathering material for his biography of Byron, to make sure Mary didn't give too much away.

Norman Abbey: a tale of Sherwood Forest by 'A Lady' was published in 1832. It is a rollicking yarn set at the time of the Restoration, and Byron's sister, Augusta Leigh, insisted on reading it hot from the press, to make sure it contained nothing libellous: however, she failed to notice her own debut as 'Donna Isadora'!

Ruins of Annesley Church

Mary Chaworth-Musters died in 1831, soon after her home, Colwick Hall, was sacked by rioters. Mary Ann's *Poems: Sacred, Dramatic & Lyric* (1833) is dedicated "To a Departed Spirit – a Sister Muse".

Mary Ann Cursham died in Derby in 1881 and is buried at Skegby with her parents.

Places to visit

Sutton-in-Ashfield: Cursham's Academy was on High Pavement, near the end of Hardwick Street, now an industrial park.
Annesley: There is a good view of the Hall from the A611 and the ruins of All Saints Church are accessible from the M1 slip-road.
Colwick Hall: where the two friends spent their literary evenings, before Mary Chaworth-Musters' tragic death.

Cecil Day Lewis 1904–1972

The poet and novelist Cecil Day Lewis (whose surname should be hyphenated like his father's, but he wanted to be different) was born in Ireland. His father, the Rev. Frank Day-Lewis, was vicar of Edwinstowe from 1918 until his death in 1937 and they lived in the recently-built third vicarage. Day Lewis attended Sherborne School in Dorset and then Wadham College, Oxford, returning home during the holidays; but he was not allowed to mix with the boys in the choir or the Scouts because they were of a wholly different class to the vicar's family.

In his autobiography, *The Buried Day* (1960), he describes some of the marked changes in Edwinstowe during those years:

> When my father moved to Edwinstowe, it was a country village. Before he died, it had become a mining town. But from the start, for all our sylvan surroundings, I was made aware that we were living in a colliery district. The prevailing wind brought the acrid smell of slag-tips from the Mansfield collieries to overcast the scent of our roses in summer: day and night the long coal trains clanked along the embankment which carried them above the fields on the far side of the village, visible from our front windows: wandering about in Sherwood Forest, which lay behind the vicarage only a few

A frost came in the night and stole my world.
(Poems 1943–1947)

hundred yards away, I could hear already the hooters from the mines and the distant rattle of the pit-head winding gear as the cages went up and down the only sounds, except for a jay screeching or rooks cawing, or branches grinding together, which broke the brooding and exhausted silences of the ancient woodland. "

In his 1938 poem, 'The Three Cloud-Maidens', he writes of the "winding Trent" and "the soiled valley" (*Collected Poems* 1954).

In 1935 Day Lewis began writing detective novels as 'Nicholas Blake' – twenty in all. He was Poet Laureate from 1967 until his death in 1972.

Places to visit

Edwinstowe: Once more a pleasant village now that the mines have gone, and gateway to Sherwood Forest, dear to the heart of many Nottinghamshire authors.

Caroline Dexter 1819–1884

Caroline Harper was born in Nottingham, the daughter of Richard Harper, a watchmaker and jeweller, and his wife Mary Simpson. She received at least some of her education in France before marrying the painter William Dexter (1817-1860) in 1841 at St Nicholas' Church on 29th July 1841. Both gave their address as Mortimer Street. After this they returned to France where Caroline is supposed to have known the author George Sand. By 1848 they were back, living in George Street, Nottingham, where William worked as a portrait and animal painter and Caroline as a teacher of languages.

In 1851 Caroline created a sensation when she appeared wearing the costume of a Bloomerite at the Great Exhibition in London, accompanied by William in similar attire. The press had a field day. Their egalitarian views may well have been acquired during their sojourn in France.

Laura felt her fingers glued to the window-glass...
('Our Portrait Gallery Photographed' – in *The Interpreter*, 1861)

William Dexter left for Australia in 1852 and Caroline joined him three years later. In 1858 she published *The Southern Cross or Australian Album and New Year's Gift*, "The First Ladies' Almanack Published in the Colonies." Her vignettes of Australian life, poetry and other items, illustrated by William, were a novelty, but subscriptions were not exactly forthcoming and the Dexter marriage was on the rocks. They separated, Caroline moving to Melbourne while William remained in Sydney where he died of tuberculosis in 1860.

Caroline reinvented herself as Madame Carole, clairvoyant, mesmerist and herbalist for women, joining forces with the feminist physician Harriet Clisby. Together they began a new magazine for women, *The Interpreter*, in 1861. One of Caroline's contributions was a serial novel based in Nottingham and she pays tribute to 'Festus' Bailey, Kirke White, Spencer Hall, Millhouse and Miller and Mary Wortley Montague. Unfortunately, the magazine folded after two issues and the novel remains a tantalising two chapters.

Caroline later married William Lynch, an Irishman twenty years her junior; with his wealth she became a patron of local writers and together they founded the National Gallery of Victoria.

Places to visit

St Nicholas' Church: the church has been 're-ordered' of late, but is still an elegant and significant historic building worth a visit.

Mortimer Street was another of those narrow streets between Castle Road and Castle Gate demolished for the construction of Maid Marian Way.

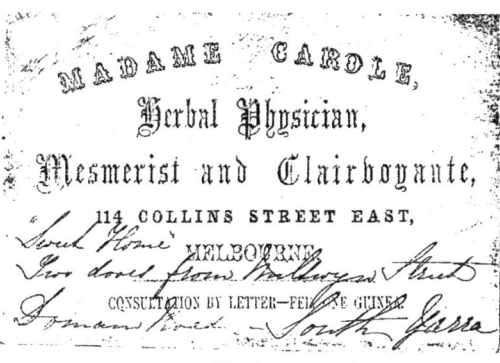

Madame Carole's calling card

Robert Dodsley 1703–1764

Robert Dodsley was born in Ratcliffe Gate, Mansfield. His father was master of the Grammar School, but did not care to make provision for his son's education, apprenticing him instead to a stocking weaver. Disliking this occupation, and already exploring his capabilities as a writer, Dodsley cancelled his indentures in 1732 and got a job as footman to the Hon. Mrs Lowther. His first volume of poetry, *A Muse in Livery*, inspired by his experiences, was published by subscription the same year.

He was soon writing plays and *The Toy Shop*, a "dramatick satire" was performed at Covent Garden. It was so successful it was thought to be by Alexander Pope writing under a pseudonym – which attracted the attention of the great poet, who then became his patron. Dodsley was able to set himself up as a bookseller in Pall Mall, and was supported by Pope and other well-known authors of the day.

A Grain of Goodness will preponderate against an Ounce of Wit.
(*The Toy Shop*)

Dodsley was a versatile author and went on to publish plays, poetry, literary criticism and songs; but his most 'home-grown' work is *The King and the Miller of Mansfield* (1737), a short farce based on an old ballad set in Sherwood Forest. It is a tale of hidden identity: Richard II and his courtiers are hunting in the forest and the King gets separated from the party, whereupon he is arraigned by John Cockle the miller, who is one of His Majesty's Keepers, on suspicion of poaching. The King does not reveal his identity but agrees to stay at the miller's house for the night.

The miller's son, Dick, arrives home from London during the evening and begins to tell the company about the corruption he has witnessed at court, painting a satirical picture of London society. Enter Dick's ex-lover, Peggy, who tells how she was duped and seduced by a Lord Lurewell. Finally, the Keepers arrive, having arrested the wandering courtiers who, of course, greet the King and all is revealed. Lurewell is made to pay Peggy a large amount of compensation and Dick still wants to marry her. The Miller begs the King's pardon and is knighted for his honesty, because "Virtue shall find protection from the throne." *Finis*.

Although simply a satire about privilege, *The King and the Miller* was alleged to be politically threatening to Walpole's government, resulting in the law that the Lord Chamberlain must vet all plays before performance. There is a sequel to the play, *John Cockle at Court* (1738).

Dodsley died of gout at the home of his friend Mr Spence in Durham and is buried in the cathedral churchyard.

Places to visit

Mansfield: Dodsley's birthplace, with an inscription over the window, still stands on Ratcliffe Gate next to the Brown Cow pub. It is an interesting area with a number of old buildings and yards still to be seen.

Dodsley's birthplace, Ratcliffe Gate, Mansfield

John Drinkwater 1882–1937

The poet and playwright John Drinkwater was another bird of passage who alighted in Nottingham for a year or so. Born in Leytonstone, son of Albert, a schoolmaster turned actor, John often went on tour with his father. When he left school at sixteen, Albert, thinking to he was doing the best thing for his son, got him a job as junior clerk at the Nottingham branch of the Northern Assurance Company on Victoria Street. John remained there from 1898 until 1901, and his experiences of the city and its suburbs are recalled in his memoir, *Discovery* (1932).

Drinkwater found the job tedious and often felt "adrift in an intellectual backwater. " He was also very poor and describes how he would often go down to the market-place at lunch time and buy three ha'porth of rotten fruit for his lunch. At first he was in lodgings, but later rented a small semi-detached cottage in Attenborough belonging to John and Elizabeth Perkins who lived next door. Here he felt more at home, joined a book club, played cricket and went walking in the Trent meadows where he marvelled at the "shimmering purple and yellow crocuses."

> **"I discovered my first poet in Byron."**
> (*Discovery*)

"I discovered my first poet in Byron," he wrote.

> Also I used to gaze with an instinctive curiosity at the little butcher's shop over which Henry Kirke White was born in the Shambles, since demolished. Later, my first literary commission was to edit his poems. . . when I have no doubt but what my early and quite vague affinity lent a sentimental tone to my criticism. (*Discovery*).

He would later write about Byron in *The Pilgrim of Eternity* (1925).

He became involved in Nottingham's lively amateur theatre scene, making his first appearance on 24th April 1900 in an adaptation of *Tom Jones* at the Mechanics. In 1901 the firm moved him to Birmingham where he met Barry Jackson and others who were producing plays, and he began to write for the theatre himself, though it was several years before he was able to give up his day job. In 1917 he became manager of Birmingham Repertory Company. He was also a fine lyrical poet, closely associated with the group known as the Dymock Poets.

The old Northern Assurances office, Victoria Street, Nottingham

Drinkwater died in Kilburn, London, in March 1937 and is buried in Piddington churchyard, Oxfordshire.

Places to visit

Victoria Street, Nottingham: The elegant old *Nottingham Journal* and Northern Assurance offices on Victoria Street, now occupied by Massers, solicitors.

Attenborough: A pleasant village to explore. The Perkins' cottages originally stood next to Vale Cottage either on Church Lane or the main road.

Sue Dymoke 1962–

photo © Graham Lester George

"I was born in Stevenage in 1962 but have lived in Nottingham since the early 1980s when I moved up here to study English, fell in love, began a teaching career and never left.

"I have always written poetry. Throughout my schooling, in Hertfordshire state schools, poetry was always there to read, listen to and write – just as it should be for every child. The first piece of writing I completed was a poem about the moon. Writing it seemed the natural thing to do. I repeatedly watched the first moon landing on a huge black and white television at infant school, listened to Walter de la Mare's poem 'Silver' during many rainy playtimes and became fascinated by the mysteries of sound and space that both the moon and poetry seemed to offer me.

"It was not until I began to put down proper roots in Hyson Green, teach full-time and travel on rush-hour buses that the city crept into my writing. Early poems featured a bus journey along Alfreton Road, Nottingham Saturday nights and a living sculpture exhibition at Nottingham Castle. They appeared in magazines like *The North* and *The Echo Room*. My first of six pamphlets, *A Sort of Clingfilm* (1987), was published by Wide Skirt Press. Through these publications I came to know and perform with many emerging poets, particularly those based in Huddersfield. I became UK poetry editor for Slow Dancer Press and helped organise poetry evenings in Nottingham. Poetry events and opportunities to meet with other Nottinghamshire writers were rare – very different from today.

"When I began to write poetry seriously I was teaching English full-time and developing a keen research interest in how poetry was taught. When I moved into Higher Education, my academic publications began to reflect this concern. These include *Drafting and Assessing Poetry* (2003), and two edited collections about poetry pedagogy published by Bloomsbury: *Making Poetry Matter* (2013) and *Making Poetry Happen* (2015).

"I have lived in Sherwood for many years now with my partner, David Belbin, and we grow vegetables on an allotment behind our house. I still write some poems inspired by bus journeys and aspects of city life, including our tremendous local green spaces like the Arboretum. My fascination with the sounds and rhythms of Nottingham and the surprising semi-rural world which co-exists with the urban have led me to write about the magnificent ash tree on East Lane at the back of our plot, the trenches dug for new water pipes, the foxes which sometimes seem to own the land, the bats, frogs and blackbirds that thrive here. Such poems can be found in two full collections: *The New Girls* (2004) and *Moon at the Park and Ride* (2012) published by Shoestring Press."

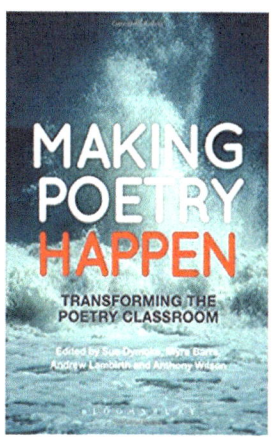

Joan Adeney Easdale 1913–1998

In Nottingham she was known as Sophie Curley, an eccentric bag-lady preaching free love in the Market Square and raving in the streets; nobody suspected that she had once been a poet, published by the Hogarth Press.

Joan Adeney Easdale was born in Manchester, the daughter of Robert Carse Easdale and his wife Ellen Adeney. She wrote from an early age, beginning her first collection of poetry at the age of fourteen. It was published by the Hogarth Press in 1931 as *A Collection of Poems* and quickly followed by *Clemence and Clare and Other Poems* in 1932. Through this she became friendly with Leonard and Virginia Woolf and other members of the Bloomsbury Group.

Her last publication with the Hogarth Press in 1939 was *Amber Innocent*, a long poem which she had worked on for seven years. It is a dream-like sequence owing much to Joan's own journey and pre-empting in some ways her later mental illness.

> **Amber trod the darkened stair, the elemental lion's lair...**
> (Amber Innocent)

In 1938 Joan married research scientist James Meadows Rendel and they had three children. During the war she found it difficult to write but made some very original biographical programmes for the BBC. They moved to Australia and here she began to experience serious psychotic episodes; the marriage floundered and she was advised to return to England for treatment in 1953.

From 1954–1961 she was treated for paranoid schizophrenia in a sanatorium in Surrey. One day she discharged herself and simply went off the radar, living rough and on the road, desperately poor and often alone. In the late sixties she appeared in Nottingham where she re-invented herself as Sophie Curley and became a familiar sight on the city streets and in the bars – a Nottingham 'character' who refused to behave herself! Her daughter Jane and granddaughter Celia never lost sight of her entirely, and in 2008 her remarkable story, pieced together by Celia Robertson, was published as *Who Was Sophie?*

Joan/Sophie died on 10th July 1998 and is buried in Wilford Hill Cemetery, Nottingham.

Places to visit

Wilford Hill Cemetery: where Joan is buried. Take the right-hand path from the Loughborough Road entrance and on approaching the hill, look down to the right, where her distinctive headstone stands proud of the rest. There are also some great views over Nottingham from this graveyard.

Joan Easdale's grave, Wilford Hill Cemetery, Nottingham

Michael Eaton 1954–

"I was born in Sherwood and still live near the Forest. Reading Social Anthropology at King's College, Cambridge provided a firm foundation for both the study of mythical story-telling and the practice of documentary-dramas, which have included, for television, *Why Lockerbie?*, *Shoot To Kill* (Best Drama, Broadcasting Press Guild; Royal Television Society; BAFTA-nominated); *Shipman* (about the Nottingham-born murderous doctor) and, for radio, *The Conflict Is Over* (on the Northern Ireland peace process) and *Washington 9/11* (for the tenth anniversary of the September 11th attacks).

"My first feature film, *Fellow Traveller*, concerned a fictional exiled blacklisted Hollywood screenwriter writing a children's version of Robin Hood (Best Screenplay, British Film Awards, 1989). Original television drama I've written includes *Flowers of the Forest* and *Night Shift* (Best Drama, Community Relations Council Film Awards, 2000) as well as *Signs and Wonders*, the story of a vicar's daughter from a Nottinghamshire pit village joining a sinister new religious movement in Los Angeles.

"I have had a long-standing relationship with Nottingham Playhouse: the first commission was a community drama, *Leaves Of Life*, about the history of Newark-on-Trent; *Angels Rave On* was about a fictional Nottingham 'rave church'; *The Families of Lockerbie* was an examination of the trial of the so-called 'Lockerbie bomber'; *Left/Right* was a short dialogue between the Lions in front of the Council House written for the theatre's fiftieth anniversary and *Charlie Peace – His Amazing Life and Astounding Legend*, directed by Giles Croft and designed by Eddie Campbell, was about the notorious portico thief and murderer who holed up in Narrow Marsh when on the run in the 1870s – it premiered in 2013 and my book about this Victorian criminal was published by Five Leaves in 2017.

"From 2006–2012 I was Visiting Professor for the MA in Creative Writing at Nottingham Trent University and was commissioned to write a history play for the 170th anniversary of the School of Art: *All Schools Should Be Art Schools*.

"As a dedicated Dickensian I have adapted several works of the Inimitable for the radio including *The Pickwick Papers*; for Dickens's bicentennial year of 2012 I co-curated a major retrospective of cinematic versions at the BFI Southbank, wrote the Arena documentary *Dickens and Film* and five short plays about Boz and London for Radio Four's *The Special Correspondent For Posterity* and in 2016 I adapted *Great Expectations* for the West Yorkshire Playhouse under the direction of Lucy Bailey.

"My short film on Nottingham Castle's collection of classical antiquities from the Temple of Nemi was included in their exhibition *The Treasures of Diana*; subsequently I translated Ernest Renan's play *The Priest of Nemi* for Shoestring Press, which has also published *Head Hunters*, originally a play for Radio 3 about the anthropologist Alfred Haddon who made the first ethnographic films in the Torres Strait in 1898 and was the subject of my documentary *The Masks Of Mer*.

Rowena Edlin-White 1948–

photo © Ed Herington

"I'm a Nottingham native, born in 1948 to a couple of penniless actors. Dad soon had to get a proper job and sold paint instead. Until I was eight we lived over the shop on Derby Road – a period fictionalised in *The Revenge of the Christmas Fairy* (1997). Even at that age I prowled the city centre on my own and came to know it very well. I was a voracious reader with an over-developed imagination and was encouraged to write by Phyl Cooper, my first, brilliant teacher at Douglas Primary School. When I was twelve I sold a poem to the *Guardian Journal* for the princely sum of 7/6 and thought I'd made it. How wrong can you be?

"Sometimes you have to go away to appreciate what you left behind: I left for drama school at twenty and worked in the theatre and TV until 1980 when a period of severe depression stopped me in my tracks. Reluctantly, I dragged myself back home 'for a rest' and unintentionally began a whole new life in Nottingham.

"I longed to be a publisher – I'd been greatly inspired by the little magazines and independent presses of the 'seventies. With a friend, Dee Duke, I began *The Spinster's Almanack*, a quarterly journal for textile buffs – it was a big hit in America and we published it for twenty-five years. I also began writing for money and my first three mainstream books – a children's novel, *Clo and the Albatross* (1996) and two anthologies – came out in a rush in the mid-'nineties. Once again I thought I'd made it, but authorship seldom works like that. As I waited for the Booker

Prize, Dee and I wrote and published the *Woolgatherings* series for spinsters and dyers, which were popular for years. When the spinsters and dyers turned to other things, we decided to go into local history and *Graces's Diary* (2005) and *Spinster of No Occupation* (2007) followed, as well as a plethora of pamphlets and short stories under the Smallprint label.

"I'm a true daughter of Nottingham, I have never regretted coming back, I love the old girl and this book is my tribute to her. We have a tremendous literary legacy in this county and, always a snapper-up of unconsidered trifles, I've very much enjoyed grubbing in archives, attics and graveyards to recover some of the more obscure and forgotten voices of our past – especially the women."

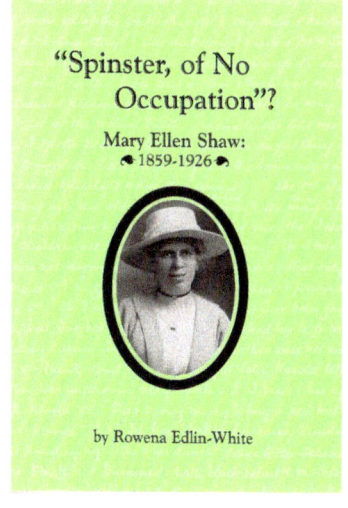

Jonathan Emmett 1965–

"I was born in Leicestershire in 1965, the son of a factory fitter and a primary school teacher. I loved books from an early age and some of my earliest memories are of visiting the library at Enderby, where I grew up. The picture books that I borrowed then, such as *Where the Wild Things Are* by Maurice Sendak and *The Cat in the Hat* by Dr Seuss have greatly influenced the stories I now write.

"I came to Nottingham in 1984 to study architecture at the University and have lived here ever since. I qualified as an architect, but after a few years working in the profession, I left to become a stay-at-home dad and to try my luck at a new career as a children's author, illustrator and paper-engineer. I didn't make it as an illustrator, but succeeded as an author and paper-engineer! My first book, a chapter fiction story called *Doohickey and the Robot*, was published in 1999.

"Most of my writing is for picture books, a couple of which were inspired by my Nottingham home. The city square that's used as a giant playground in *Dinosaurs After Dark* was based on Nottingham city centre with its town hall, fountains and nearby train station. When I wrote the story in 1998 the skyline around the square was filled with tower cranes, which also feature in the book. *Ruby Flew Too* was inspired by a swan's nest at Highfields Park. I used to run to the park, round the lake and back home again. One day I spotted a solitary egg lying in the nest. There's a story to go with that, I thought and the opening line,

"Once upon a time, upon a nest, beside a lake" popped into my head. I substituted ducks for swans and the story of Ruby "the duckling that hatched last but went on to fly the furthest" grew from there.

The story I've written that probably has the strongest connection with Nottinghamshire is an environmental detective novel for children that I wrote when I was still working as an architect. The eponymous detective's name was taken from a signpost and will be familiar to anyone who knows the countryside south-east of Nottingham. The story, which has never been published, was called *Tollerton Plumtree and the Great Waste Scandal!*"

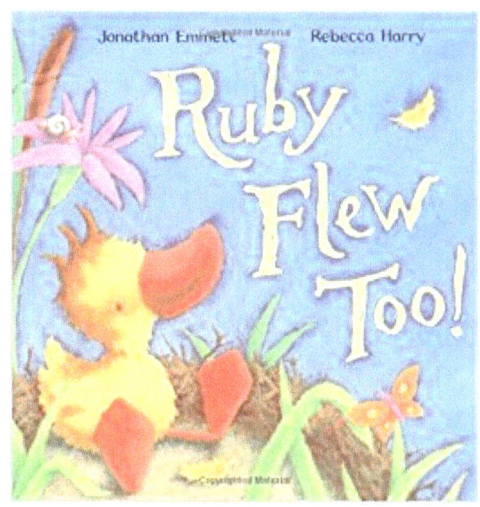

Rose Fyleman 1877–1957

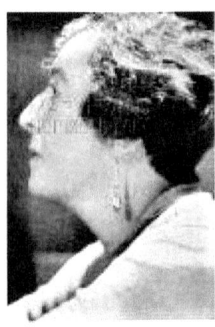

Famous for "There are fairies at the bottom of our garden," Rose Amy Feilmann was born in Nottingham to John Feilmann, a German Jewish immigrant in the lace trade, and his wife, Emilee Loewenstein. Rose attended University College but didn't finish her course; instead, she trained as a singer in Paris, Berlin and London. On her return she taught music in her sister Gertrude's private school at 10, Pelham Terrace, and in 1912 the family moved to 29, Newcastle Drive. When the First World War broke out, many Germans who were British subjects felt safer changing their names, and the Feilmanns became Fylemans.

Rose was forty when she began her writing career and the famous fairy poem was published in *Punch* magazine. She continued to supply poems for *Punch* and her first collection, *Fairies and Chimneys*, came out in 1918, the first of many in neat little books issued by Methuen, as well as short stories and plays for children. She is identified with these, but she was a versatile author. *A Small Cruse* (1923), bearing the familiar fairy insignia, contains some much darker poems, shot through with the cruelty and horror of old folk tales and ballads.

> **I met a fairy yester-eve**
> ('Reality')

Fyleman is at her best in *A Princess Comes to Our Town* (1927), a fantasy set in Nottingham. Princess Finestra leaves Fairyland to put off the evil day when she must marry a boring old prince, and comes to live among Real People for a while – with the author, on Standard Hill. Fyleman paints a convincing picture of

1920s Nottingham, remarking on such things as the new Council House which was being built at the time. Her descriptive passages are particularly good and the illustrations by Gertrude Lindsay of the Arboretum, the Castle and the Market Square are unmistakeable.

One of the funniest episodes involves the statue of Queen Victoria (then in the Market Square) coming to life after dark and exploring the city in a fire engine.

Finestra is an impulsive young woman: but a mysterious man appears in various guises whenever she and the narrator get into hot water, and he turns out to be the very person she has been avoiding. He wins her heart when he saves her from a fire-eating dragon at the Goose Fair.

Rose Fyleman moved to London to live in the late 1920s so maybe this fairy-tale was a final, affectionate tribute to her native city?

Places to visit

The Park: A stroll around The Park is hard to beat. Newcastle Drive, where the Fylemans lived, is especially atmospheric when the old gas-lamps come on at dusk.

Trent Bridge: Have a word with Queen Victoria – she went walkabout again in 1953 and settled in the Memorial Gardens at Trent Bridge.

Winifred Marshall Gales 1761–1839

Born in Newark on 10th July 1761, the daughter of John and Elizabeth Marshall, Winifred began writing as a young child, publishing her first novel, *The History of Lady Emma Melcombe and Her Family*, when she was seventeen.

On 4th May 1784 she married Derbyshire-born Joseph Gales (1761–1841), then apprenticed to the printer James Tomlinson in Newark. The Gales moved to Sheffield where they opened a bookshop and from 1787 published the *Sheffield Register*, a liberal newspaper. They became Unitarians and took up various radical causes including parliamentary reform and the abolition of slavery. Winifred gave birth to four children in Sheffield and continued to write: *Lady Julia Seaton* was published in 1788.

In 1794 Joseph's political activism caused him to be indicted for conspiracy and he left for Hamburg whilst Winifred stayed behind to sell the business, eventually joining him in America. In 1795, in Philadelphia, they began another newspaper, *Gales' Independent Gazetteer*. They finally settled in Raleigh, North Carolina, publishing the *Raleigh Register* and opening another bookshop with stock imported from England.

> **Egerton indulged in the luxury of sad sensation.**
> *(Matilda Berkely)*

Winifred's *Matilda Berkely or Family Anecdotes* (1804) was hailed as the first novel by a resident in North Carolina. It was assumed to be autobiographical, because the action begins in the Midlands, but other than that there seem to be no grounds for the assumption. Typical of its time, it is a complicated love-tangle, concerning two families where the wife has married against the wishes of her family and has been cut off from them. Matilda, the heroine, is an orphan with a fortune, whose innocent eyes are opened when she is thrust into London society along with her penniless companion Eliza. A lost brother, a shipwreck, incarceration in a convent and a startling scene-change to Russia ensue, but all is revealed at the end. For a provincial girl, Gales seems to be pretty familiar with high society, so she may have had a 'season' in London before she married.

The tolerance and liberalism the Gales cherished became difficult to maintain in North Carolina, so in 1833 they moved to Washington D.C. where their son Joseph edited the *National Intelligencer*. Winifred died there in 1839, while Joseph returned to Raleigh and died two years later.

Places to visit

Newark: Tomlinson's Press was on Church Street.

Newark Church and Church Street

Rosie Garner 1957–

"I can still sit in my parents' garden and listen to the bell on the town clock tolling the hours and the quarter hours. On a quiet day I can take the thirty-five minute walk back to my own house and listen to it again, in my own garden. 'Little John' has a calm assured tone I've found deeply reassuring my whole life and, I realised very recently, I would find it hard to live anywhere beyond the bell's range. I don't know if this is a good or a bad thing but yes, I am a Nottingham person. The town is in my bones and in my head.

"Me and Nottingham go back a long way. My great-great-grandfather had a little shop on Bridlesmith Gate. From it, he witnessed Byron's funeral procession snaking down to Market Square, and later, he stood on Hounds Gate watching the rioters burn down Nottingham Castle. He sympathised with their cause but not the violence, and I can understand that.

"So Nottingham has had an effect on my writing from the beginning. My earliest Nottingham literary influence? A Ladybird book about Robin Hood. I remember every illustration in that book vividly. For a long time I thought I was Robin Hood. Then it was Ned Ludd, which makes sense. Between the two of them they have informed my politics and probably my writing. I am a quixotic socialist with mythological leanings, and I suspect my poetry shows it.

"As a teenager, it was *Sons and Lovers*. I fell so hard my boyfriend threatened to dump me unless I stopped 'seeing this Lawrence'. He seeped into everything I wrote for years. And now? Nottingham is packed with writers I like and admire – which is not the same as being influenced by. Right now the living writer with the greatest effect on my own work is Jon McGregor. I feel incredibly at home in his writing. There is something about it that lets me carry on.

"I have often been asked to write about Nottingham and I did, after all, write an entire poetry collection on Nottingham bus routes (*Poetry on the Buses*, 2005), but I've never really seen myself as a Nottingham writer. Other people do, and that's good, but I just see myself as a writer who doesn't get out much."

Rosie Garner's collection *The Rain Diaries* was shortlisted for the East Midlands Book Award in 2010.

Abigail Gawthern 1757–1822

Abigail Anna Frost, born in 1757, was the second daughter of Thomas Frost, a grocer of Rotten Row near the Market Place. She married her cousin, Francis Gawthern, a white-lead manufacturer, at St Peter's Church in 1783 and they settled in an elegant house on Low Pavement. Abigail also inherited her father's estates which included Holme Hall near Newark, which the family used as a country retreat.

Abigail Gawthern is celebrated for her diary which she kept from 1751 to 1810. It was discovered in a Norfolk bookshop in the 1960s, purchased by Nottinghamshire Public Libraries and edited by Adrian Henstock. It is a real historic gem, as Abigail describes life at the heart and hub of Georgian Nottingham.

Cultural life flourished: "Aug 12, 1790: Mrs Jordan acted at the Playhouse in 'The Country Girl'; she performed delightfully." "Sep 7, 1807: Mrs Siddons acted this evening in 'Macbeth' at the Nottingham theatre..."

Captain Fothergill intoxicated and behaved rude to Mr Ray.
(*Diary, 18th April 1804*)

Balls and assemblies took place at the Assembly Rooms just across the street, and tea-drinking was the fashionable thing for the upper crust: "Aug 21, 1798: Lord Byron, the two Miss Parkyns, and the two Master Smiths at Wilford spent the day here; Miss Edwards drank tea with us."

And of course there was lots of delicious gossip! Births, deaths, murders, marriages and elopements are all faithfully recorded, as well as social *faux pas*, such as, "18 Apr 1804: at a sandwich party at Mr

Thomas Smith's, Bromley House, above 50 people; Captain Fothergill intoxicated and behaved rude to Mr Ray. "

Nottingham at this period was politically volatile and the Gawtherns witnessed the bread riots, Luddism and other disturbances. Even elections were dangerous: "Jun 17, 1790: Great rioting this evening; the mob broke Mr Smith's windows, and Mr Green's in Wheeler Gate... and one man was killed, which was Mrs Marshall's son in St Peter's churchyard, who was merely standing as a spectator."

Abigail died on 7th January 1822 and is buried in St Mary's Church with her husband, who predeceased her in 1791.

Places to visit

26, Low Pavement, Nottingham: Abigail's home is still there to admire.

Holme Hall: Situated near Newark, currently a hotel.

26, Low Pavement, Nottingham

Ann Gilbert 1782–1866

Ann Gilbert was born in Islington, daughter of the Rev. Isaac Taylor, Congregationalist minister and engraver. All the members of the family were authors, artists and intellectuals, known collectively as The Taylors of Ongar. With her sister Jane she published one of the first collections of poems and songs written specifically for children, *Hymns for Infant Minds*, in 1805, which ran through many editions.

In 1813 Ann married the Rev. Joseph Gilbert, who in 1825 became the Minister of Friar Lane Chapel. When they first came to Nottingham they lived in a wing at the Castle, later moving to Castle Gate. She remembered standing on the roof and watching the Castle burn during the Reform Riots in 1831.

> **Dread spirit of inclosure come–thy wretched will be done!**
> ('The Last Dying Speech of the Crocuses')

As Dissenters, the Gilberts held similar political views to the Howitts (see pages 130–136) and in 1834 they joined forces in campaigning for the dissolution of the Church of England. Both families were members of the Nottingham Subscription Library at Bromley House and were much involved in the literary and intellectual life of the town.

Ann continued to write poetry and hymns, as well as a two-volume *Autobiography* which is of considerable interest. Like many poets of the period she was captivated by the crocuses that transformed the Meadows each year and in 1852, when enclosure threatened the area, she wrote 'The Last Dying Speech of the Crocuses', the last verse of which reads:

> Spirit of giant trade! We go; on wings of night we fly,
> Some far sequestered spot to seek, where loom may never ply.
> Come line and rule–come board and brick–
>   all dismal things in one–
> Dread spirit of inclosure come–thy wretched will be done!

Ann died in 1866, joining Joseph in their distinctive Gothic tomb in the General Cemetery at Canning Circus.

Places to visit

Castle Gate: The Gilberts' home was, for many years, at 33, Castle Gate. See drawing by Annie Laurie Gilbert on page 91.

General Cemetery: The Gilbert grave is on the left of the path adjacent to Talbot Street.

The Gilbert grave, General Cemetery, Nottingham

Anne Gilbert 1830–1908

Anne Gilbert's grave, General Cemetery, Nottingham

Born Anne Gee, in 1851 she married architect Isaac Charles Gilbert, a son of Ann and Joseph Gilbert to whom Watson Fothergill was once assistant. The family lived on Clinton Street and then at 6, Arthur Street, off Waverley Street, where Anne Gilbert kept a private school. Their eldest daughter, Annie Laurie Gilbert (1851–1943), was a local watercolour artist who captured many scenes of old Nottingham.

> **There were besides many tea-gardens**
> (*Recollections of Old Nottingham*)

Anne was the author of *Recollections of Old Nottingham* (1904), based on a lecture delivered by her at Addison Street Church Literary Society on 10th March 1901. It provides a valuable historical resource in its description of the streets, shops, markets and surroundings of Nottingham in the first half of the nineteenth century. She wrote:

> "No town had a neighbourhood richer in country rambles, whether of meadow or field or stream or woodland. The working-man had his garden on the Hunger (said to be a corruption of Hangar) Hills; his master having his near his own house, for most of the houses in the chief streets had gardens at the back. There were besides many tea-gardens, the resort of the middle classes and others; those at Radford Folly, St Ann's Well, Blue Bell Hill, the Coppice, the Whey House near the Trent, Old Lenton, and others recur to me."

Anne Gilbert died in 1908.

Places to visit

6, Arthur Street, off Waverley Street: where Anne had her school. The Addison Street Chapel was demolished in 1978.

General Cemetery: Anne's is a low grave to the right of Josiah Gilbert's pink pillar; she is buried with her husband Isaac.

6 Arthur Street, Nottingham

Josiah Gilbert 1814–1892

Another son of Ann and Joseph Gilbert, Josiah was an artist, traveller and author. He wrote *Cadere or Titian's Country* (1869), *Landscape in Art before Claude and Salvator* (1885) and edited the *Autobiography and Other Memorials of Mrs Gilbert, Formerly Ann Taylor* (1874).

Places to visit

General Cemetery His grave is marked with an unusual pink marble column close to that of the Mathesons.

Josiah Gilbert's grave, General Cemetery, Nottingham

The house in Castlegate, Nottingham once inhabited by the Rev Joseph Gilbert and his wife, Ann Taylor.

*By their granddaughter
Annie Laurie Gilbert
(in her 88th year.) 1939*

From Ann Taylor Gilbert's album

A sketch of the Gilbert house on Castle Gate, from St Nicholas' churchyard

Sidney Giles 1814–1846

William Sidney Giles was born in Mount Street, Nottingham, "of humble parents" and lived for some years in Sneinton. He was a friend of Spencer T. Hall and attended the literary gatherings at Richard Howitt's, where his poetical abilities were encouraged. He never published a collection but regularly contributed sonnets and poems to the literary journal, *Dearden's Miscellany*, typical of the Sherwood Forest Group:

> Man's word I trust not now, nor woman's smile
> But only Nature ; and the wild, the free,
> The bounding joyous river, most of all
> Keeps with affectionate bands, my heart on thrall.
> ('To the Trent', 1839)

By 1841 he was living in Leicester, working as a bookbinder, and that year he married Jemima Cartwright, the daughter of a dyer. By 1846 he was dead at the age of 32, probably from cholera, and was buried at Gallowtree Gate Congregational Chapel, leaving his widow and two children "scantily provided for," according to Wylie (1853).

> **The bounding joyous river**
> ('To the Trent')

Hall said that he was, "one in whom gentleness and tenderness of spirit are associated with the most fervent, honest, and pure affections, and an active imagination." Hall's beautiful sonnet which begins, "Glad as a poet's thought – as wild and free –" is addressed to his friend.

An epitaph by Hall appeared in the *Nottingham Review* in January 1847, but it is unclear whether it ever appeared on a headstone; the Chapel closed in

1921 and the burials were transferred to Welford Road Cemetery in Leicester.

> Come, Nature's lover! Let thy tear
> Fraternal on this verdure fall:
> A poet's bones are mouldering here–
> His mind earth could not keep in thrall.
>
> Oh, truest love poor Sidney bore
> For all that's noble, pure, or kind;
> And we may search the wide world o'er,
> But not a friend more faithful find.
>
> How warm his heart! His wit, how bright!
> His thoughts what beams of morning light!
> Alas, that here so soon was run
> A course with so much hope begun.

Places to visit

Mount Street, Nottingham: now largely obliterated by Maid Marian Way but once more of a thoroughfare between The Park and Chapel Bar.

Welford Road Cemetery, Leicester: Staff at the Visitor Centre will direct you to the memorial stone which reads: "In Remembrance of all those buried in Gallowtree Gate Congregational Chapel graveyard between the years 1824–1871. Removed to this spot in 1823 after the closing of the Chapel."

One of the last remaining original buildings on Mount Street

Elizabeth Glaister 1840–1892

Elizabeth Glaister was born in Sussex, the eldest child of the Rev. William Glaister. Her father had become Rector of Beckley in 1837 and married Elizabeth Burrill of Broughton Sulney (Upper Broughton). William died in 1861 and it seems likely that Elizabeth and her mother came back to Nottinghamshire because her brother, Canon William Glaister, Vicar of Grantham, was then a curate at Southwell. They settled on the Burgage for the rest of their lives.

Elizabeth began writing in her thirties, producing five novels, of which *The Markhams of Ollerton: A Tale of the Civil War 1642-1647*, was the first to be published in 1873. The story draws on local history and tradition: it takes place during the occupation of the Minster by Cromwell's soldiers, when Catherine Bertie (*née* Markham), whose husband is fighting at Newark, hides in the *parvise*, the little room above the North Porch, and gives birth to a child. She remains in hiding for ten weeks, cared for by her servant Mary Kelsterne and her aunt, Mrs Bernard, housekeeper at the Bishop's Palace. The two woman slip in and out unnoticed with food and medicines until Newark is relieved and Captain Bertie released.

The author obviously knows every nook and cranny of the Minster, and if at times the novel reads

> **Katharine did not care much for antiquities...**
> (*The Markhams of Ollerton*)

like a guide book, it is not surprising, as Elizabeth Glaister wrote the first printed guide to the Minster and also the text for the Southwell volume in Cassell's *Popular Cathedrals of England*. She was also an expert on ecclesiastical embroidery.

Her other novels are: *A Constant Woman* (1878), *The Perfect Path* (1884). *Bernard and Marcia: A Story of Middle Age* (1888) and *Two and Two: A Tale of Four* (1890).

Elizabeth died in 1892 and a substantial obituary appeared in the *Grantham Journal*. The *Southwell Diocesan Magazine* noted that "She was not a bit like other people," and mentions her knowledge of architecture, painting and her exquisite art-needlework. She was obviously well-loved and fully involved in the life of the church in Southwell.

Places to visit

The Glaister grave at Southwell Minster

Southwell Minster: Look up at the *parvise* with its little windows and chimney above the North Door which inspired *The Markhams of Ollerton* – even better, read the book and use it to explore the Minster.

Ollerton Hall, home of the Markhams, has been unoccupied for many years and is currently on the "at risk" register.

Elizabeth Sarah Villa-Real Gooch 1757–1807

image © Houghton Library, Harvard University

This novelist, poet and memoirist was born in Edwinstowe in 1757. Her father, William Villa-Real, was from a wealthy Sephardic-Jewish family, her mother Elizabeth Hallifax of Mansfield. They lived in a house near the river which was later rebuilt on higher ground and named Villa Real. William's death in 1759 left Elizabeth a wealthy heiress.

Marriage at eighteen, to fortune-hunter William Gooch, produced two sons – then, for an alleged indiscretion, he hustled her out of England and abandoned her in France. Alone in a foreign country, her character destroyed, Elizabeth was prey to every passing seducer and sponger and soon heavily in debt. Returning to England, she was several times arrested; but whilst in the Fleet Prison she began to write about her unfortunate experiences. *An Appeal to the Public, On the Conduct of Mrs Gooch* (1788) was followed by *The Life of Mrs Gooch, Written by Herself* (1792). She maintained:

> **I had never even read a novel… I was as inexperienced as a girl of ten.**
> (*The Life of Mrs Gooch*)

> "Were Mercy, that godlike attribute, held out with a lenient hand to support the tottering steps of the daughters of indiscretion, there are many, I doubt not, who would rise superior … to those who have so rashly condemned them " (*The Life of Mrs Gooch*)

Shunned by her family, deprived of her children and fortune, she resorted to the stage, assuming the names of Mrs Jackson, Mrs Freeman and others; though the theatrical portrait above bears her own name.

Her novels, drawing on her early life, include: *The Contrast* (1795), *The Wanderings of the Imagination* (1796), *Fancied Events, or the Sorrows of Ellen* (1799), *Truth and Fiction* (1801) and finally, *Sherwood Forest* (1804). She always hoped to return to her "first and long-lost home!"

In later years, Elizabeth enjoyed a congenial relationship with a Captain Lindley who treated her with love and respect. She died in Plymouth in 1807 and is buried there at St Andrew's Church.

Villa Real Farm, Edwinstowe

An excellent article about the Villa-Real family by Sarah Murden and Joanne Major may be found at georgianera.wordpress.com.

Places to visit

Edwinstowe: Villa Real Farm is on the A6075 Mansfield Road – currently a metal construction business.

Hodsock Priory, Blyth: Two group portraits of Elizabeth's grandmother, Kitty Villa Real, and her children, including William, are on display.

Catherine Grace Frances Gore 1798–1867

This prolific 'silver fork' author revealed very little about her origins, but it is known that her birth name was Moody and she was brought up (and maybe born) in Retford in a merchant's family, moving to London with her family after her father's death. In 1823 she married an army officer, Captain Charles Arthur Gore, and they had ten children together.

She was probably already writing before her marriage, as her first book, *Broken Hearts*, was published in 1823. She went on to produce some seventy novels and plays between 1823 and 1861. The Gores moved in fashionable London, and also lived in Paris between 1832 and 1840, and it was the doings of high society that she wrote about – hence the term 'silver fork'. The critic William Hazlitt dismissed such novels as pandering to "the admiration of the folly, caprice, insolence, and affectation of a certain class," but it was obviously a very popular and successful genre at the time, read mostly by women. Titles like *Theresa Marchmont, or The Maid of Honour* (1824), *The Ambassador's Wife* (1842) and *The Two Aristocracies* (1857) give some idea; but *Women as They Are, or The Manners of the Day* (1830) and *Mrs Armytage, or Female Domination* (1836) also suggest an exploration of women's roles at the period.

> **And not one filial thought of her!**
> *(Reflections... of a Young Lady)*

Gore also wrote the odd poem, and eleven plays, including *The School for Coquettes* (1831) and her comedy *Quid Pro Quo*, which won a £500 prize and was produced at the Haymarket Theatre in 1844.

Captain Gore died in 1846, and serious financial problems must have encouraged Catherine's prodigious literary output. She died in Hampshire on 29th January 1861 and is buried with her husband in Kensal Green Cemetery. Her obituary in *The Times* said that she was "the wittiest woman of her age."

Places to visit

Retford: The White Hart Inn (now The Herbalist), a coaching inn in Gore's time – the transport hub of Retford. One of many fine buildings which survive from the period.
Bromley House Library which still has three shelves of Mrs Gore's best-selling titles!

The White Hart Inn, Retford

Ray Gosling 1939–2013

Ray Gosling was born on 5th May 1939 in Northampton, but Nottingham became his adopted home.

He attended the University of Leicester for a year, during which time he set up a youth club for Teddy Boys and managed a band. He describes this in *Sum Total* (1962), the memoir which caused Philip Callow to seek him out; it is a rambling but splendid stream-of-consciousness testament to the early sixties.

The Leicester experiment came to grief and Gosling moved on to Nottingham, settled in Shakespeare Street and immersed himself in the political and cultural life of the city. In 1964 he wrote:

> **one solitary tomb to a ... boxer called Bendigo.**
> *(Personal Copy)*

The political scene is jumping here just as the flower beds on the traffic islands are splendid and colourful; very fine, uplifting: makes your morning eyes feel glad. The New Left Club brings in people from the corners of the world to speak beneath the fluorescent brightness of the Mechanics Institute. There is the famed Jordan's International Bookstore for all your socialist literature – tucked away in a back street, hidden behind a front of second hand paper backs, thrillers and all, gad what, Comrade. (*Anarchy 38*, April 1964 – reprinted by Five Leaves Bookshop)

In the sixties he became involved in the politics surrounding the demolition and redevelopment of St Ann's, moving into the area and acting as an advocate for the people who wanted to stay. His description of the seven-year campaign is told in *Personal Copy* (1980).

Ray made and presented many radio and TV documentaries and was always an activist, including fighting for gay rights.

He died on 19th November 2013.

Places to visit

St Ann's, Nottingham: There are still corners of old St Ann's – visit the little cemetery alongside Victoria Park where Bendigo is buried: Ray explored the area when he first came to Nottingham and mentions it in *Personal Copy*.

Nottingham Trent University houses Ray Gosling's massive archive.

picture © Gillian Elias

Memorial to Bendigo, Victoria Cemetery, Nottingham

Gwen Grant 1940–

"I was born in Worksop, a small mining town at the northern end of Nottinghamshire, in 1940 and, certainly, my whole writing life has been coloured by my Nottinghamshire roots. Life for me as I was growing up was full of interest because of the deep individuality and humour of the people around me. I still find this the case today. It was never a bygone conclusion that I would be a writer. People from my background generally did not become writers and although I loved writing and poetry, it was years before I realised that despite not being dead, as I thought all writers and poets were, I could actually think about becoming a poet and writer myself.

"A great deal of my work was and still is influenced by where I live and I very much wanted to catch the spirit of the people, the time and the place when I wrote the first book of my trilogy, *Private – Keep Out* (1978). This book is set in Worksop, as is the third book of the trilogy, *One Way Only* (1983). The second, *Knock and Wait* (1979), is about the year I spent in Kent at an Open Air School.

"*The Revolutionary's Daughter* (1990) was a novel written about the Miner's Strike in the 1980s. Living in a mining town, I felt so strongly about this and about the way these men and their families were treated that ,again, I wanted to explore their passion and commitment.

"Nottinghamshire is not a place where you can adopt a take-it-or-leave-it attitude. In my experience, it's a place and a people you fall in love with and stay in love with. Oddly enough, the Nottinghamshire writer who was an enormous influence on me felt exactly the opposite. D.H. Lawrence couldn't wait to get away from the place where he was born.

"Some other books of mine are: *Bonny Starr and the Riddles of Time* (1987), set in the house where I was born and in the school I went to, is an exploration of good and evil, of time and of what time does.

The Lily Pickle Band Book (1982) and *The Lily Pickle Eleven* (1987) both came about because I was standing on my then widowed mother's doorstep when this scraggly band turned the corner and came down the street. Instant love on my part.

"I've been short-listed for literary awards many times and won the Nottinghamshire Libraries Acorn Award for my picture book *Jonpanda* (1992)."

Graham Greene 1904–1991

The novelist Graham Greene spent even less time than Barrie in Nottingham. Like Barrie, he came to work for the *Nottingham Journal*, which had by then moved its offices to Upper Parliament Street. He worked as an unpaid trainee from 1st November 1925 until 1st March 1926 – just four months – not long at all, but it proved to be a significant period for the young Oxford graduate in both a personal and literary sense.

He lived first in lodgings on Hamilton Road but soon moved, along with his dog Paddy, to better digs at Ivy House, All Saints Terrace, close to the Arboretum. It wasn't what he was used to and to be fair, he wasn't seeing foggy old Nottingham at its best in the winter. However, images and characters from this brief sojourn would turn up in several of his novels and a play. *A Gun for Sale* (1936) is set in 'Nottwich' where the assassin Raven comes to seek out his betrayer, Cholmondeley:

There was no dawn that day in Nottwich.
(Gun for Hire)

> There was no dawn that day in Nottwich. Fog lay over the city like a night sky with no stars. The air in the streets was clear. You had only to imagine that it was night. The first tram crawled out of its shed and took the steel track down towards the market. An old piece of newspaper blew up against the door of the Royal Theatre and flattened out... Along the line a signal lamp winked green in the dark day and the lit carriages drew slowly in past the cemetery, the glue factory, over the wide tidy cement-lined river. A bell began to ring from the Roman Catholic cathedral. A whistle blew.

Ivy House features in this, in *Brighton Rock* and *It's a Battlefield*; and Greene's nosy Nottingham landlady, Mrs Loney, made appearances as Mrs Prewitt in the former and Mrs Coney in the latter.

The old *Nottingham Journal* offices

Greene found Nottingham something of a cultural desert, though he did meet Cecil Roberts, who had also worked at the *Journal* and had by then become a successful novelist earning £400 a year. Greene also became a Catholic in order to marry his fiancée; Father Trollope at the Cathedral prepared him for baptism and he left town the following day.

See David Belbin's essay for more on Graham Greene in Nottingham (page 271).

Places to visit

All Saints Terrace: David Belbin, Michael Eaton and several others, including me, have endeavoured to find 'Ivy House' (there was no All Saints Terrace in Greene's time). The best guess is one of the houses on Goodwin Street.

Upper Parliament Street: The old Watson Fothergill *Nottingham Journal* and *News* offices, where there is a plaque to Greene on the wall in the entrance.

Spencer Timothy Hall 1812–1885

Hall, a Quaker, was born at Brookside Cottage, Sutton-in-Ashfield, 16th Dec 1812. He had to work from childhood, getting little schooling, but reading whatever he could. At sixteen he ran away from home with "a small bundle of books and clothes and thirteen pence halfpenny in cash" and got an apprenticeship on *The Mercury* in Nottingham, lodging in Olive Row, Mount Street. He joined the Artisans' Library, attended literary gatherings at Richard Howitt's pharmacy and began contributing poetry to newspapers. He founded a small periodical, *The Sherwood Magazine*, before moving to York to work on the *Herald and Courant*. In 1841 he published *The Forester's Offering*, a collection of prose and poetry, followed by *Rambles in the Country* as the 'Sherwood Forester' (1842).

> **Thou fine old town – thou Nottingham of my youth!**
> *(The Peak and the Plain)*

Hall became a mesmerist, giving lectures in England and Scotland, then took up magnetism and homeopathy. He lived in London, Nottingham, Derby, the Lake District (where he ran a hydropathical establishment) and Ireland, but he continued to identify himself with the 'Sherwood Forest Group' of writers (see page 257 for more on this group) and it is thanks to his *Biographical Sketches of Remarkable People* (1873) that we know so much about them.

Hall loved following old paths and rivers and walked many miles for his topographical books like *The Peak and the Plain* (1853), a sensitive description of rural life in the 1830s–50s, and *Days in Derbyshire* (1863). With Christopher Thomson he inaugurated the 'Old Sherwood Gatherings' at Edwinstowe in the 1840s, where tribute was paid in song and verse to the Forest, which was steadily shrinking as a result of enclosure.

In *The Peak and the Plain* he sadly describes returning in 1838 to the Nun-Brook at Maplewell Close, west of Sutton-in-Ashfield, which like St Ann's Well had once been a popular place for picnics. The field had been sold, the public right of way closed, the well destroyed and trees uprooted.

Hall's birthplace

Hall married Sara Blundstone in 1859 but she died within the year. In 1861 he married Mary Julia Grimley and they had at least four children. He died penniless at Fylde 26th April 1885 and is buried at Layton Cemetery, Blackpool. Charles Plumbe paid for the headstone which celebrates "The Sherwood Forester."

Places to visit

Sutton-in-Ashfield: Hall's birthplace stood at the corner of what is now Brook Street and Woods Hill.

Sherwood Forest: Obtain a copy of *The Peak and the Plain* and explore the old paths with Hall, especially around Sherwood Forest.

William Hallam 1797–??

Born at Bonsall, Derbyshire on 20th July 1797, Wylie (1853) says Hallam was "A respectable machinist and model maker [for medallions etc.]." Apprenticed in Mansfield, he left the area at the age of about nineteen and for some years lived in Oxford and Birmingham. In 1851 he was living at 1, Greyfriar Gate, Nottingham with his wife Mary Ann and six children, and they were still at the same address in 1854.

So far as we know, his only volume of poetry is *Pleasley Vale and other Poems or The Wanderer's Sketch of Home* (1852). It is a reflection on the home of his youth to which he returned after some thirty years. He notices the changes in the landscape as he walks from Mansfield to Pleasley and remembers how the "truant urchin, catering for a meal" would collect nuts and berries from the hedgerows; the rural entertainments when the day's labour was over; and the exploration of local historical sites like the Roman villa discovered by Hayman Rooke in 1786.

> **Sweet Pleasley Vale, to meditate on THEE.**
> ('Pleasley Vale')

He is impressed by the works of the Hollins family (later Viyella) which occupy the Vale, bringing employment and prosperity to the area. The book is dedicated to William Hollins Esquire, who also heads the list of subscribers to this little book. Other subscribers include Nottingham poets Henry Hogg and Edward Hind.

A friendly review in the *Nottinghamshire Guardian* 15th April 1852, states,

> We see nothing in *Pleasley Vale etc.* that could call forth severity, even from the most wanton critic. On the contrary, there is much in it that will please and

improve the mind of the reader; and it is written with a degree of smoothness and facile accuracy highly credible to any "humble mechanic".

Places to visit

Pleasley Vale: the immense factories commented upon by Hallam are still there but now house small businesses, and what must have been an area of great activity and noise is much quieter. There are pleasant walks to be had through the Vale and along the old railway line, through what is now a conservation area.

Hollins factory, Pleasley Vale

John Harvey 1938–

photo © Molly Boiling

"I was born in London in 1938 and first came to live in Nottingham in 1965, dividing most of my time between those cities ever since. First as a teacher and then as a writer, I've found frequent inspiration in the Nottinghamshire-based work of D.H. Lawrence and Alan Sillitoe and, more recently, Jon McGregor. I was awarded an MA in American Studies by the University of Nottingham in 1978 and an honorary doctorate, D. Litt, in 2009.

"Beginning in 1989 with *Lonely Hearts*, which was named by *The Times* as one of the hundred best crime novels of the last century, my series of Nottingham-based novels featuring Detective Inspector Charlie Resnick, concluded in 2014 with *Darkness, Darkness* which is partly set during the Miners' Strike of 1984–85.

"An essay, 'Resnick, Nottingham and All That Jazz', is included in the collection, *Minor Key* (Five Leaves, 2009), which brings together a number of short stories and poems associated with the city of Nottingham and/or jazz. A further collection of short stories, *Going Down Slow*, was published by Five Leaves in 2017.

"My dramatisation of 'Darkness, Darkness', developed with Jack McNamara of New Perspectives Theatre Company, was staged at Nottingham Playhouse in 2016."

Elain Harwood 1958–

"I write about twentieth-century architecture. My interest in modern architecture really came from the fact that the most interesting public buildings in Nottingham and Beeston date from the 1950s and 1960s, and buildings like the county's schools and the Nottingham Playhouse represented all that was most progressive and innovative culturally when I was growing up in Beeston and Chilwell in the 1970s.

"I joined English Heritage (now Historic England) in 1984 and began working as a researcher there in 1987 just as the listing of post-war buildings was beginning, so my love of these buildings gave me a head start.

"My first major work was a study of 1960s' theatres, and I met the architect Peter Moro when preparing the listing of Nottingham Playhouse in 1994. This work led in turn to a major book studying post-war architecture by building type, *Space, Hope and Brutalism*, finally published in 2015. The interest in theatres also encouraged me to start a PhD on the subject, which I later changed into a detailed study of London's South Bank, including the Royal Festival Hall where Moro first made his name as the architect of the interior.

"Meanwhile, I was invited to write the *Pevsner City Guide* to Nottingham's architecture, published in 2008. It was a revelation to be able to explore and research the city centre in intricate detail, for while I lived in Nottinghamshire until 1980 I really did not know the city save for its shops and later its pubs. I discovered the extensive collections of Nottinghamshire Archives and the richness of the nineteenth-century city, led by Thomas Hine and Watson Fothergill, but also a testament to a wealth of shadowy figures who had trained at the School of Art, now part of Nottingham Trent University. They and their buildings became my friends.

"I was later to use Nottinghamshire Archives for a book on post-war schools, and an unpublished report on the county's post-war public houses. I've led tours of the city's pubs, and of surviving cinema buildings in the county. Although I'm based in London, it means a lot to me to have a second base outside it, even if it means I belong to neither one place or the other.

"I'm now writing a book on Britain's new towns for Historic England, and the contrast of those planned towns with the adhoc development of Beeston and especially Chilwell really resonates with me."

Paul Augustus Herring 1870–1938

Paul Herring was born in Nottingham in 1870. He was a regular contributor to the *Nottinghamshire Guardian* and *Evening Post* for over forty years, as well as writing 'light' fiction, which his obituary states enjoyed "a considerable vogue" in Britain and America. He was largely self-educated and worked as an assistant librarian at Nottingham Central Free Library from the 1890s.

The Magic of Miss Aladdin – a Humorous Romance (1906) begins in Australia. The heroine, Linnet 'Aladdin' Lane, is the daughter of a gold digger; the hero, Godfrey Starling aka 'Ned Nugget' the bank robber, son of minor baronet. Both are incurable romantics. Linnet paints a portrait of Ned entitled 'The Romance of the Great Road', makes a great deal of money and leaves for England to visit her Uncle Cornelius in Copplestone.

Meanwhile, Ned has a weird experience in the desert with a magician, Hassan, who sends him to find a magic gem, the Blue Ray. When he recovers, he sheds his alter ego and goes home – to the family seat in Copplestone.

'Copplestone' is familiar:

> The cheerful texture of the winding village street was the result of long collaboration between Nature and Time. It was more texture than a colour – a texture woven of very homely material in quiet sympathy with the village industry – they made stockings on hand-frames, and all the villages around followed the same old-fashioned trade. . . The stocking frame was

> **Miss Aladdin caught her first intimate glimpse of Copplestone.**
> (*The Magic of Miss Aladdin*)

invented by a parson belonging to the old village of Calverton, which hides behind those hills... In that way lay Woodborough... and a few miles over footpaths and cornfields took one to Arnold...

This surely has to be Lambley.

Cornelius is custodian of the village library which contains mostly adventure books. He leads 'The Shipwreck Club' at the local pub and he and his cronies enact stories of outlaws, highwaymen and Luddites. Time-slips occur because of the Blue Ray and soon they are living in the past for real. Eventually the church sundial turns everything back to normal and Godfrey and Linnet agree to marry.

Miss Aladdin is a quaint mix of *Arabian Nights* and Mitford's *Our Village*, with plenty of literary allusions and puns. Herring also wrote *Bold Bendigo – a Romance of the Open Road* (1927), in tribute to Nottingham's bare-knuckle fighter, as well as *The Wrong Mr Chamberlain*, a political farce; *Sir Toby and the Regent* (1929); and a thriller, *The Murder of Margaret Midnight* (1932).

He died on 15th June 1938 at 2, Robinson Road, Mapperley.

Places to visit

Lambley: Explore this lovely village not far from Nottingham.

photo © John Wilson

The 'Mass Dial' (sundial) at Holy Trinity Church, Lambley

Anthony Hervey 1797–1850

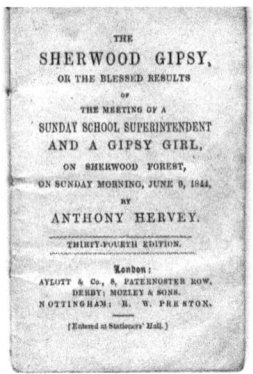

Anthony Hervey was a lace-maker from Carrington and Missionary to Collin's and Labray's Almshouses. He was author of a penny tract called *The Sherwood Gipsy*, subtitled: "The Blessed Results of the Meeting of a Sunday School Superintendent and a Gipsy Girl, on Sherwood Forest June 9th 1844."

Tracts were stories of religious conversion, often ending with an affecting deathbed scene and an exhortation that the reader should examine him or herself, repent, and follow Christ. Alternatively, they might be an account of a godly life which readers might care to emulate. They were printed in their thousands, and for many poor people were the only books they ever had.

> ... to inhale the fresh air from the hills of Sherwood.
> (*The Sherwood Gipsy*)

Hervey described how he was walking one June morning on Mapperley Common "to inhale the fresh air from the hills of Sherwood," when he came upon a Gipsy encampment and got into conversation with a girl called Matilda Harrison. She was intelligent and literate and Hervey quoted poetry to her, as well as portions of scripture. The Gipsies were moving the following day, so he gave her a Bible, some tracts and his address. The following February she wrote to tell him that she had come to faith, but was very ill, and in March he heard she had died, blessing their meeting on Mapperley Common.

Hervey's account of Matilda's conversion was in its 34th edition by the time he died on 26th March 1850, when some details of his life and death were added, including the fulsome inscription on his headstone in the General Cemetery. Hervey's little tract is a mere crumb in the literary history of Nottingham but nonetheless representative of a very popular genre.

Places to visit

Mapperley Common was an area of fifty-seven acres between the top of Coppice Road (now Ransom Road) and The Wells Road, a wild, unlevel district covered with gorse and thorns where cattle were put to graze and Gipsies camped (Mellors 1926). A year after Hervey's encounter, the common was declared 'waste', enclosed and sold for building.

General Cemetery: For Hervey's grave take the middle path from Canning Circus down and through the small car park. Keep straight on at the junction in the paths, and count three graves down and then three graves in on the left. Hervey's handsome slate headstone faces down towards Waverley Street.

Hervey's grave, General Cemetery, Nottingham

George Hickling 1827–1909

George Hickling, or 'Rusticus', as he was known to his readers, was born and lived in Cotgrave and employed as a framework knitter for I. & R. Morley. In his Preface to *Echoes from the Woodlands* (1892) he writes:

> In offering this book to 'The People,' I may say that it has been written for them by one of themselves – an uneducated man who never had the advantage of literary society, having lived in an isolated village all his life.

'Rusticus' found an audience in the *Nottingham Journal* and published three volumes of poetry. Henry Brown, introducing *Echoes from the Woodlands* writes:

> **... my childhood's home where I was born.**
> ('The Voice of Nature, a Pastoral')

Truly the poet has shown throughout a life of labour how it is possible for a man to rise above his surroundings, and to win, in social life, the respect of his neighbours for his diligence. . . From his thirteenth year 'Rusticus' has been an assiduous artisan and toiler; and, moreover, has always been a thinker.

He lived close to the church and describes his home affectionately and at great length in 'The Voice of Nature, a Pastoral':

> 'Twas such a cottage, standing by the church,
> O'er shadowed by the aspen and the birch,
> That was my childhood's home where I was born,
> And where I felt life's early, beaming morn,
> The ample roof, o'ergrown with lichens green,
> Was just discerned the leafy boughs between.
> About the eaves the sparrows rear'd their young,
> And perched above, the robin sang his song;

His other collections are: *The Pleasures of Life and other poems* (1861) *Echoes from Nature or The Song of the Woodland Muse* (1863).

Places to visit

Cotgrave: The church was substantially rebuilt after a fire in 1996 but its outer shell and surroundings must still be much as Hickling knew them. In spite of his description it is hard to decide the exact location of his cottage today.

Cotgrave Church

Walter Hilton 1340–1396

The date for Hilton's birth is approximate. He is believed to have been educated at Cambridge, after which he was ordained and became a hermit. However, the eremitical life did not suit him; he joined the Augustinian order and came to live as a Canon at Thurgarton Priory.

He was, and is, best known as the author of *The Scale [or Ladder] of Perfection*, a book of spiritual instruction of particular interest to anchorites (male) or anchoresses (female), solitary religious people who nevertheless were not hermits, but lived within the community, attached to a church. The book begins "Ghostly [spiritual] Sister in Christ Jesus...", so did he have anyone particular in mind?

Julian of Norwich (1342–1429) was a well-known anchoress of the period. She lived confined in a cell built onto St Julian's church, but windows gave her access to the church interior and the services, and also the common street. Pilgrims or anyone else could approach her from the street and ask for prayer or advice. Julian was literate, and may well have read Hilton's book, but there were many other anchoresses like her recorded.

> **Ghostly Sister in Christ Jesus**
> *(The Ladder of Perfection)*

Hilton's book was written in the vernacular – in English – and circulated in manuscript form long before being printed in 'black letter' by Wynkyn de Worde in the 1650s, when it went through several editions. It appealed not only to anchorites but to ordinary lay Christians who cherished an interior spirituality.

Hilton died on 24th March 1396.

Places to visit

Thurgarton: The remains of the monastic buildings are in private ownership, but the Priory Church of St Peter in the village is worth a visit. Hilton was probably buried with other brothers in the Priory grounds, but there is a modern memorial to him on one of the pillars in the church.

Thurgarton Priory, 1726 engraving

Edward Hind 1817–1872

Born 7th November 1817 in a house close to the Castle Wharf where his father Benjamin was an iron and coal merchant, Hind is loosely associated with the Sherwood Forest school (Wylie, 1853). Spencer Hall provided an introduction to his *Poems* (1853), many of which celebrate local beauty spots, but not with the same tone of regret as others of the group. This poem, 'Colwick Lane', seems to have been written as a song:

Colwick Lane

Come away to Colwick wildwood –
Come away down Colwick Lane;
As we wandered there in childhood,
Let us ramble there again!
By the hill-side steep ascending,
Over boughed by arches green,
Darkly overhead impending,
Shading all the pleasant scene!

There retreating – here advancing,
See the ever-shifting view;
Rich plantations round us glancing,
Dark against the beaming blue!
Here, the high park opening o'er us,
Showing nature's secret charms;
There, the low park spread before us,
Clasps us in its sylvan arms!

> **Come away to Colwick wildwood, Come away down Colwick Lane.**
> (*Poems*)

Past the hall, and steeple hoary,
Girded by encircling trees –
Past each high wood's stately glory,
Waving grandly in the breeze;
Past the village – onward roaming,
Over meadows, bright and still,
Till we pause beneath the gloaming,
By the white cot on the hill.

Other works include *Prometheus Bound – a Life-Drama*, which was highly thought of, and *Ethel's Hope*, a narrative using many different forms of poetry and prose which demonstrate his versatility. *My Magazine* (1860) is, to my mind, his most interesting book: poetry, polemic, short plays and autobiography reveal the struggles of the warehouseman-poet who suffered intermittent mental illness and whose good-natured father bankrupted the family at least twice.

In 1860, Hind's address was Wightman Terrace, St Ann's Well Road. Later he and his wife Emma Street moved to Woodborough Road where she died in 1869. Edward Hind died 30th Sept 1872 leaving three young children and is supposed to be buried in St Mary's churchyard.

Places to visit

Colwick Woods: for sure, and the area at the foot of the Castle where the old wharves used to be.

Colwick Woods

Muriel Hine 1874–1949

Muriel was the daughter of architect George Thomas Hine, who designed Mapperley Hospital. Her grandpapa was the more famous T.C. Hine. They lived affluently in Wollaton, but the result of an unwise investment forced the family to downgrade to 73, Raleigh Street. In the 1890s they moved to London.

Educated at Queen's College, London and in Paris, Muriel became a prolific author of popular fiction, including a handful of novels based on her own early life in Nottingham, which she calls 'Lacingham.' *A Great Adventure* (1939) covers this period. Although it carries a disclaimer that all characters "are entirely imaginary" this is barely true: George Henty is an architect in his father's business and his wife is an unimaginative, jealous, woman, embarrassed by her eccentric in-laws at 'Oxford House'. She believes reading is selfish and a waste of time:

> **Reading could be a drug, she decided...**
> (*A Great Adventure*)

> A coal fell into the grate, startling her, and she glanced at her husband, who had not stirred, deep in his book. Reading could be a drug, she decided, above all, to a Henty.

She is harsh with her daughter Gina, stamping on any imaginative activity as "untruths" and allowing her no time to herself. It is only after George loses his money and they move to 'Ivanhoe Street' that Gina is allowed to attend the Girls' High School. Encouraged by her headmistress, Miss Ironside, she begins to write for publication and forms a close alliance with her Aunt Aggie (Annie Hine), an ardent suffragist. *A Great*

Adventure creates a vivid picture of Nottingham in the 1880s, with all its social innuendoes.

Another Lacingham book, *Wild Rye* (1931), describes the trials of seventeen-year-old Jenny Rorke, despatched by her unscrupulous father to live off the goodwill of her maternal grandparents, who are based on the elder Hines. Jenny is seduced by the local doctor's son and her grandmother dies of a heart attack, leaving her at the mercy of her cruel, sanctimonious Aunt Effie. In *Jenny Rorke* (1932), Hine rescued her heroine and gave her a new, satisfying, life running a vineyard in Italy – as well as the chance of revenge.

73, Raleigh Street

Hine often explores the 'woman question', toying with female utopias, as in *The Island Forbidden to Man* (1946), and the changing role of women in World War II (*The Prodigal Daughter*).

She married cricketer and businessman, Sidney William Coxon, and they lived in fashionable Chelsea where Muriel died in 1949. She continued to write best-selling fiction (at least thirty-three novels), plays and even song lyrics, to the end of her life.

Places to visit

73, Raleigh Street: This may be modest, but it retains the style and dignity one would expect from T.C. Hine, who also designed All Saints Church.

The Park: The T.C. Hine home on the corner of Oxford Street and Regent Street features in *A Great Adventure* and *Wild Rye*.

Henry Hogg 1831–1874

Born on 20th October 1831 and baptised at Radford, son of Joseph Hogg who was in the hosiery trade, Henry Hogg was educated in Nottingham and became a solicitor. He published two volumes of poetry: *Mournful Recollections* (1849) and *Songs for the Times* (1856), the latter being the more interesting in its subject matter, as the following extracts demonstrate. For example, he wrote about the exploitation of labour in 'England's Slavery':

> Labour is dignified and grand,
> And elevates our race;
> But there are thousands in the land,
> That groan beneath a cruel hand;
> Driven like a servile band,
> In slavish fetters base.
>
> Body and soul completely crushed,
> Beneath the murderous yoke;
> Cheek white, that should with health be flushed;
> Heart dead, whence feeling might have gushed;
> Conscience into stupor hushed
> That once in warning spoke.

> **Labour with stout workmen fills, Mine and forge, and factory.**
> ('The New Age')

In 'The Fallen', he highlights the double sexual standard, and in 'The New Age' regrets that industrialisation comes at a price:

> Old romance is fled away,
> And the age of chivalry;
> Shepherd pipes no longer play
> In deep vales of Arcady.
> Mail-clad knights no more are seen,
> Outlaws fail from forest green,
> Nymph, and fawn, and fairy queen,
> Have departed utterly.

Now we hear the whining wheels,
Of the vast machinery;
Labour with stout workmen fills,
Mine, and forge, and factory.
Merchants store their merchandise,
Art her busy fingers plies,
Steam propels and language flies
To the world's extremity.

Hogg died on 19th June 1874 at his home on Elm Avenue and is buried in the General Cemetery.

Places to visit

General Cemetery: Hogg's grave is almost opposite Robert Millhouse, to the left of the path.

Henry Hogg's grave, General Cemetery, Nottingham

Charles Hooton 1810–1847

Hooton was born in Upper Parliament Street on 10th May 1810. He had a short but exciting life, beginning his career as editor of the *Leeds Times*, then moving to London 1836–37 where for brief periods he edited *The True Sun* and *The Woolsack*. His novel *Bilberry Thurland* was serialised in *The Spectator* during this time.

He emigrated to America, first to Texas where he spent nine months in the woods, hunting and fishing, before moving on to New Orleans, New York and Montreal, working on newspapers. His health was ruined by 'swamp fever' while abroad and he continued to suffer from it for the rest of his life. He was awarded £20 from the Literary Fund. Back in England, he used his experiences to write articles for magazines and a series of ballads illustrative of American life and literature for the *New Monthly Magazine*.

> **Colin looked. A beautifully-complexioned girl was on the stage.**
> (*Colin Clink*)

A novel, *Colin Clink*, was published in 1841. It is the lively tale of Colin, the Squire's illegitimate son, as he makes his way through the world. The shady sides of both country and city life throw up several eccentric characters worthy of Dickens – Mr Veriquear the rag and bone man is a prime example. The good-natured Colin unravels several dastardly plots and is finally adopted by his true father as the heir of Kiddal Hall. Although set in

Yorkshire, the plot shifts at one point to the depths of Sherwood Forest.

In 1847 Hooton began another novel, *Launcelot Widge*, but his premature death left it unfinished. There was supposedly a manuscript of his autobiography, but the whereabouts are unknown.

Wylie (1853) bore witness that Hooton was, "of a kindly disposition, open and sincere, generous, unsuspicious, and frank-hearted; an enthusiastic lover of the noble, the beautiful, and the true, both in sentiment and conduct..." He goes on to compare him with the poet Thomas Chatterton, "who perished in his pride" which doesn't sound so good.

Hooton died at thirty-six from a huge overdose of morphine, on 16th February 1847, at his father's house

255, Mansfield Road

which was next-door-but-one to the Forest Tavern on Mansfield Road. The inquest found that he had been in the habit of using opiates to allay the symptoms of his fever, and had accidentally exceeded the dose. *Launcelot Widge* and *St Louis Isle or Texiana* were both published after his death.

Places to visit

The Forest Tavern on Mansfield Road is now The Maze (number 257). The building next to it looks as though it might originally have been two dwellings, so Hooton probably died in the left-hand portion of number 255. Raise a glass to this colourful author in the pub. He is buried in the General Cemetery in Nottingham.

Margaret Anastasia Howitt 1839-1930

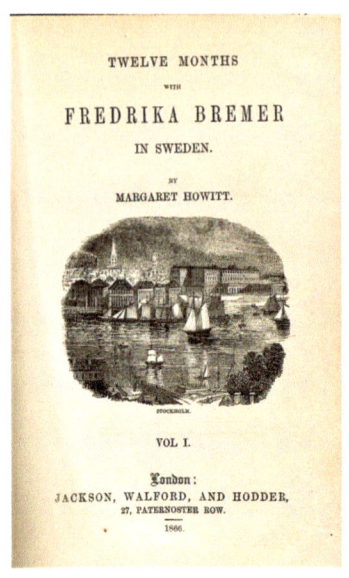

Margaret was William and Mary Howitt's youngest child, born in Esher, Surrey, 2nd August 1839. As well as editing her mother's autobiography, she wrote at least one book for children – *Birds of a Feather or the Two Schoolboys*. In October 1863, she went to Stockholm for eighteen months to stay with the famous writer and feminist Fredrika Bremer, whose works had been translated into English by her parents. Bremer made sure that Margaret had every opportunity to experience Swedish culture, from the peasant market-women in the streets to the aristocracy. Bremer was a social reformer who had drawn attention through her novels to issues affecting women in Sweden (*Hertha* was particularly influential). Bremer died in December 1865 and a year later Margaret's book, *Twelve Months with Fredrika Bremer in Sweden* (1866), was published.

> **The king when he meets Miss Bremer bestows an especial greeting upon her.**
> *(Twelve Months with Fredrika Bremer)*

In 1870 she accompanied her elderly parents to Italy and in 1880 she and her widowed mother built a home at Meran, in the Tyrol, called Marienruhe. Mary died there in 1888 and at some point Margaret returned to England. She died on 8th April 1930, her home being Fern Cottage,

Launceston, Cornwall. She was the last of the family to die and is thought to be buried at St Cuthbert Mayne (Roman Catholic) Church, Launceston.

MARIENRUHE.

Marienruhe, where Mary and Margaret Howitt lived after William's death (thought to be drawn by Anna Mary Howitt Watts)

Mary Howitt 1799–1888

Born Mary Botham in Coleford and brought up in Uttoxeter, Mary and her sister Anna received little stimulation as children. At the local dame school they were not allowed to sit with other children lest they be 'contaminated by the world'. What they did have, in abundance, was access to the natural world. The 'characters' they met in the Staffordshire countryside would reappear later in Mary's fiction. She had some formal education in Croydon and Sheffield but not enough to satisfy her – both sisters had a great desire for books, and through a local family were introduced to Scott and Byron, and some sensational novels.

Mary's grandfather John Botham was related to the Howitts of Heanor and through this connection Mary would meet and marry their son William, whom she found "more than a scholar – a born genius, and most agreeable." He was widely read and soon brought Mary up to date with the literature of the day. They began married life in Hanley but moved to Nottingham in August 1822.

> I walk again amid the crocuses of the Nottingham meadows...
> (*Autobiography*)

They began writing together for the *Staffordshire Mercury*, as they walked 500 miles through Scotland and the Lake District, absorbing the landscape in the manner of the Romantic poets. Two volumes of poetry, *The Forest Minstrels* (1823) and *The Desolation of Eyam* (1827) followed, written collaboratively. The first of their seven children was born in 1824, so while William tramped the countryside, Mary had to fit writing in with domestic duties. She wrote children's stories, including *Woodleighton* and *My Uncle the Clockmaker*, set in familiar surroundings and peopled with local characters. Gift books and annuals provided a ready market for poetry and sketches, and Mary's famous 'Spider and the Fly' comes from this period.

They left Nottingham for Esher in 1836 then moved to Heidelberg for a few years. Mary learnt Danish to translate Hans Christian Andersen's fairy tales, and Swedish to translate the novels of Fredrika Bremer. In the 1870s they settled abroad and Mary was received into the Catholic Church – a far cry from her plain Quaker upbringing. Her autobiography and letters edited by her daughter Margaret are excellent resources.

William and Mary Howitt are frequently discussed as a pair, and for good reason: they were both prolific authors who sometimes collaborated, particularly on poetry and translation, and together produced nearly 200 books. But for various reasons they also pursued their own interests into different genres and deserve individual entries. They were both from Quaker families and were married in 1821.

Places to visit
See the entry for William Howitt on page 136.

Richard Howitt 1799-1869

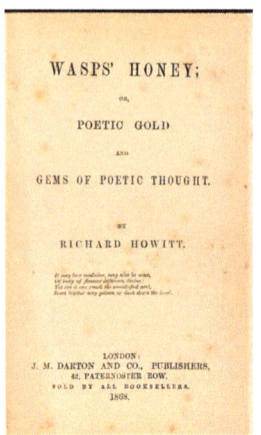

Born at Heanor, a younger brother of William, Spencer Hall called him, "a true poet, a just critic, a cheery companion, and a young man's mentor." Richard ran the pharmacy on the corner of Lower Parliament Street and Newcastle Street from about 1823. A sociable bachelor, he kept open house for the poets and authors of the Sherwood Forest Group, including Thomas Bailey, Robert Millhouse, Samuel Plumb, Thomas Miller, Sidney Giles, Joanna Williams and Jane Holmes: "[T]he little cluster would sit conversing, concocting quaint ballads, or firing original epigrams or sonnets at each other, for hours together," Hall remembered fondly. Hall himself thought nothing of walking fourteen miles for a single night's conversation, returning the same night "through the thick, dark woods of Annesley" (*Sketches*).

Howitt went to Australia with his brothers Godfrey and William in 1839 and wrote *Impressions of Australia Felix* (1845), about the experience. He returned in 1844 and retired to a small farm in Edlingley, "at a corner formed of two roads," where Hall last saw him preparing a bucket of mash for the cattle whilst composing a ballad.

Blithe gipsy of the summer!
('To the Cuckoo')

Richard was no mean poet and published *Antediluvian Sketches* (1830), *The Gypsy King* (1840) and *Wasp's Honey or Poetic Gold and Gleams of Poetic Thought* (1868).

Mary Howitt described his death in her *Autobiography*:

"On February 5, 1869, Richard Howitt breathed his last. His tenants and his poor neighbours, according to country custom, one by one visited their old friend and champion, as he lay robed for the tomb; and as they stood beside the coffin, each one laid his or her hand in blessing upon the cold brow, in the belief that this 'laying on of hands' gives rest to the dead. His relatives accompanied his revered remains, in a mist of soft rain, across the district of old Sherwood Forest to his grave in the burial-ground of the Society of Friends at Mansfield."

Places to visit

Parliament Street, Nottingham: The site of the pharmacy may still be seen to the right of the Victoria Centre.

Edingley: The site of the farm is uncertain.

Mansfield: The Quaker Burial Ground where Richard lies is sadly now beneath the new bus station and the tarmac of Quaker Way. A memorial plaque to those interred has been placed at the bus station, on which Richard Howitt's name appears.

Newcastle Street, Nottingham, where Howitt's pharmacy stood

William Howitt 1792–1879

William was born in 1792 in Heanor, "an obscure rural nook linked to the outer world by the carrier's cart." His father was a colliery manager and his upbringing was much less severe than his wife Mary's. He was one of seven brothers and they lived in a large house near the parish church. After attending Ackworth School in Pontefract and a Friends' school at Tamworth, William continued with his studies and dreamed of emigrating. An admirer of Rousseau, his father decided he would be an architect and apprenticed him to a carpenter in Mansfield, where his favourite retreat was Sherwood Forest. On the day he was released, he tore up his indentures and scattered them to the wind as he walked home to Heanor.

He spent the next few years studying languages, chemistry and medicine and enjoying the outdoor life, but after meeting Mary, the woman "destined to be my best friend, truest companion, and wife," he was inspired to get a job and became a chemist. Soon after they moved to Nottingham, his brother Richard took over the pharmacy on Lower Parliament Street and William and Mary relocated to South Parade. They became part of the literary community and William became involved in local politics, supporting the Reform Bill and the disestablishment of the Church of England. He wrote a highly controversial book, *The History of Priestcraft*, which the Artisans' Library refused to buy.

> **The enclosure system has been one of unexampled absurdity...**
> *(Rural Life of England)*

William spent his time travelling around recording his observations of country life and traditions which were beginning to disappear, and his *Rural Life in England* is an important work, as is *A Country Book for the Field and Forest* (1859), which has Nottingham interest. He also wrote *Homes and Haunts of the British Poets* and other similar guides. He tried his hand at publishing a periodical, *Howitt's Journal*, but it failed financially.

Several Howitt brothers travelled widely, and William spent two years in Australia where he bumped into William Dexter, Caroline's husband, rabble-rousing in Bendigo! In their seventies, he and Mary left England for good, spending their summers in the Tyrol and wintering in Rome. They walked, gardened and climbed mountains, though Mary, at least, kept writing. When William died in 1879 she was thankful for her pension from the Swedish government in gratitude for her translations of Bremer.

Portrait sculpture, Nottingham Castle

The Howitts are buried in the *Cimitero acattoico* or non-Catholic Cemetery, in Rome.

Places to visit

Nottingham Castle: There is an impressive double sculpture of William and Mary in the colonnade.

South Parade, Nottingham: The Howitts' home stood on the site now occupied by Wetherspoons.

Heanor: The Howitt house at Heanor has gone but they are remembered in street names, a school and a good little archive in the library.

Lucy Hutchinson 1620–1681

Lucy's father was Sir Allen Apsley, Governor of the Tower of London, and it was there that she was born on 29th January 1620. Her mother, the former Lucy St John, was determined to give her daughter every educational advantage: the child could read perfectly at four and preferred Philosophy, Latin and Greek to dancing, music and embroidery. Her father died when she was ten, and she and her sister Catherine moved to Richmond with their mother. When Lucy was eighteen, John Hutchinson, a law student, visited Richmond; Lucy was away but he heard from her sister all about her academic accomplishments and liked what he heard. When she came home she liked him too and they were married in 1638.

> "The hardy soldier doth all toils sustain..."
> (*Verses*)

John Hutchinson was the eldest son of Sir Thomas Hutchinson of Owthorpe and Lady Margaret Byron. When the Civil War began, the Apsleys and Hutchinsons found themselves on different sides. Lucy's brother and cousins were in the Royalist army, whilst she and her husband supported Parliament. At the age of only twenty-seven, John found himself Colonel of the troops defending Nottingham from the Cavaliers. They left Owthorpe Hall to be sacked by the King's troops and moved into town, where John became Governor of Nottingham Castle in June 1643. Lucy played an invaluable part during the assault, patching up the wounded of both sides and making sure prisoners were treated humanely. After the Battle of Naseby they returned to Owthorpe where they repaired the damage and lived quietly until Cromwell's death, when John, as a signatory on the King's death warrant, was arrested. He died of fever in 1664 whilst imprisoned at Sandown Castle in Kent.

Lucy Hutchinson is renowned for her *Memoirs of the Life of Colonel Hutchinson*, and her account of the defence of Nottingham Castle is important enough, but she also wrote what is thought to be the first epic poem by a woman in English. *Order and Disorder* is based on the book of Genesis and bears comparison with Milton's *Paradise Lost*; five cantos were published in 1670 but it was not published in full until 2001. Add to this more poetry and translations from Ovid and Lucretius and we have a fuller picture of this brilliant woman.

Lucy Hutchinson died at Owthorpe in 1681.

Places to visit

Owthorpe: The Hall was demolished in the nineteenth century, but the little church of St Margaret contains the Hutchinson family vault. There is an ornate memorial to John, but none to Lucy.

Owthorpe Hall

William Ivory 1963–

"Nottingham and the wider county is at the heart of everything I write – even something like *Made in Dagenham*, in which the striking Ford workers were based massively upon the women I had grown up with in Southwell and the bigger City, fourteen miles beyond.

"I like to think my work is spiky, a little bit abrasive but, if you bother to delve deeper, heartfelt and about something – much like the area. Nottingham doesn't greet with open arms and frequently a good deal of its welcome is undercut with dark, put-you-in-your-place humour, but that's only because Nottinghamians know that friendship is useless unless it's prepared to endure, and encompass not just the good but the difficult times, too. So it won't flatter and fawn, for fear of attracting flatterers and fawners back; it'll test you out instead – your robustness and your spirit. It will deliver a big dollop of unfettered, unfiltered existence (which does tend to be messy and unconsciously funny, too, but often, alongside that, renewing and life-affirming) and if it finds you worthy, then it'll offer itself up, warts and all still, but secure in the knowledge that you understand, this is for life now, and from here on in, your back is always covered, you'll always have a bolt-hole – no matter what state you're in.

"Many of the characters I write, my heroes at least, have this in their heart.

"Anyway, here's a scene. It's the nearest I've got to encapsulating the essence of the place – *and* the way in which it feeds so readily into my work."

INT. PORK FARMS - DAY

Two men stand on a production line, overseeing pork pie output.

DAVE: Do owt good at the weekend?

GAV: I did. I went to this new massage parlour that's opened up in Sherwood. Opposite where the bus station used to be.

DAVE: Oh...I didn't know there was one.

GAV: (nods) Oh, yeah. You go in and all the girls are lined up at the bar and you pick one you want and then you pay twenty quid. Then you get half a bitter, a beef curry and a wank.

DAVE: For twenty quid? That's amazing.

GAV: Aww. There wan't much meat in the curry.

THE END

Sarah Jackson 1977–

photo © Lee Garland

"When I arrived in Nottingham in 2009, I found myself immersed in a lively literary scene, discovering and rediscovering a host of local voices: Jon McGregor, Alison Moore, Alan Sillitoe, Matthew Welton, Gregory Woods, and the many voices of colleagues and students at Nottingham Trent University. This list continues to grow. While I don't think of myself as a 'Nottinghamshire writer' (I try not to think of myself as any particular 'sort' of writer), my work remains bound up with the region and its people. Nottingham's rich literary heritage and support for local writers – not to mention its plentiful supply of caffeine – have fuelled much of my writing over the last few years. 'Light over Ratcliffe' and 'Ten O'Clock Horses', for instance, which both appear in my poetry collection *Pelt* (Bloodaxe, 2012), were directly inspired by the history of Ruddington, where I live, and the nearby landscape. Much of my second book, *Tactile Poetics: Touch and Contemporary Writing* (Edinburgh University Press, 2015), was written and edited in Bromley House Library over the last couple of years, and I cannot help but think that something of the spirit of that place feeds into what I have to say. But I think I most frequently read and write outside the city, working at its edges – East Midlands Parkway, Bunny Hill, a phone box in Hoveringham or the café in IKEA – and it is Nottinghamshire's liminal spaces that really resonate in my work.

"I'm currently developing a project inspired by telephones, and this means thinking about the ways that reading and writing involve the operation of a vast switchboard of different voices – emerging, historical, local and global. During a recent visit to the old telephone exchange in our village museum, I found myself listening out for the ghostly echo of literary voicemail, and the one Nottinghamshire writer whose voice keeps on returning to me is D.H. Lawrence. His story, 'The Rocking Horse Winner' (1926), is filled with uncanny exch-

anges. Even the house in which the protagonist lives seems to have something to say: 'The whisper was everywhere, and therefore no one spoke it. Just as no one ever says: "We are breathing!" in spite of the fact that breath is coming and going all the time.'

"Nottinghamshire, for me, is full of such whispers – whether we speak about them or not – and the future of my writing is bound up with the act of listening to the voices all around me."

Sarah Jackson edited *Ten Poems on the Telephone* (Candlestick Press, 2017)

Jane Jerram 1815-1872

Born Jane Elizabeth Holmes in Radford in 1815, Jane was a member of the Sherwood Forest Group. Spencer Hall met her at Richard Howitt's and mentions that Mary Howitt loved her as a daughter. Jane's own family have not been identified with any certainty but she draws upon her childhood for two short sketches in *The Child's Own Story Book* (1837). She mentions living near the River Trent and that she and her sister Rebecca would play in the meadows full of crocuses, and ramble around Wilford, Bridgford and Clifton Grove.

> ".. the forget-Me-not, by the side of our own blue Trent.
>
> (*The Child's Own Story Book*)

She married William Jerram of Derby at St Mary's Church by Archdeacon's License on 15th October 1836. The license gives no details of her parentage, nor do the notices in the newspapers, so the marriage may not have been approved. The couple went to live with William's family at Bannells or Bannils Farm in the hamlet of Bearwardcote in the parish of Etwall, where they had at least four children. Spencer Hall visited them and wrote in *Sketches* that:

> [Jane] shone not less as an industrious farmer's wife, managing her dairy, than she had in her books by the firesides of thousands of her country-people, – her intellectuality, as well as her devotion to every duty, producing a marked effect upon the scattered neighbourhood.

Her books include *The Pale Star, My Three Aunts, My Father's House, The Pearly Gates, The Child's Own Story Book* and *Mama's Stories*. She was also a poet, according to Hall, but so far I have failed to uncover any poetry by her (there is a poet by the name of Jane Elizabeth Holmes, roughly contemporary with Jerram, who is sometimes confused with her, but she died much earlier).

Jane and her husband both suffered some kind of paralysis and Hall tried to get Jane a pension from the Civil List, but without success. By then the Jerrams were living at Litchurch, close to Derby.

They died within a day of each another, Jane on 8th and William on 9th May 1872 and are buried in Nottingham Road Cemetery. The inscription on their headstone mentions Jane as being the "Authoress of 'My Father's House,' etc."

Places to visit

Bearwardcote: There appear to be no surviving traces of Bannells Farm, but this area of countryside near Etwall makes pleasant walking.

Nottingham Road Cemetery: The Jerram grave is a few paces beyond the British Legion War memorial, in section A20. The well-preserved slate headstone is engraved on both sides, their daughter Catherine Barrowcliffe being on the reverse.

Lucy Joynes 1782–1851

Lucy was baptised at St Mary's in November 1782, the daughter of William and Mary Joynes. William Joynes became Clerk to St Nicholas' Church and the family settled close by, on Gillyflower Hill.

In 1818 Lucy opened a 'Ladies' School' on Gillyflower Hill, moving ten years later around the corner to Castle Gate, where she remained until her death.

Her first book, *Occasional and Miscellaneous Poems*, was published by Sutton & Son in 1820. She had begun to record, in verse, notable events in Nottingham: for example, 'The Explosion' describes the "dreadful catastrophe" which occurred on 28th September 1818 on the Boat Company's Wharf below the Castle, when a cargo of gunpowder exploded with ten fatalities. She recalls how her pupils shrieked with terror at the sound of the blast.

A hymn for the opening of The Methodist New Connexion Chapel on Parliament Street in 1817 and several more hymns are included in *Original Poetry for Infant and Juvenile Minds* (1838). She also rustled up a special one, 'For the Time of Pestilence', to be sung on The Day of Humiliation in the churches on Tuesday 25th September 1849, when cholera was raging throughout the district.

She is loosely connected to the Sherwood Forest Group but the closest she comes to mentioning the encroachment of the built environment is the loss of pleasant walks in the vicinity of the Castle and the Park in 'South-West of Nottingham':

> **Rise Nottingham! – among the counties rise; Illustrious in benignest enterprise.**
> ('Invocation')

Embracing piles of timber, brick and stone,
Now stretch afar, ay, so the rocks might groan;
And hanging street o'er street, with upward swell;
And plat, with peopled roads a-parallel.

... That hill! Late hung with rural tapestry,
Sparkling parterre, and bower and walnut-tree:

... Holly and haw, wild plum, and eglantine.
And storied cliffs with gaudy ridges spread
With lichens, gilliflowers, and roses white and red...

Joynes is an eye-witness to changes within an already urban landscape and she seems to positively relish the advent of modern conveniences like gas lighting and the railway. Her 'Historical Chart of the Borough of Nottingham' charts these events, as well as extreme weather, epidemics and royal visits. She died a woman of substance, leaving the rents and profits of a leasehold house on Gillyflower Hill, various fine furnishings and valuable goodies to her nephews and nieces. She died on 25th April 1851, aged sixty-eight, and was buried at St Nicholas' Church, Nottingham.

View of Nottingham from *Original Rhymes* (1844)

Places to visit

Castle Road: Stroll up Castle Road from Castle Boulevard; this originally led to Gillyflower Hill. Lucy's property in the vicinity was demolished around 1858, to build St Nicholas' Schools.

Bromley House Library owns a framed copy of the famous Historical Chart – ask to see it in the Ethel Harrington Room.

Fred Kitchen 1891–1969

Kitchen was born in Edwinstowe in 1891, his parents left soon after for Yorkshire where his father worked as a cowman on a big estate. After his father's death the family settled in the village of Maltby and after leaving school, he began hiring himself out to work on farms, mainly with heavy horses and cows. He also spent a few years on the railways and at the pit-top.

In 1927 he took a job as cowman near Worksop, moving in 1930 with his boss to Kilton Forest Farm, Forest Hill. Towards the end of the 1963 edition of his classic account of farming 'the old way', *Brother to the Ox*, he describes how, having cherished a love of good literature for many years, he joined a WEA class in 1933 and was encouraged to write, publishing his first book in 1940.

> **Hail, Birkland oaks of Edwinstowe, Where now the touring trippers go –**
> ('The Sherwood Oak')

This book has many fine lyrical descriptions:

> There is something fascinating, almost evil, about the grass-reaper; unlike the binder that waits for the corn to die and then reaps, it cuts through life, sweeping down the slender moon-pennies and toppling them over into long lines of swathes. It chatters its way through tangles of wild vetches, desecrating beds of royal purple, and leaves behind it long lines of trembling grass, cocksfoot, and white clover. By seven o'clock the sun gets higher and all the grasses shimmer in drops of crystal, and the skylark dries his dewy wings in the sun, and in the shady wood the pigeons croon a drowsy note, and all the air is full of scents and hazy mists and humming bees.

In 1946 Kitchen settled on a small-holding in Bolsover near Chesterfield and began public speaking and writing articles for papers. He wrote more than a dozen books about the countryside he loved, including a collection of poems and prose, *Songs of Sherwood* (1948), with descriptions such as this, from 'The Sherwood Oak':

> Hail, Birkland oaks of Edwinstowe,
> Where now the touring trippers go –
> Whose youthful branches have withstood
> The strains and stress since Robin Hood
> Ranged the close confines of thy wood.
> Now, while the woodman's axe strikes keen,
> Tell of the things that thou hast seen,
> From Birkland to Bilhaugh.

Places to visit

Sherwood Forest: Pay homage to the ancient oak trees that remain, especially the Major Oak, thought to be more than 800 years old, which won the title 'England's Tree of the Year' in 2014.

David Herbert Lawrence 1885–1930

Born in Eastwood in 1885 and arguably the most controversial of our native-born authors, Lawrence was one of five children of Arthur John Lawrence, a 'butty' at Brinsley Pit, and his wife Lydia Beardsall. 'Bert' Lawrence was a sickly child and dogged by poor health all his life. A brief period working as a clerk at Haywood's surgical appliance factory in Nottingham was curtailed by illness, after which he trained to be a teacher at University College, Nottingham, and taught in Croydon between 1908 and 1911.

During this time Lawrence was writing, drawing inspiration from his Eastwood background – "the country of my heart," as he famously called it. His first novel, *The White Peacock*, was published in 1911. Some of his greatest novels: *Sons and Lovers*, *The Rainbow*, and *Women in Love*, and numerous short stories, drew upon his deep Nottinghamshire roots – and he had no compunction about creating thinly-disguised characters based on his friends and acquaintances. In 1912 he eloped with Frieda, wife of his old Professor, Ernest Weekley. They eventually married but, having transgressed the social code, were forced to live abroad until his early death.

> **The country of my heart.**
> ('Nottinghamshire')

Lawrence's novels, poetry and paintings were too explicit for their time and in wasn't until the 1960s controversy surrounding *Lady Chatterley's Lover*, that his other work began to be reassessed and reprinted. Lawrence was a genius whose Nottinghamshire roots show through in nearly all his work. For a taste of the local dialect of the period, you can't do better than his plays, *A Collier's Friday Night* and *The Daughter-in-Law*.

Lawrence died on 2nd March 1930 at Vence in France and his ashes lie in a small chapel in Taos, New Mexico.

Places to visit

Eastwood: There are many places to visit which can be recognised in Lawrence's books. The D.H. Lawrence Birthplace Museum is the place to go. Here you can pick up a copy of the Blue Line Trail which leads to four houses where the Lawrences lived and other significant sites. In Eastwood Cemetery, about half a mile along Church Street, the Lawrence burial plot is clearly signposted and D.H.L. is recorded on the headstone. Other places within a few miles include Newthorpe and Moorgreen (*Women in Love, White Peacock*), Felley Mill (*White Peacock*) and Cossall village. Haggs Farm at Underwood, home of Jessie Chambers (Miriam in *Sons and Lovers*) is private property and not accessible.

Nottingham: A plaque, a few yards up Castle Gate on the left, indicates the site of Haywood's factory – Lawrence's first job and Jordan's in *Sons and Lovers*. The old University College building where he studied is on the corner of Shakespeare Street and Sherwood Street, and up at the Castle is a fine bust by Diana Thomson FRBS. On the University of Nottingham campus, the arts centre beside the lake is called the D.H. Lawrence Pavilion, and a bronze statue of Lawrence (right), also by Diana Thomson, may be seen in front of the Law School.

William Lee 1899–1951

Lee was director of the engineering firm, Lee & Hunt Ltd., and in the 1930s lived in Edwalton. He had many poems published in the *Nottingham Journal* and was connected with the Midland Group of artists. His *Poems* is dedicated to artists William Kiddier and Bernard Page, and has a preface by Noel Denholm Davis, the portrait painter. He often wrote on music, cricket and the countryside and some of his poems were set to music by Maynard Grover.

He served with 7th Sherwood Foresters in World War I, having joined up at sixteen. He was a passionate patriot but also had a hatred of warfare. He was also sensitive to the changing landscape of Nottinghamshire, and several poems in *Woodland Warriors* hark back to the Sherwood Forest Group's belief that the countryside is pure and good whilst the city is filthy and corrupted. 'The Dying Forest' in *Poems*, was "Written on hearing of a proposed Railway through Sherwood Forest". On a more cheerful note, his paean to cricket (*Nottingham Evening Post*, 29th June 1934), dedicated to Nottinghamshire Cricket Club, was for many years on the wall in the pavilion at Trent Bridge Cricket Ground.

> **Beneath the shade of old ancestral trees**
> ('Cricket')

Cricket

Oh you who bring a magic to the green
Of ancient village; here where have been
Beneath the shade of old ancestral trees,
Nodding and drowsing, sitting at their ease,
The watchers of the game. A murmurous sound
Dreams slowly round the wide and sunlit ground
As ball meets bat and soars into the air;
Flies into waiting hands and lingers there.
Game of our Fathers; golden-hearted men
Have played and lived it. People alien
Know not its charm; an English game withal
Played by the sons of England. Leaves may fall
And other games be crowned; but in our heart
May it abide, nor ever to depart.

Lee published several volumes of poetry including: *Poems* (1926), *Manna from the Moon* (1938) and *Woodland Warriors and Other Poems* (1931).

William Arthur Lee died in 1951.

Places to visit

Trent Bridge cricket ground: Soak up the atmosphere where Lee spent many happy hours.

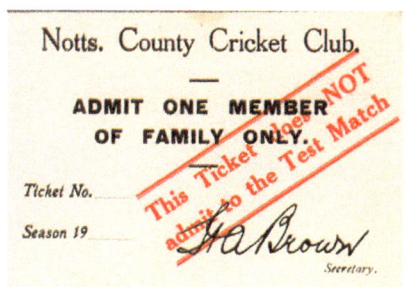

Hilda (Winifred) Lewis 1896–1974

Born in London, Hilda Lewis came to Nottingham in the 1920s with her husband, Professor Michael M. Lewis who worked for the University of Nottingham. Her first book, *The Ship that Flew* (1939), was written for her son Humphrey during a family holiday and ranks among the best children's books of the period.

Historical novels became Lewis' speciality and *Penny Lace* is her tribute to the history of lace manufacture in Nottingham and its suburbs. It begins in 1890 when Nicholas Penny, a twist-hand at Heriots, a large family lace business, meets the boss's daughter Heriot Ware. Heriot, heir to the factory whose name she bears, loves the mechanical side of the business, whilst Nicholas has ambitions to be a 'mester' with his own lace factory. Heriot marries him against her family's wishes, thereby losing her inheritance. Nothing daunted, Nicholas re-invents himself as a gentleman, gradually building up a vast business of his own – but out at Long Eaton where Union rates and conditions don't apply. He sweats his workers and spares no-one – including his wife – to get what he wants. An illegitimate child, Penny's daughter Nicolet, who is as ruthless and self-willed as her father, a suicide, bankruptcy and secrets which must never be told, make it a real page-turner.

Sensational plot-lines aside, the great thing about this novel is its authenticity. Lewis did a great deal of research helped by a local lace manufacturer, John

> **Clean patterns.
> Quality yarns.
> And a reputation
> for value.**
> *(Penny Lace)*

Granger, to whom she dedicated the book. For a starter history of the lace trade in the Nottingham of that period, it is very good indeed. *Penny Lace* was reprinted in a Bromley House edition by Five Leaves in 2011.

Lewis wrote at least one other adult novel with recognisably local features: *More Glass than Wall* (1950) takes place in 'Brantham' during the Second World War, and is something of a soap-opera involving seven families in 'Park Crescent' and 'The Hall', which has been turned into a hotel for the duration. It could be Wollaton, or simply an amalgam of Nottingham places.

Hilda Lewis wrote around twenty books. She died in 1974.

Places to visit

The Lace Market, Nottingham: Unfortunately Nottingham no longer has a dedicated lace museum, but a stroll round the Lace Market gives some idea of the vast lace factories Nottingham once contained. The stately Adams Building on Stoney Street, now part of New College Nottingham, has a restaurant open to the public.

David Love 1750–1827

Here's David's likeness for his Book.
All those who buy may at it look.
As he is in his present state.
Now Printed from a Copper plate.

Love was born in 1750 in Torriburn near Edinburgh, the son of a collier who bound his wife and children to a coal owner for seven years then absconded with the money. As a child David led his blind mother through the towns and villages, selling books door to door. He went down the mine but badly injured his arm in an accident and became a teacher. Eventually he stuck with what he did best – writing and selling ballads and hawking books. Over the next ten years he married his first wife and joined the South Fencibles at Dalkeith, recruiting for the American War, moving with the regiment with his wife and six children until his discharge.

In London he wrote pamphlets reporting trials and prisoners' dying speeches for three years. His wife died in Rugby and he carried on to Nottingham where he found great demand for his books and pamphlets. He would sing his ballads on street corners and at fairs and more than once got thrown into prison for public disorder. He met his second wife in Nottingham, who also died in Rugby and was buried with the first.

> **This place I lov'd exceeding well, And many books I here did sell.**
> (*The Life... of David Love*)

After more travelling, David settled in Nottingham again, marrying his third wife at St Mary's in 1810, but trade was not good and the family spent time in the workhouse – though he did write a poem about it! They took a house at 66, Plumb-street, Turncalf Alley, but the Overseers insisted they return to Scotland; instead they went to London, where David published the *Cries of London*. They came back to Nottingham by canal boat and lived at Knotted Alley, then Butcher's Close.

The *Life, Adventures and Experience of David Love, Written by Himself*, was published by Sutton and Son around 1823. He became a local character known as Old David, or Old Glory when he was peddling religious material. He died in Close Alley on 12th June 1827 aged 77 and was interred in the Old Burying-ground of St Mary's, Nottingham.

An anonymous epitaph reads:

> Long were his verses, and his life was long,
> Wide, as a recompense, his fame was spread;
> He sold for half-pence (all he had) a song,
> He earned by them ('twas all he wished) his bread.

Places to visit

Nottingham: Armed with a copy of the Town Map of Nottingham 1820 (available at the Archives), explore the old Lace Market. Plumb-street was roughly where the Midland Station stands; Knotted Alley was in Broad Marsh; Butcher's Close is now Poplar Street and Close Alley is roughly where the Manvers Street flats are.

Stephen Lowe 1947–

"I was born in a two-up two-down in Sneinton in 1947. My father had returned from the War with meningitis and TB and for most of my childhood was in and out of sanatoriums. My mother was a machinist, struggling to bring up two kids. After an experimental treatment my father went 'stone deaf' but refused to learn to sign or lip-read. Home life was tense – and served as the source for my autobiographical play *Moving Pictures* at London's Royal Court Theatre (published in a collection by Methuen). There were no books at all in the house.

"Two things transformed my life – the first, joining the youth group at the Co-operative Arts Theatre where I was stunned and stirred by the plays of Arthur Miller, Tennessee Williams and overwhelmed by the musicals. The opening of the new Nottingham Playhouse was a dream come true. The second salvation – my sacred library card. Reading *Sons and Lovers* convinced me it was possible to be a writer. The first play I directed at university was *The Daughter in Law*. Lawrence had smashed open the door for us backstreet kids. He, and of course, Sillitoe. Radical, non-establishment voices.

"It's not so much the bricks and mortar of the city that fascinates me. It's the radical history of the people, the famous and the forgotten, that inspires me. Its people have become the heroes of my plays: Lawrence in *Empty Bed Blues* and *Divine Gossip* (RSC); Cloughie in *Old Big 'Ead in the Spirit of the Man* (Nottingham Playhouse); the working women at the end of the War in the award-winning *Touched* (published by Nick Hern Books); the much-maligned Luddites in the musical *Paradise* as well as BBC TV dramas – Warren Clark in *Ice Dance*, inspired by Torvill and Dean, Nigel Hawthorn as a Jewish survivor in *Flea-Bites*, set at Goose Fair, and *Cries From a Watchtower*, filmed on Sneinton Market.

"As a writer you can live in one of two places – home or anywhere. I tried anywhere – quite nice – but when home is so rich in tales the choice was easy to make. In 1983 I moved back to Nottingham with my partner Tanya Myers to set up Meeting Ground Theatre Company, opening all our plays here as well as touring nationally and abroad."

In 2013 Stephen was awarded an honorary doctorate for services to the arts by the University of Nottingham, where his archives can be found.

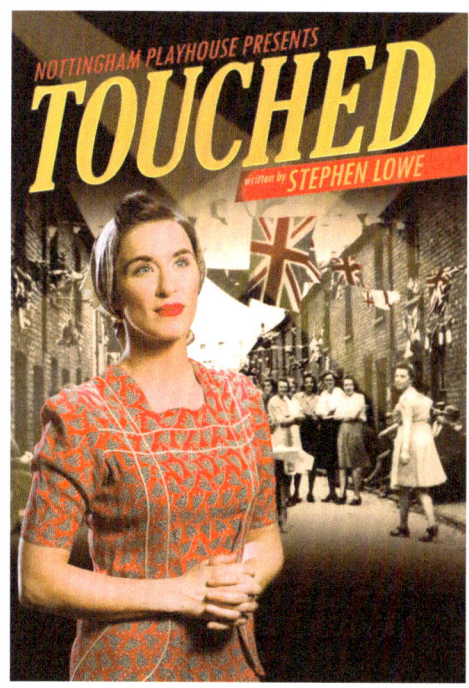

John Lucas 1937–

photo © Graham Lester George

"Although I was born in Exeter in 1937 and spent the years 1947–1964 in the south of England – I write about this period in *Next Year Will Be Better* (2010) – I think of myself as a Midlander. With my artist wife (Pauline Lucas), small son, and soon-to-be-born daughter, I arrived in Nottingham in the late summer of 1964 and I've been here ever since. Not exactly a home-coming, given that the Midlands where I'd lived during my early childhood was a village in rural Leicestershire – it features in my novel, *Waterdrops* (2012) – but whenever I'm away for any stretch of time I find myself thinking about my adopted city. My first pamphlet-collection of poems, *About Nottingham*, was written when we were in America, 1967–8, and in 1984–5, when I had the grandly-named Lord Byron Visiting Professorship of English at the University of Athens – the glory was all in the title – I was working on a book called *England and Englishness* (1990). This grew out of my earlier writing on provincial poets and novelists, including George Crabbe, John Clare, Elizabeth Gaskell, Thomas Hardy, Arnold Bennett and, inevitably, D.H. Lawrence, a selection of whose poems and non-fictional prose I made for Routledge and Kegan Paul (1987).

"My first full collection of poems, *Studying Grosz on the Bus* (1989), which included a clutch of poems about Nottingham appeared four years after Basil Haynes and I had published *The Trent Bridge Battery: The Lives of the Sporting Gunns*, about a great working-class Nottingham family of footballers,

STUDYING GROSZ ON THE BUS

Poems by John Lucas

PETERLOO POETS

cricketers, and in the case of George, a full-blown eccentric.

"'A certain provincialism of feeling is invaluable,' Hardy confided in a notebook. 'It is the essence of individuality.' Hardy is protesting about the atomistic 'crowd'. Better by far the quirks of individuals. But it's a false antithesis. Crowds come apart to reveal individuals, as Dickens, my great hero, knew – none better. My delight in living in Athens for a year grew with the realisation that, teeming, dirty city though (or perhaps because) it was, Athens was also a place of wondrous individuals. (The Greeks call them 'characters'. Bennett's Stoke called them 'Cards'.) It was this that prompted the book I wrote about Greece, *92 Acharnon Street* (2011).

" 'The city will always pursue you.' Cavafy is right. The city I know best features in all my collections of poems, including the latest, *Portable Property* (2015), as it comes into my second novel, *Some of These People* (2016). There's no escaping Nottingham."

John Lucas' new novel, *Summer Nineteen Forty-Five* was published in 2017 by Greenwich Exchange.

Annie Matheson 1853–1924

Annie was born in Blackheath in 1853, eldest child of the Rev. James Matheson and his wife Elizabeth Cripps. Her father came to Nottingham first as assistant, and then in 1856 as successor, to the Rev. Joseph Gilbert at Friar Lane Congregational Chapel. Matheson was well-known for promoting higher education and setting up reading and debating groups for people from all walks of life. He was also a suffragist.

Annie began contributing to periodicals in her early teens, developing into a well-published poet, essayist and biographer. She was twenty-five when her father died in 1878 and the family moved back to London. Her first book of poetry, *The Religion of Humanity and Other Poems*, was published in 1890. She worked as a teacher and journalist and settled at Maybury Hill, Woking. She championed the cause of working women and her deeply ironic poem, 'A Song for Women', describing exploitation by sweated labour, was printed as a leaflet by the Women's Protective and Provident League, the first trade union for women. The last verse is a challenge to all women to act on behalf of the "starving girl" whose plight she has described:

> **Wild snowdrops... from the little village of Papplewick**
> (*By Divers Paths*)

> O God in heaven! Shall I, who share
> That dying woman's womanhood,
> Taste all the summer's bounteous good
> Unburdened by her weight of care?
> The white moon-daisies star the grass,
> The lengthening shadows o'er them pass;
> The meadow pool is smooth as glass.

In her essay 'Poetry and the Labour Party' (*Leaves of Prose*, 1912) she writes,

> I have had the high honour of living in the closest intercourse with labouring people and I know that their lives, which in pathos are ever on the edge of tragedy, often breathe the very spirit of the deepest poem.

Annie published eight books of poetry and prose, and for children wrote excellent biographies of Florence Nightingale, Elizabeth Fry and Joan of Arc. She also wrote prefaces for new editions of novels by George Eliot and Mrs Craik. Annie Matheson died in London in 1924, leaving many projects unfinished. Her ashes were brought back to Nottingham and buried with her parents and infant sister in the General Cemetery.

Places to visit

Nottingham: The Mathesons had homes on Castle Gate, Forest Road West, Bilbie Street and Larkdale Street – all unnumbered on the Census or since demolished.

General Cemetery: The Matheson grave has a plain slate headstone and is about twenty yards down from Millhouse, tucked behind the pink pillar of Josiah Gilbert.

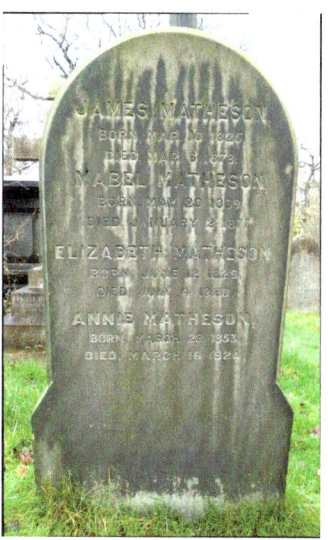

The Matheson grave, General Cemetery, Nottingham

Pat McGrath 1954–

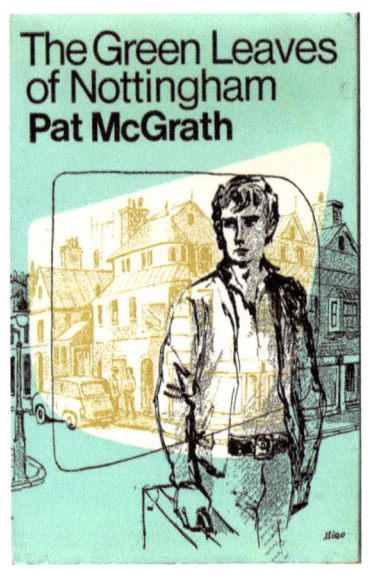

Pat McGrath was born in Nottingham but moved to London around 1970. He wrote *The Green Leaves of Nottingham* at the age of fourteen. It is an edgy novel set in the Radford area: Jamie Howe comes home from Borstal, meets up with Dion Kilgrady, another former inmate, and they get involved in organised crime. Things quickly spiral out of control, culminating in Jamie shooting the serial killer Ernest Keft.

'The Green Leaves' is the name of the local pub, against whose back wall a younger Jamie once held court with his gang and upon which he longs to be recorded as a local legend:

> Taken away by the devil,
> Why did he raise such a fuss?
> He proved that he was a rebel,
> He roused the rebel in us.

He and Kilgrady try hard to be rebels, only to be crushed by much more dangerous criminals, and the book ends with Jamie about to be sent down for murder.

Robin Hood looms up out of the fog at me
(People in the Crowd)

Alan Sillitoe wrote the introduction to this remarkable first novel: "The Nottingham of this story is of course authentic... the message underneath rings true enough. The pages burn along at a young man's rate..." He should know.

A play based on the book was produced during the Nottingham Playhouse 1971–2 season.

McGrath followed this book with *People in the Crowd* (1978), a collection of short stories, again with a Nottingham background, including St Ann's, Broad Marsh, Radford and the city. This is from 'After the Rainfall':

> Walking along Maid Marian Way I stop to light a cigarette. I turn my jacket collar up and turn off into the narrow lane, walking up towards the hidden castle. The black bronze statue of Robin Hood looms up out of the fog at me in the freezing cold morning that makes my hands burn red. The lights of the lorries, vans, cars roll past, exhaust fumes manifesting dirty green in this grey oblivion. It's Nottingham trying to find its way through the foggy morning, it's me trying to find my way through my foggy life.

McGrath has written at least one more book, *Daybreak* (1979).

Places to visit

Maid Marian Way which ruthlessly chopped its way through one of the oldest parts of Nottingham.

Arthur Mee 1875–1943

Born in Stapleford on 21st July 1875, the second of Henry and Mary Mee's ten children, Arthur is remarkable for his inventive educational publishing. His father was an engine-driver on the railway and a strict Baptist. In 1889 the Mees moved into Nottingham, to what is now 311 Woodborough Road. At fourteen, he went to work as a copy-holder for the *Nottingham Evening Post* and, ambitious for greater things, taught himself shorthand in order to report on political speeches and the like. By 1891 he was a junior reporter on the *Nottingham Daily Express* and sub-editor of the *Evening News*. He worked seven days a week including Christmas for £2 per week.

> **Sherwood Forest has given the world immortal chapters of romance.**
> *(The King's England: Nottinghamshire)*

Mee began to submit articles of general interest to *Tit-Bits*, a popular paper published by Newnes, and this served to increase his meagre salary. He became adept at collecting facts and figures which, by 1902, amounted to some 250,000 items. In 1896 he joined the staff of *Tit-Bits* for around £1,000 a year. In 1903 he moved to the *Daily Mail* at the invitation of Sir Alfred Harmsworth and soon began a series of educational part-works, beginning with *The Harmsworth Self-Educator*. *The Harmsworth History of the World* followed, and then in 1906 *The Children's*

Encyclopedia, which was a great success, written in plain language with colour illustrations. Even after the final number in 1910, it continued to be published in hardback well into the 1940s.

My Magazine for children and *The World's Greatest Books*, as well as many informative books for children and adults, bore Mee's name. *The King's England* series of county guides, begun in the 1930s, still make interesting reading – the Nottinghamshire volume was written by Mee's sister Lois and her husband Claude Scanlon.

Arthur Mee died suddenly on 28th May 1943 and his ashes were scattered at his home, Eynsford, at Sevenoaks in Kent.

Places to visit

Stapleford: The Arthur Mee Centre is on Church Street. This was originally Stapleford School which Mee attended as a boy and where he was inspired by his teacher George Byford. There is a blue plaque commemorating Mee.

Blue plaque on the Arthur Mee Centre, Stapleford

Stanley Middleton 1919–2009

photo © Sue Dymoke

Stanley Middleton was born in Bulwell, the son of a railwayman. He was educated at High Pavement School and then – with the help of scholarships and grants – at the University of Nottingham. He graduated early in anticipation of being called up for war service, after which he obtained a teaching qualification and returned to High Pavement, where he taught English until he retired. He lived in Nottingham for the rest of his life.

Middleton's first novel, *A Short Answer*, was published in 1958; after this he wrote virtually one a year and his fourteenth, *Holiday*, was joint winner of the Booker Prize in 1974. Middleton didn't look to his Bulwell roots for inspiration, he became an author of the better-off suburbs: his characters are teachers, solicitors and middle-class professionals leading unsensational lives in 'Beechnall'; then something – or somebody – intrudes into this routine ordinariness and everything jolts a bit and has to be re-configured.

> **... terraced houses on a fine, left-curving, cobbled road**
> ('Bulwell')

Of his phenomenal output – some forty-six novels – several, *Harris's Requiem*, for example, draw on his considerable musical knowledge; whilst his solid Methodist Bible upbringing and his deep love of Shakespeare (which he taught memorably) are evident in the odd turn of phrase and some of his titles, coming naturally and unobtrusively to his pen. Beechnall aside, Middleton remembered his roots in a short essay, 'Bulwell', recently republished by Five Leaves in its Bookshop Occasional Papers series:

> There the town crouched, then, in its hollow. When I became a reader and discovered D.H. Lawrence, born not five miles away as the crow flies, the effect was startling. And much as I resented his 'miserable Bulwell' in *Strike Pay* he more than made up for it with a sentence in *Sons and Lovers*, a sentence I greatly admired and often copied: '... there was a patch of light at Bulwell like myriad petals shaken to the ground from the shed stars; and beyond was the red glare of the furnaces, playing like hot breath on the clouds. (*Places: An Anthology of Britain*, Ronald Blythe, 1981).

Stanley Middleton, by his own admission, was a Nottingham writer through and through. He is one of our great authors of recent times. Ronald Blythe writes, "He continues to stand alone; there is no other writer at all like him." (*Stanley Middleton at Eighty*, Five Leaves, 1990).

The old High Pavement School building, Forest Fields, Nottingham

Places to visit

Bulwell: Look up to see the traces of long-gone chapels and factories; walk around the park and explore the 'edges' of the town, which in Middleton's childhood was called the 'Forest', and is now a golf course.

Sherwood: The area around Caledon Road is typical Middleton country, where he lived.

Stanley Street, Forest Fields: The old High Pavement School building on Stanley Street where Middleton taught for many years.

Thomas Miller 1807–1874

Miller was born 31st August 1807 in Sailor's Alley Yard, Gainsborough and he and the Chartist poet Thomas Cooper were boys together. Miller received his education courtesy of the White Hart charity while Cooper was a Bluecoat Boy. "Tom and I were all for learning, and excitement, and for doing something to win fame," wrote Cooper (*Life*).

Thomas' first apprenticeship to a shoemaker was a failure, so he moved to Nottingham in 1832 where he was apprenticed to Mr Watts, a basket-maker, in the basement of Bromley House. He became friends with the Howitts, the Baileys and Robert Millhouse. Later he had a shop in Swann's Yard (now home to the publishers of this book) and, on Saturdays, a stall on the corner of the Exchange and South Parade. Here he would declaim poetry between basket sales.

> ... the Ship, one of the oldest public houses in Nottingham.
> (*Gideon Giles the Roper*)

He wrote several novels set in and around Nottingham: *Royston Gower* (1838), *Fair Rosamund* (1839) and *Gideon Giles the Roper* (1841).

Gideon Giles begins in the village of Burton Woodhouse in Lincolnshire. Giles loses his job and sets off on foot to find a new one calling at various rope-makers all the way to Nottingham. He travels via Newark to Torksey; to Martin (sic), then by Knaith Park and Lea toward Gainsboro'; by way of Bole, Wheatly, Welham and East Redford (Retford) he arrives in Worksop via Babworth and Clumber

Park; then from Norton to Warsop to Mansfield and finally to Nottingham.

Memorial plaque at Nottingham Castle

> Poor Gideon! He passed the hut [The Hutt] on the lonely road, and neither thought of Byron, or Newstead, but with weary feet and a heavy heart descended Red Hill at the hour of sunset; he walked towards Sherwood, and was compelled to rest...

He enters Nottingham by Forest Hill as St Mary's clock strikes nine, goes down Mansfield Road, and finally reaches, "the Ship, one of the oldest public houses in Nottingham" in Pelham Street. Miller would have known the Old Ship well – the landlord, Nathaniel Warren, had a soft spot for poor authors. Poor Gideon walks all the way home again in the morning – without a job.

Miller loved Nottinghamshire, especially the romantic lure of the greenwoods, but he left for London in the 1830s where he made a passable living as a writer and bookseller. He died on 24th October 1874 and is buried in West Norwood Cemetery.

Places to visit

Nottingham Castle: There is a memorial plaque to Miller by Ernest Gillick in the colonnade.

Torksey to Nottingham: It would be an interesting, if strenuous, day's walk to follow Gideon's fifty-odd mile journey, but could be better enjoyed in short stretches. Stop at Gainsborough to pay homage at Miller's birthplace where there is a blue plaque.

Robert Millhouse 1788-1839

Millhouse was born in poverty in Mole-court, Milton Street and died in much the same condition at 32, Walker Street, Sneinton. The second of ten children, he began work at the age of six. However, he received some basic education at Sunday School, discovered the great poets and began to write himself. From 1810-14 he served with the Nottinghamshire Militia in Plymouth and Dublin and in 1812 sent home his *Poem of Nottingham Park*. Some of his poetry is highly patriotic, for example, *Song of the Patriot*, published in 1826; but many of his sonnets and songs are addressed to local haunts he had loved as a boy but had disappeared.

> **The Maze of Old is gone!**
> ('Written ... on Sneinton Plain')

The sonnet 'To Larkdale' recalls:

> First of my Childhood haunts! In youthful hours,
> Oft have I trac'd thy winding path with glee,
> When May-flowers spread their bosoms to the bee...

Larkdale was one of the ancient paths from the town up to the ridge which became Forest Road. Another sonnet, 'Written on the site of the once ancient labyrinth on Sneinton Plain', laments:

> Unfeeling Avarice! Couldst thou not forego
> One Rood, where youth might point to other years?
> The Maze of Old is gone!"

This feature, a favourite destination for Nottingham townsfolk, near St Ann's Well, had been ploughed up.

The long poem, 'Nottingham Park', nostalgically refers to what is now the Park Estate, which in Millhouse's youth, was another cherished green space open to the public.

His three volumes of poetry were published by subscription. Millhouse was poor but had many friends. In his final illness they supported him financially and Dr Godfrey Howitt attended him *gratis*. His last words to his friend, Spencer Hall, were, "My name, Spencer, is linked with Sherwood Forest, of which my children will live to be proud. Your turn will be next... go forth into the world, my lad, and may God, and a dying poet's blessing, go with you!" The Sherwood Forest Group saved up for three years for his headstone and Hall wrote the affectionate epitaph:

> When Trent shall flow no more and blossoms fail,
> On Sherwood's plain to scent the springtime gale;
> When the lark's lay shall lack its pulsing charm,
> And song forget the Briton's soul to warm:
> And love o'er youthful hearts hath lost its sway,
> Thy fame, O Bard, shall pass – but not till then – away.

Places to visit

Nottingham Castle: Millhouse's portrait plaque in the colonnade.

General Cemetery: From the Canning Circus entrance follow the right-hand path beside the wall. About 200 yards along, there is an elaborate white marble headstone with a harp carved at the top and Hall's poem on the slate below. The cemetery lies alongside Millhouse's beloved Larkdale.

Millhouse's grave, General Cemetery, Nottingham

Nicola Monaghan 1971–

"I write as Nicola Monaghan but also as Niki Valentine. I was born in Radford, and raised on council estates further out of town: Aspley, Bilborough, Broxtowe, Top Valley. We moved quite a lot in the hope of finding an elusive 'somewhere nice'. I lived away from the East Midlands for years, in large, cosmopolitan cities like London, Paris and Chicago. I came back to Nottingham in 2002 to study for an MA in Creative Writing at Nottingham Trent University. That was when I realised what an interesting place it was, and renewed my love for my home city, where I've lived ever since.

"I identify strongly as a Nottingham writer. Much of the fiction I write is set in the area, and the region informs the characters I write about and the kinds of stories I tell. I was a big fan of D.H. Lawrence as a teenager and, later, Alan Sillitoe. I met Alan, and we sparked up a correspondence and friendship. He was such a lovely bloke, and so supportive of my career. As can be seen from my MA dissertation, with my first novel *The Killing Jar* (2006), my intention was always to create something that fitted within the working-class Nottingham tradition. I also used dialect in my story and found inspiration from both of these local writers, as well as others further afield, such as Irvine Welsh.

"Not all of my books have such a strong sense of the region where I live, but I do find Nottingham an inspiring place to be a writer. In 2005, I met Jon McGregor, and we discussed the idea of a space for writers in Nottingham. The next year the Nottingham

Writers' Studio came to be. There's a real groundswell of creativity in the area, and the studio is at the centre of this. There's a wonderfully vibrant spoken word scene in the city, as well as a surprising number of novelists and storytellers.

"I've also written *Starfishing* (2008) and a novella, *The Okinawa Dragon* (2008). As Niki Valentine, I have written *The Haunted* (2011) and *Possessed* (2012). I've self-published a collection of short stories called *The Night Lingers and Other Stories* (2014) and a novella series called *The Troll* (2015) – these are both set in Nottingham."

Lady Mary Wortley Montagu 1689–1762

Born Lady Mary Pierrepont in London on 15th May 1689, she was the daughter of Evelyn Pierrepont and his first wife, Lady Mary Feilding; the following year her father became the 5th Earl of Kingston-upon-Hull. Mary's mother died when she was eight and she and her siblings were brought up at Holme Pierrepont Hall. The family also owned Thoresby Hall which had a fine library which Mary used extensively: "I used to study five or six hours a day in my father's library, and so got that language [Latin] whilst everyone else thought I was reading nothing but novels and romances." By the time she was fourteen she was not only an accomplished student but a compulsive writer.

> **While vain coquets affect to be pursued**
> ('The Lady's Resolve')

She met her husband, Edward Wortley Montagu, when she was about fourteen; he was eleven years older than her and a second son, so his prospects were not great and her father thought she could do much better. They conducted a secret correspondence for ten years and as they seldom met and were almost never alone, this was their courtship. They finally eloped in August 1712:

The Lady's Resolve, Written on a Window, Soon after her Marriage 1713

Whilst thirst of praise and vain desire of fame,
In every age, is every woman's aim;
With courtship pleas'd, of silly toasters proud.
Fond of a train, and happy in a crowd;
On each proud fop bestowing some kind glance,
Each conquest owing to some loose advance;

While vain coquets affect to be pursued,
And think they're virtuous, if not grossly lewd:
Let this great maxim be my virtue's guide;
In part she is to blame that has been try'd –
He comes too near, that comes to be deny'd.

Mary is famous for her letters, but she was also a critic, travel writer and poet, who collaborated with Alexander Pope, with whom she later had a spectacular falling-out. Edward was appointed ambassador to Constantinople in 1716 and in Turkey Mary witnessed inoculation for smallpox, which she would later vigorously promote in England. In 1739 she left her husband to travel independently in Europe and did not see him again before his death in 1761.

Lady Mary died in London on 21st August 1762, a genius, wit and pioneer of medicine, and an independent woman before her time.

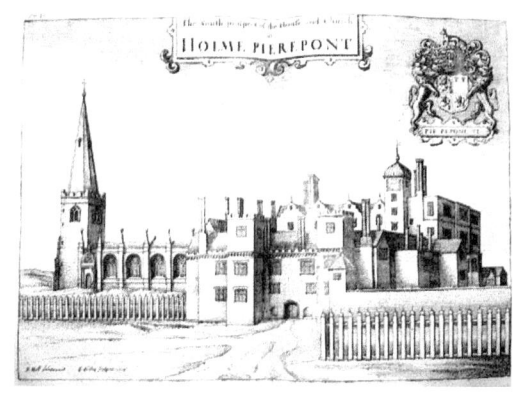

Holme Pierrepont Hall

Places to visit

Thoresby Hall, Ollerton: Now a hotel, but the courtyard and gallery are open daily to the public.

Holme Pierrepont Hall, Nottingham: Open at various times during the year – check the website: www.holmepierreponthall.com

Elinor Mordaunt 1872–1942

Evelyn May Clowes was born at Cotgrave Place on 7th May 1872 and christened at the Parish Church. She was the fifth of eight children of St John Legh Clowes of Broughton Hall, Lancashire, and the Hon. Elizabeth Bingham, daughter of Lord Clanmorris of County Mayo. They were not wealthy: Cotgrave Place was owned by the Manvers family and Clowes farmed there from 1870 until 1876, before moving on to Cheltenham.

In 1897, Evelyn accompanied a cousin to Mauritius, and married a planter, William Wiehe. The marriage failed, and by 1902 she was living in Melbourne, Australia with her son Godfrey. Here she reinvented herself as Elinor Mordaunt, the name on her first book, *The Garden of Contentment*, published that year. In 1915 she changed her name permanently by deed-poll.

She lived in Melbourne for nearly a decade, writing, painting and doing anything she could to support herself and her son. Later she became a compulsive traveller, visiting the islands of the South Pacific and the Dutch East Indies. She thought nothing of taking passage on a leaky tramp steamer or trading ship, relishing the rough-and-ready voyage as much as the destination. *The Venture Book* and *The Further Venture Book* (both 1926) recount her adventures, and the places inspired many of her short stories.

> "I'm only going to Africa. I'll be back tomorrow."

She died on 25th June 1942 in Oxford, her richest legacy being her travel books, novels and short stories – and the reputation of having had a writ issued against her by Somerset Maugham for *Gin and Bitters*, her satirical rejoinder to his book, *Cakes and Ale*.

The Tales of Elinor Mordaunt is a great introduction to her work: thirty-eight short stories, with many an uncanny twist, which span her career.

In her autobiography *Sinabada* (1937), Elinor describes her earliest years in Cotgrave with great affection.

Places to visit

Cotgrave Place is a private house in the grounds of the Golf Course on Main Road, Cotgrave, but the surrounding countryside is still recognisable from Elinor's memoirs.

Cotgrave Place

Katharine Morris 1910–1999

Born 22nd May 1910 in Nottingham, Katharine was the daughter of Robert Ernest Morris, a lace manufacturer, and his artistic wife Katharine, née Dymoke. They lived in Albert Grove, Lenton, but some time after 1914 the family moved to Little Firs, Bleasby, opposite Manor Farm. Robert's business suffered as the lace trade diminished, and his wife wrote stories for children's papers. Katharine, known then as Mollie, had her first story published, aged nine, in *Tiger Tim's Weekly*.

When her first adult novel was rejected Mollie approached the author Lionel Britton, who advised her to write about what she knew – village life. The result was *New Harrowing* (1933) which was published to some acclaim in Britain and the US.

New Harrowing begins in Lenton at the end of WWI when Sally and David Howard are orphaned. They go to a cousin, Janet Stirling, who lives at Martin's Hollow, a farm at 'Collerton', near the Trent. Here they grow up with Janet, their Uncle Sampson, blinded in the War, and cousin Andrew, also a war veteran, who comes and goes from his medical studies in Nottingham and his practice in London. The seasons go round and the children grow up; Sally falls in love with Charles, son of the local squire, but finally admits she loves the much older Andrew. He has only a short time to live due to shrapnel wounds; they do not marry, but she goes to London to care for him. None

> **The skyline is empty, the hillside is dumb.**
> ('The End of the Rookery')

of the relationships are straightforward or conventional, but eventually Janet and Sampson marry and turn up again in *Country Dance*. There is a nice description of Newark Market, and of walking to early communion on Christmas morning.

As Katharine Morris, Mollie published four more novels set in the Trentside villages: *The Vixon's Cub* (1951), *Country Dance* (1955), *The House by the Water* (1957) and *The Long Meadow* (1958). She portrays proud, hard-working rural communities where the seasons dictate peoples' lives and where relationships can smoulder and ignite. Her descriptions of the area are still recognisable.

Katharine served in the Women's Auxiliary Air Force during World War II, followed by welfare work in Hamburg. The remainder of her working life was spent in social work in Kensington and Chelsea. She retired to her childhood home in 1975, where she painted, sculpted and wrote poetry. She died on 22nd August 1999 and is buried with her parents in Bleasby churchyard.

Places to visit

Bleasby: Katharine's home, Little Dower House, is on the corner opposite Manor Farm Tea Rooms. It is privately owned but the nameplate on the gate lists the titles of Katherine's books.

Peter Mortimer 1943–

"I never truly knew my native city till I left it – it's half a century since I upped sticks. Now, the city's many physical changes mean I can get lost in parts of the centre. Yet on another level, I am in tune with it and understand it more than I ever did in those initial twenty-one years. And certain loyalties remain. Each Saturday afternoon Notts County's is still the first football result I seek out (I spent many years dreaming of signing on for the team). But on a slightly more intellectual level, I recently had the luxury (not afforded to many) of properly analysing my relationship to Nottingham.

"In 2011, I spent a month on Sherwood Council Estate, living in the same street in which the Mortimers resided until I was nineteen. I wanted to move into the erstwhile Mortimer council house itself, but this proved impossible, so I settled for five doors away, where the resident family were refreshingly relaxed about a total stranger moving into the spare room.

"The book resulting from those four weeks and their significance, *Made in Nottingham* (Five Leaves), was often uncomfortable to write but established my relationship with the city for the rest of my life.

"Nottingham and I can now get on. I accept the city as part reality, part myth, part fable. At times, the knowledge it belongs to my lost youth, never to be recaptured, deflates me. Other times I am energised by what the city taught me, by how it released me into the world to become a real person, yet is happy to welcome me back on any return visit.

"On a recent trip I stood under the giant conker tree in Woodthorpe Park. I would once climb this, and some years ago my young son Dylan also climbed it on our visit from Tyneside. That ascent by Dylan and his lobbing down of the conkers to tumble noisily through the branches forged a link between two times, two generations.

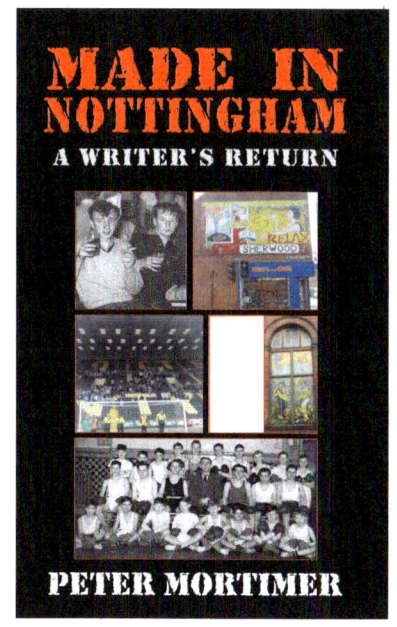

"I knew then that we must always leave the place of our childhood, but we never abandon it, and that we can visit the past but never live in it.

"Nottingham will never have the passionate sense of place known to Novocastrians. But neither will it run Newcastle's risk of nostalgia and sentimentality. It is a more practical place. It gets on.

"Writing *Made in Nottingham* was an emotional and intellectual experience, the gathering together, distilling, respecting and making sense of the past without indulging or sentimentalising it. There is no nostalgia, but there is deep feeling for those remembered hills between Sherwood and the city centre.

"The sight of a Pork Farms pork pie, Richard Green singing the corny song, 'Robin Hood' (played as Forest run out), the unexpected sound of a flat Nottingham accent ('nah then, serre!')... All these are to be kept in their place. And all are to be cherished."

Tanya Myers 1958–

"I was born in the Potteries in 1958 and settled in Nottingham in 1985 with my playwright husband Stephen Lowe and our two daughters.

"I am a theatre maker. Theatre is a collaborative craft fusing design, sound, music, lighting, film and, of course, performance. When writing I hope to fire the imagination of other artists. I always cradle future audiences in my mind, aware that one day we will share an embodied communion of moments.

"I have wrought performance for street, playgrounds and old factories in and around Nottingham, as well as conventional studios and theatre spaces in the UK and abroad. My plays include *Dance for Girls* (1986), a play exploring ancestral possession; *Pushing On* (1987), a large-scale street performance written and choreographed for Wheeler Gate in Nottingham for women, babies and wheel-chair users; and *Florence* – three generations of women, mother, daughter and myself seeking sense in my grandmother's suicide.

"I believe my plays mark 'rites of passage', written because they have to be written – marking personal transitions in my own and other's lives close to me. Often reflecting transitions such as loss, birth and trauma, they may serve as voyages of psychological healing. I wrote *Story Chair* after 9/11 to encourage local children to talk about their fears and dreams; *Shoes* (2004) was for my eldest daughter – exploring individuation, leaving home, a mother letting go – set on an ocean shore in a junk yard of shoes. Writing raw – sometimes it is difficult to analyse immediate meaning – but compelled by unconscious needs, I seek to touch emotional nerves of performers and audience alike. For the 1994 UK tour of *Falling Angels*, months were spent talking to Nottingham people from all faiths and creeds, researching attitudes to intercultural marriage, digging deeper into relationship questions of volition and commitment. Nottingham offers a perfect maelstrom for such honest dialogue – communities and individuals being eclectic yet accessible.

"*Small Waves* is about exile. Inspired by my Bosnian friend who lived in St Ann's – it's about self-acceptance, depression and a search for home within. *Promise to my Mother*, commissioned by Babel Sound – a prayer written prior to my mother's death – was translated into 120 languages and played through 100 speakers to visitors from all over the world.

"*Inside Out of Mind* is a play sourced from narratives of carers and nurses observed by ethnographic researchers working in dementia wards in Nottinghamshire. The poetry from accents and practise inform the dynamic and musicality of the text. Those nurses and carers originally observed are now transformed into theatre observers and hopefully empowered and valued by being placed centre-stage."

Julie Myerson 1960–

photo © Barney Jones

"I was born at the Firs Maternity Home in Sherwood in 1960 and lived in and around Nottingham – Mapperley Plains, Mapperley Park, Caythorpe, the city centre, Epperstone – until I left school. My mother's family weren't from Nottingham, but her Hungarian mother worked for a while in one of the lace factories and then ran a café at Trent Lock.

"My father was Managing Director of a knitwear factory in Ayr Street which had been started by his grandfather Alfred Pike. I remember vast rooms where ladies in overalls and slippers pedalled their feet on loud whirring machines. Also the dim-lit billiard room with its huge, green baize table, a man called Mr Lichfield who (mysteriously) had his name etched in the glass of his office door and the huge containers on wheels which my sisters and I loved to play in when we came round after school.

"I used a fictional version of Alfred Pike Ltd in my first novel *Sleepwalking* (1994). And *Out of Breath* (2008) was very much inspired by the years we spent out in the country at Caythorpe and later at Epperstone, where I'd get up at dawn and roam the fields looking for moorhen nests and digging up old bottles and clay pipe heads.

"*Not a Games Person* (2005) is a memoir covering my schooldays at the Wyvil School, Mountford House and Nottingham High School and is largely set in Nottingham. And in *Home: The Story of Everyone Who Ever Lived in Our House* (2004) I spent time going back to almost every house I had ever lived in as a child in Nottingham, partly as a way of trying to make sense of writing about the history of our house in London. But despite all of this, I haven't yet set a whole novel in Nottingham and I'm not sure why.

"My mother finally moved away from Nottingham ten or so years ago and, with no family there any more, I haven't been back in a while. I find that the older I get and the more distant the memories of my time there, the more I'm haunted by the place. There's an almost sinister kind of mystery to the city centre – all those caves and catacombs beneath the forest – and I love the flat, dusky-mauve beauty and bleakness of the countryside. It's a landscape that could easily provide inspiration for a future book – I just need to get there slowly and in my own time."

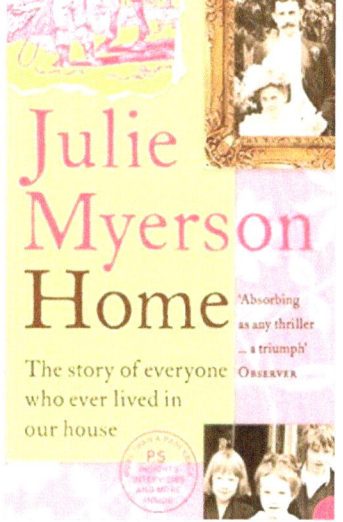

Henry Normal 1956–

"After stacking shelves at Fine Fare on Bracebridge Drive, Bilborough, I got a job in 1974 as an insurance broker's clerk in the centre of Nottingham. At lunchtime I would scour the local bookshops for comedy books. I read all the *Monty Python* books, the *MASH* series, Spike Milligan's books, any cartoon (*Honeysett* being my favourite), even James Thurber and Alan Coren. I read books of TV and radio scripts – I loved the Marx Brothers' scripts. I read some non-comedy books, including Alan Sillitoe's *Saturday Night and Sunday Morning* and *Loneliness of the Long Distance Runner*. I could relate to both of these, having been born in St Ann's and with my dad and my brother both working at Raleigh.

"I applied for a job as a trainee at Sisson and Parker's – a posh old fashioned shop that sold Parker pens and desk tidies along with books. I loved Sisson and Parker's, but the interviewer apparently didn't love me. He asked me only one question: 'Do you play football?' I told him I did and loved to watch Forest. I never heard from them again.

"What was it he saw in me that meant I wasn't the type that would be right to work with books? Was it my working-class Nottingham accent? My Burtons suit? My schooling? It made me set my jaw to succeed. I was determined to make my way in the world and do it by being myself.

"I joined a writers group at Angel Row Library that was part of the Worker Writers Federation. Once a year at Nottingham University all the UK groups had a conference, where I read some poems which seemed to go down well. This encouraged me to keep writing and performing, which I did at any chance I could in the pubs around Nottingham. Eventually I felt confident enough to try the local cabaret, Spotz, and managed to get a second booking.

"Widening my horizons, I started to perform around the country. I must have performed at almost a thousand events. I learned my trade on bills with the band Pulp, alongside Seamus Heaney and John Cooper Clarke, in factories, schools and hospitals. By the time I reached the Edinburgh Festival I was good enough to be offered my own Channel 4 TV show.

"Now living in Manchester, I met Caroline Aherne and Steve Coogan. I co-wrote, script-edited and associate produced all the *Mrs Merton* shows, and co-wrote all the early Coogan shows, other than *Alan Partridge*. I also co-wrote two *Mrs Merton* books and a *Paul and Pauline Calf* book – the sort of books I used to read as a young man in Bilborough.

"Along the way I changed my name to Henry Normal to always remind me where I'd come from. I was lucky enough as a boy from a council estate to work with great actors like Alan Rickman and Sigourney Weaver, and national treasures like Joanna Lumley and Dame Judi Dench. I even stood next to Gorbachev once.

"Last year, after thirty years of working in television, the last seventeen of which I ran Baby Cow Productions, I retired. We'd just been nominated for several Oscars for *Philomena* and had won every other award possible, most several times. This year I was given a special BAFTA for my services to the UK TV and Film industry.

"I've written several poetry books, and I'm writing a full length book on autism for Byron's publisher. It strikes me as ironic now when I think back to the job interview at Sisson and Parker's and wonder, if I'd got that job where would I be now?"

Eliza Sarah Oldham 1822–1905

'Death of a Drunkard' from *The Haunted House*

Eliza was born into the Sutton family of publishers and booksellers on Bridlesmith Gate, Nottingham. One of her brothers was the poet Henry Sutton. The Suttons were friends with the Howitts, and Eliza went to school with Anna Howitt. Later, she attended boarding school at Dalestorth House near Mansfield and studied art in Nottingham and Manchester.

In 1861 she was an art teacher, living in Painswick, Gloucestershire, with William Oldham, a radical free-thinker thirty years older than herself. The following year they were married and Eliza published a short temperance story, *The Haunted House*. Two years later, she won first prize from the Scottish Temperance League for her full-length novel, *By the Trent*, which remained in print into the 1900s.

Another drink, Mr Morris?
(*By the Trent*)

This book draws on areas she knew well: Wilford village is 'St Wilfrid's' in the book and Nottingham is 'Trentham'. Set in the 1830s, the plot carries a strong temperance message. The author skilfully interweaves the stories of several families to support the ideal of teetotalism at a time when it was considered fanatical. John Broadbent and his sister, Clara, live at St Wilfrid's. John is a fervent abstainer, rescuing and rehabilitating those he can, mostly in the poorer areas of Trentham. However, it is not just the poor who need help: Stephen Morris, a popular preacher in a fashionable church, needs a drink even to get into the pulpit. Oldham charts his awful descent into alcoholism, disgrace and finally, madness.

The Lee family, who live opposite St Mary's churchyard, are a decent family destroyed by drink. Mark Lee is a blind basket-maker whose youthful excesses have brought him to his present state; his daughter Veronica is a lace-mender working for a pittance and her sister Letitia is a prostitute. The characters are not irredeemable: Letitia, with whom Oldham sympathises, longs for a different life and eventually succeeds. The descriptions of this area after dark are truly Dickensian.

Dalestorth House

Every poet in Nottingham was in love with Wilford, which Oldham uses to represent an idyllic, pastoral way of life. The book finishes with singing and dancing at the Labourer's Institute beside the river and only water is drunk – from the Trent!

The Oldhams remained in close contact with the Howitts, and Eliza's friendship with Anna lasted more than fifty years. Eliza died in 1905 at Painswick in the house which she had named 'Howitt Villa'. She is buried with William at Kingston on Thames.

Places to visit

Nottingham: The Sutton's shop was on the corner of Bridlesmith Gate and Bottle Lane, demolished in 1852.

Lace Market: There are still some ancient corners around St Mary's Church and one can picture some of the scenes described.

Dalestorth House: Now a guest house and garden centre, on the corner of Skegby Lane (B6014) and Beck Lane.

John Oldham 1653–1683

Some authors passed through, some came to quietly die. It has been suggested that Oldham was consumptive and I do wonder if he had some kind of presentiment that Holme Pierrepont would be his final post. Born 9th August 1633 at Shipton, Gloucestershire, the son of a non-conformist minister, he studied at Edmund Hall, Oxford where he distinguished himself in Greek and Latin. By 1674, having nothing else in view, he became an usher at the free school in Croydon, a lowly, ill-paid job, progressing in 1678 to the position of private tutor to the grandsons of Sir Edward Thurland.

> **A plague of this fooling and plotting of late**
> ('The Careless Good Fellow')

He had already begun his short, brilliant career as a poet, his earliest traceable poem being a tribute to his friend Charles Morwent in 1675. He moved swiftly on to long, clever, satirical poems on the iniquities of contemporary society. John Dryden admired him, others thought him a mite crude, but whatever he wrote he did it with passion.

In 1682 he was invited by the young fourth Earl of Kingston to come to Holme Pierrepont as his chaplain, but Oldham declined to be dependent upon the gentry, agreeing instead to be the Earl's house-guest. It wasn't long before he sensed his end, expressing his fears in an anguished piece of prose, 'A Sunday-Thought in Sickness', and he died of smallpox on 9th December 1683.

If Oldham were writing today, he would find much to satirise in modern society, as the first verse of his song, 'The Careless Good Fellow' suggests:

> A plague of this fooling and plotting of late,
> What a pother and stir has it kept in the State;
> Let the rabble run mad with suspicions and fears,
> Let them scuffle and jar, till they go by the ears;
> Their grievances never shall trouble my pate,
> So I can enjoy my dear bottle in quiet.

Kingston paid tribute to his friend in an elaborate memorial – possibly designed by Grinling Gibbons – in the parish church. The fulsome Latin inscription asserts that "no one was more filled with holy rage, no one in themes was more sublime, or in words more happily daring!"

Places to visit

Holme Pierrepont Church:
Open at appointed times or borrow the key from the Hall. Oldham's fantastical memorial hangs from the pillar immediately inside the church door, you can't miss it.

Oldham's memorial at Holme Pierrepont Church

Geoffrey Palmer 1912–2005

Born in Edwinstowe, the son of Ivy and William Rabbitt, Geoffrey grew up at Kirkstall Lodge, a house built by his maternal grandfather. He attended Brunts Grammar School and University College, Nottingham, after which he worked as a teacher in Lowdham. As a Conscientious Objector in World War II he drove ambulances and began his own theatre company, entertaining the troops in the Far East. By this time he had changed his name to Palmer and met his partner, actor Noel Lloyd (1924–1998), with whom he would write and edit many books. His first and only adult novel, *To Church on Sunday*, was published in 1940.

After the war, Palmer returned to teaching, becoming Headmaster of Highbury Quadrant School in London. On his retirement in 1976, he and Noel opened the Compton Bookshop in Islington.

Geoffrey and Noel wrote more than thirty books together, including biographies, 'Observer' books, anthologies of ghost stories and other series for young people. They are remembered locally for a trio of children's adventure books set in and around Sherwood Forest: *Mystery in Sherwood* (1962), *The Greenwooders* (1963) and *Greenwooders' Triumph* (1964).

> I'm a descendant of Robin Hood.
> (*Greenwooders' Triumph*)

The Greenwooders are six children growing up in 'Edwinton' who know Sherwood Forest very well.

Tony and Felicity are the vicarage children, Stephen's father is the local doctor, Sam is the son of a farmer, and twins Peter and Pauline live at the Post Office. In *Mystery in Sherwood* – the only full-length adventure – a stolen box, strange goings-on in the Forest and a secret passage leading to a cache of treasure hidden at the Reformation, put several members of the gang in real danger. In the final frame Tony is almost killed after being imprisoned in the church bell-tower, but is saved by scribbling a message on a page torn from his I-Spy book – those were the days!

The other two books are made up of shorter adventures, and modern readers may be surprised that these children, aged between nine and thirteen, have such a lot of freedom and are allowed to take serious risks; for example in *Greenwooders' Triumph* when the River Medding (Meden) bursts its banks and the gang come to the rescue in a flimsy rubber dinghy. Firmly set in an Edwinstowe of the early 'sixties, these books are still very enjoyable.

Noel and Geoffrey spent their last years trading as Hermitage Books in Eye, Suffolk. Noel died in 1998, Geoffrey in 2005.

Places to visit

Kirkstall Lodge is at 40, High Street, Edwinstowe, next to the library, where you may still borrow signed copies of the *Greenwooder* books.
Sherwood Forest: of course!

Helena Pielichaty 1955–

"I moved to Nottinghamshire from Sheffield in 1985 when my husband found a job at Meritina, part of the former Nottingham Manufacturing Company, in Newark. My daughter was a baby at the time so I didn't immediately look for another teaching post to replace the one I'd left in Sheffield. What I did look for was something to fill this creative urge I had. Up to this point I had never considered myself to be a writer in any shape or form. Yes, I'd kept diaries during my teenage years but I doubt that they'd have troubled the likes of Samuel Pepys or even Adrian Mole. I had also written a few short playscripts to use with my classes but that was as far as it went, so why I enrolled on the WEA Creative Writing Course at Southwell Scout and Guide Hut, I have no idea.

"The course was only for six weeks and led by someone who ran a tea shop in Tuxford and had written for radio. For our first assignment we had to 'open with a bang.' Mine, set in a comprehensive school not dissimilar from the one I'd just left, began with swearing. Feedback from my group was mixed and ran along the lines of, 'children weren't like that in my day.'

"It didn't matter. I'd written something. Yes, it was rubbish, but I had written something. It was like turning on a tap that I couldn't turn off again. I continued to write despite returning to teaching and having another baby. I sought out further classes and the East Midlands Write Away weekend courses were ideal. My first one, 'Writing for Children', was led by Gwen Grant and Helen Cresswell. I couldn't believe my luck. I'd used Helen Cresswell's *Ordinary Jack* in class and Gwen Grant's *Private – Keep Out* was already a classic. That weekend was a defining moment in my writing career. Both tutors said I 'had something', and afterwards Gwen Grant mentored me, as she has so many fledgling Nottinghamshire writers, and set me on my way.

"My first book, *Vicious Circle*, was published by OUP in 1998. I have since had thirty-two books published and am working on the thirty-third. Without a doubt, Nottinghamshire, especially the Newark area, has greatly influenced my writing. *There's Only One Danny Ogle* and *Jade's Story* were set in Besthorpe and *Accidental Friends* in Newark. I might be from Yorkshire but my muse is definitely from Notts."

Samuel Plumb 1793–1858

Plumb was born on 11th Oct 1793 in an isolated cottage called 'The Odd Place' between Woodborough and Lambley. His father, George, a stockinger, was allowed to live rent-free on condition that he kept the deer from destroying his landlord's corn. The family moved to Southwell, to near Edingley, to Radford, and finally to Carlton-in-the-Willows in 1808.

At nineteen, Plumb began writing poetry and contributing to newspapers like Sutton's *Nottingham Review* as 'S.P.'. Spencer Hall wrote: "the charm there is in fields and woods and by riversides, having imbued his soul from childhood, began to show its effects in his maturing character." Plumb made use of the Artisans' Library in Nottingham and soon became known to Howitt, Millhouse, and others in the Sherwood Forest Group. He married at twenty-one, but his wife and infant child soon died; he made up his mind to emigrate, but was never able to afford it.

> "The old brown lines of rural liberty"
> ('On Footpaths')

Like many of the Sherwood Forest fellowship, Plumb was a great walker, and his poem 'On Footpaths' expresses his dismay as enclosure deprived the common people of these "old brown lines of rural liberty."

> With pain and indignation we behold
> Paths intersecting wood and flowery lea,
> The old brown lines of rural liberty,
> Ta'en one by one away: where, uncontrolled,
> Enjoying friendly converse, on we strolled
> Through scenes and haunts in which we loved to be,
> Fearless of lurking menial, and as free
> As is the wind. But now, oppressions bold
> With avarice leagued, upon our birthrights lay

Their grasping hands, shielded by laws severe.
These wrongs are ours, and much we think and fear
The time may come, nor distant far the day
When all these pleasant paths may disappear,
And none be left us but a
    bare highway.

Plumb continued to walk even when rheumatic and incapacitated in later years. Spencer Hall recalled, "I was stepping out of my door at Derby, when who should be stumping along the garden-path towards me but Samuel, with a little bundle in a blue cotton handkerchief, tucked under his arm, filled with manuscripts and printed slips from newspapers and asking me, in half-articulate words and with a tear in his eye, to get them published for him." (*Sketches*)

Gedling Church

Plumb died at Basford aged sixty-six and was buried on 2nd January 1859. Hall says, "Gedling Spire, one of the most picturesque landmarks in Nottinghamshire, overlooks his grave, with no other monument."

Places to visit

Gedling churchyard: where Plumb is buried.

Charles Plumbe 1813–1899

Believed to be a cousin of Samuel Plumb, Charles was born at Edingley where he was baptised on 1st August 1813, the son of Benjamin and Elizabeth Plumbe. He ran the Post Office in Sutton-in-Ashfield from 1837, and from 1844 published the first local newspaper from premises in the Market Place, *The Sherwood Gatherer*, "to which many well-known local literary men contributed." (Lindley, 1907). This was superseded in 1846 by the *Midland Gazette* which continued until 1885.

Plumbe was a good friend of Spencer Hall and involved with him in the Sherwood Forest Gatherings of the 1840s. Although predominantly a publisher and bookseller, he contributed poetry to local periodicals, a selection of which he published as *Fugitive Rhymes* (1884) under his own imprint, the Sherwood Press, dedicated to his wife Elizabeth and their children.

Appointed postmaster in Mansfield in 1863, he lived there for some years, returning to Sutton to live at Sherwood View on High Pavement, where he became Registrar of Births and Deaths.

> **... some boyish dream of bliss ...**
> (A Fragment)

In his poetry, Plumbe returns to his childhood around Edingley; in 'A Fragment' he recalls Southwell Minster, as seen and heard from Norwood Park:

> From here, where Norwood's green arcades extend
> And stately shades in foliag'd pomp ascend
> Through vista'd branches rich in Nature's smile,
> I view the towers of Southwell's ancient pile.
> I hear the music of its murmuring chime
> Ring sweetly forth to mark the lapse of Time,
> And, as each cadence rises on the gale,

Pale Mem'ry's musings o'er my breast prevail.
Each lengthen'd tone awakes some hidden spell
Whose latent powers within my bosom dwell,
Each lingering sound recalls some boyish dream
Of bliss – elusive as lightning's gleam...

When Hall died in 1885, he supplied the headstone and an affectionate epitaph for the grave of the 'Sherwood Forester':

Who, walking oft with nature, hand in hand,
Turned on her when she spoke, a raptured eye.
And then, retiring in his inmost heart,
There pondered all her teaching o'er again,
Until, o'er filled with gratitude and joy,
He tried to echo them in hymns to God,
And cheering words and work for suffering men.

Charles Plumbe died at Sherwood View on 15th August 1899. His son William carried on the Sherwood Press in White Hart Street, Mansfield.

Places to visit

Norwood Hall and Park are open to the public for special functions and Southwell's bells are audible from there. The illustration shows the Minster without its 'pepper-pots', as Plumbe knew it.

Southwell Minster, from Bailey's *History of the County of Nottingham*, 1853

Sutton-in-Ashfield: High Pavement is greatly changed but Sherwood View is thought to have stood on the corner of Crown Street, now called The Twitchell.

James Prior 1851–1922

The best of Prior's regional fiction anticipates D.H. Lawrence by at least a decade. Lawrence admired him, as did J.M. Barrie. Born on Mapperley Road, Nottingham, son of James Kirk, hat-maker, he had a private education but was to reject both the law (his father's choice) and millinery. Instead, he aspired to become a writer, cutting his teeth on short stories and plays. He married his cousin Lily in 1886, and settled at Lushai Cottage in Bingham where he continued to write as James Prior, looking to the Nottinghamshire countryside for inspiration.

Prior's best-known novel is *Forest Folk* (1901, recently republished by Leen Editions), set in and around Blidworth in the volatile era of the Luddites. Southerner Arthur Skrene, travelling to claim an inherited farm, witnesses an episode of violent machine-breaking on the Rufford Road by a group of local activists, including 'Tant' Rideout, a young farmer. Within the hour he has also met Rideout's feisty sister, Nell, ploughing the fields of Low Farm in men's clothing. She treats Arthur with hostility but he admires Nell's spirited defiance.

> It's no secret; they call it Gallers Hill.
> (*Forest Folk*)

Machine-breaking carried the death penalty, but Arthur's sister Lois saves Tant's neck by testifying in court; Nell is accused of witchcraft but Arthur saves her from drowning in a bog – the plot has all the ingredients of a rollicking historical adventure, but Prior transcends the genre by his sense of place and acute ear for dialect.

All the places in *Forest Folk* are real, from Blidworth Bottoms to Nottingham Assizes. Blidworth Methodist Chapel and Parish Church are the scenes of two untypical declarations of love between Lois and Tant, and Nell and Arthur.

Other titles by Prior include *Renie* (1895), *Ripple and Flood* (1897), *Fortuna Chance* (1910), *A Walking Gentleman* (1907) and *Hyssop* (1904). *Forest Folk* was republished by Leen Editions in 2017.

Prior died at Banks Cottage, Bingham in 1922.

Places to visit

Heywood Oaks Farm, Blidworth

Blidworth: Take the A60 Mansfield Road to Ravenshead and turn right at Larch Farm, following Main Road to Blidworth Bottoms near where 'Low Farmhouse' (home of the Rideouts) and 'High Farm' (the Skrenes' farm) are placed. High Farm is supposed to be Heywood Oaks Farm, which may be admired from the road.

Fishpool (the original name for Ravenshead), The Druid Stones and Rainworth, all mentioned in the book, are close by.

Bingham: Lushai Cottage is 19, Fisher Lane, Bingham, though it no longer bears the name. Prior is buried in the cemetery, near the railings alongside the Grantham Road.

Nottingham: Stand on the corner of Forest Road and Mansfield Road, opposite Saint Andrew's Church – this was Gallows ('Gallers') Hill where Tant Rideout narrowly escaped being hanged.

Paula Rawsthorne 1967–

"I was born in Liverpool in 1967 and came to study at Nottingham University over twenty years ago. I loved the city so much that I decided to stay. It was in this city that I first started to write stories, quite out of the blue, when I was in my thirties.

"In Nottingham I found a thriving and friendly writing community. The unique Nottingham Writers' Studio (NWS) and its dynamic Development Director, Pippa Hennessy, nurture and inspire the city's writers. I've been lucky enough to have my writing championed by so many of Nottingham's cultural community including NWS, Ross Bradshaw, Five Leaves Publications and *LeftLion* magazine. Nottingham is a city that takes pride in its authors' successes. I felt honoured to be commissioned to write a story for Nottingham's first ever 'Big City Read' and to be active in its successful bid to become a UNESCO City of Literature.

"In 2010 I was a winner of the Society of Children's Book Writers and Illustrators (SCWBI) 'Undiscovered Voices'. My young adult novels, *The Truth About Celia Frost* and *Blood Tracks*, are published by Usborne. *Celia Frost* was shortlisted for eleven literary awards, winning The Leeds Book Award (2012), Sefton Super Reads Award (2012), and the Nottingham Brilliant Book Award (2013). *Blood Tracks*, was shortlisted for several literary awards, winning the Rib Valley Book Award 2014. My third YA novel, 'Shell' will be published by Scholastic in Jan 2018. I'm currently writing my fourth novel.

"As well as novels I have short stories for adults published by Route in *Ideas Above Our Station* and *Bonne Route*. 'A Foreign Land' is published in *These Seven* by Five Leaves for Nottingham's Big City Read and my young adult (YA) story, 'A Level Playing Field' is published in the anthology, *Stories From the Edge*. My comic tale, 'The Sermon on the Mount', won a national BBC competition and was read by Bill Nighy on BBC Radio 4.

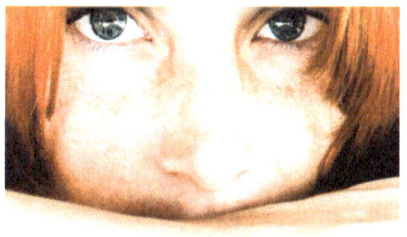

"For me, an important part of being a YA author is to work with teenagers to enthuse them about reading and writing. I'm invited into secondary schools throughout the country to do author visits and workshops and I'm also a writer-in-residence in a Nottingham school for the wonderful literacy charity, First Story. I'm a member of Nottingham Writers' Studio, SCBWI-BI and The Edge (a collective of YA writers). I feel proud to be part of my adopted city's literary community and I'm indebted to them, and to Nottingham, for their great support of my writing."

Lady Laura Ridding 1849–1939

Laura Ridding was born on 26th March 1849 in London. Her father was Roundall Palmer, later first Earl of Shelbourne, and her mother Lady Laura Waldegrave. In 1876, when she was twenty-seven, she married Rev. George Ridding, a widower, who was then headmaster of Winchester College. In 1884 George became the first Bishop of Southwell and supported by him, Laura, a keen suffragist, put a lot of energy into projects to help women and girls in Nottinghamshire, though her political beliefs were somewhat played down during George's bishopric.

After her husband's death in 1904, Laura recommenced her suffrage activities and was one of the founders of the National Union of Women Workers in 1895.

> **Jeanne was one of the same noble sisterhood.**
> *(By Weeping Cross)*

She was contributing essays and stories to periodicals like *The Monthly Packet* and *The Powder Magazine* as early as 1871. As Hannah Baud (2003) observes, "Many of Laura's published works were addressed to her fellow gentlewomen, placed as they were in ladies' journals. She advocated a wider education for ladies in order to realise their social responsibilities."

In later life she wrote three biographies: that of her husband George Ridding, of her sister Lady Sophia Palmer, and her nephew Robert Palmer.

She also found time to write one historical novel. *By Weeping Cross* (1899), which describes women's lives in Southern France in the mid-1400s through her heroine Jeanne Motte-Servolex, with more than one reference to the courage of the martyred Jeanne d'Arc.

Lady Laura died in 1939 and is buried beside her husband at Southwell Minster.

Places to visit

Southwell Minster: The Riddings lie in the churchyard to the left of the South Door to the Minster.

Laura Ridding's grave, Southwell Minster

Cecil Roberts 1892–1976

Cecil Edric Mornington Roberts was born on May 18th 1892, more-or-less where the Victoria Centre now stands, later moving with his family to Wilford Grove where he grew up.

He was a scholarship pupil at Mundella Grammar School and left at fifteen to began work as an office boy with the Corporation. When his father died, his wages were increased from eight shillings to seventeen shillings a week, as he had his mother to support.

He was already gazing poetically across the river to Wilford and Clifton Grove, and in 1912 won the Henry Kirke White Poetry Prize with a tribute to a dead school-friend: "Roll on, O Trent, though fierce thy raging flood/ Still fiercer is the grief within my heart."

> **This awful Nottingham accent! It's butter, not batter, my boy!**
> *(The Growing Boy)*

Roberts started work as an office boy and then became a junior reporter on the *Nottingham Journal*, then, at twenty-three, literary editor of the *Liverpool Post*.

His first novel, *Scissors* (1923), was inspired by a statuette of Dionysus in the Castle Museum, and lecture tours in America helped launch a highly successful career as a novelist.

He became an itinerant writer, spending much of his time in Venice, which is lovingly described in several works of fiction. He wrote more than fifty books of fiction, poetry, travel and memoirs, of which *The Growing Boy* (1967) and *The Years of Promise* (1968) should be of particular interest as they describe the literary landscape of Nottingham the early 1900s and his own development as an author.

In the 1930s, in a fit of nostalgia for his native land, Roberts bought a sixteenth-century cottage near Henley-upon-Thames and wrote a memoir *Gone Rustic* (1934) and three loosely-connected novels about it, *Pilgrim Cottage, The Guests Arrive* and *Volcano*. The settings range from Soviet Russia to a Venetian fort to the island of Santorini: intrigue, adventure and romance abound – very Cecil Roberts!

Roberts was made a Freeman of the City of Nottingham in 1965. He died in Rome on 20th December 1976 and his ashes were scattered at Pilgrim Cottage. One obituary noted that his life "often appeared to resemble a twentieth-century grand tour, strewn with places in the sun, grand seigneurs and charming hostesses..." The scholarship boy from the Meadows had travelled a long way.

Places to visit

The Nottingham Journal Offices: Next to the Coach and Horses pub on Parliament Street – Graham Greene's plaque is in the doorway.

Central Library on Angel Row: The Cecil Roberts Meeting Room is on the first floor.

Gertrude Savile 1697–1758

Another notable diarist, Gertrude was the third child – the youngest by sixteen years – of Rev. John Savile of Thornhill, Yorkshire and his wife Barbara Jennison. He died when Gertrude was three, the year his son George inherited the baronetcy of Thornhill and Rufford. Gertrude grew up at Rufford, resented and neglected by her mother and hating her financial dependence on her brother.

Her diaries begin in 1721 when she was twenty-four, shuffling back and forth between "the damping mortifications of my Brother's house" and the London home she shared with her mother. She spent her time reading novels and plays (an illuminating insight into contemporary literature), playing the harpsichord and doing hours of embroidery. Although she found company difficult due to a skin complaint, she often attended the theatre, returning again and again to favourite plays like *The Beggar's Opera*.

> **... the damping mortifications of my Brother's house.**
> (*Diaries*)

In the 1730s Gertrude received an unexpected legacy from a cousin which gave her independence for the first time, and in 1737, at the age of forty, she moved to a "little house in Farnsfield", the first home of her own.

> June 29–July 2 1742 – Journey from London to Farnsfield. Thank God a safe journey without the least accident or fright, and a pleasant one... I bless God I found all at my little home – my maid, horses, dogs etc. well, beyond my hopes or expectation, except my garden sadly neglected; scarce any fruit or anything but weeds... This summer has abounded much in Insects, as Fleas within doors, and without, wasps, earwigs and Pismires [ants] which destroys the little fruit there is.

She lived happily there for six years, returning to London in October 1744. The later entries in her diary dwell less upon personal matters than on the state of the country and politics. All in all, this is a valuable account of the period.

Gertrude died in March 1758. Her burial place is uncertain, though many of the family lie in Thornhill Church, Yorkshire.

Places to visit

Rufford Abbey where the "damping mortifications" have mostly been seen to.

Farnsfield: It is open to debate where Gertrude's house was, but still a pleasant place to visit.

Rufford Abbey

Miranda Seymour 1948–

"Born in 1948 in Nottinghamshire, I am best known for my prize-winning memoir, *In My Father's House*, in which I chart the life of an eccentric father and the extraordinary house with which he fell in love. Thrumpton Hall (now run as a business and wedding venue) was lived in by the Byron family for over a hundred years. Already the author of a biography of Mary Shelley, I am now completing a study of Victorian reputations, focussed on Lord Byron's wife, and his brilliant daughter, Ada Lovelace. One of my first books, *Count Manfred*, a historical novel, wove together the life of Byron with the story of the Nottinghamshire Riots.

"I have written biographies of Robert Graves, Ottoline Morrell and a group portrait of Henry James's English circle. My study of Anglo-German friendship, *Noble Endeavours*, was published in 2013. I have also written several novels including *The Telling* and *The Reluctant Devil*, and four children's books. A Fellow of the Royal Society of Literature, I have been President of Bromley House Library and, from 1997–2004, a Visiting Professor at Nottingham Trent University. I have also lectured at the University of Nottingham.

"Best known as a biographer and historian, I am also an essayist and critic, writing regularly for the *New York Times*, *The Guardian*, *The Sunday Times* and the *Daily Telegraph*. Five of my books have been picked for the *New York Times* Books of the Year award.

"As a writer, I have been profoundly influenced by the Nottinghamshire landscape in which I grew up.

Like many writers, I have been powerfully attracted to the wild moorland known as Clifton Pastures and to the history of the area with its wealth of Saxon and Roman remains in which my ancestral home and its unspoilt village lie.

"I count myself fortunate to have been a long-term friend of Nottinghamshire writer Alan Sillitoe and his wife Ruth Fainlight."

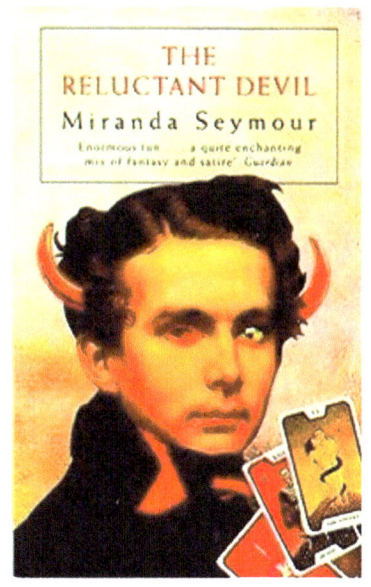

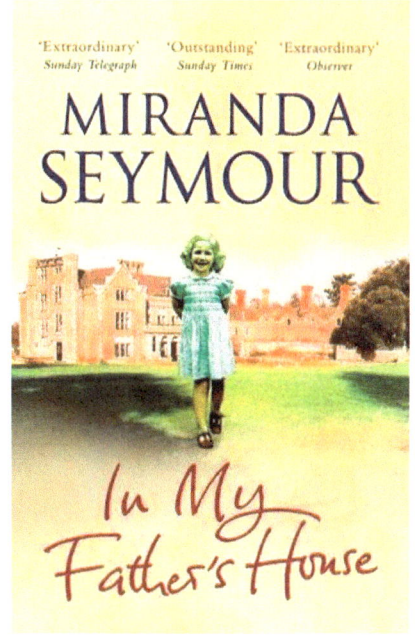

Alan Sillitoe 1928–2010

It is very hard to do justice to Alan Sillitoe in four hundred words, but I think he'd appreciate the democratic intentions...

Alan was born in Nottingham on 4th March 1928, the second of five children of Christopher Sillitoe and Sabina (*née* Burton). His father was mostly unemployed and the family moved often. Alan left school at fourteen and worked at Raleigh making bicycles until he joined the RAF in 1946 where he was a wireless operator. He was discharged in 1949 and began to write in earnest, but it was nearly a decade before his novel of Nottingham working-class life, *Saturday Night and Sunday Morning*, was published in 1958. It was a best-seller, and the film with Albert Finney as Arthur Seaton two years later fixed it forever on the Nottingham literary consciousness.

> **In the beginning was the word, and Adam was the Printer's Devil.**
> (*Raw Material*)

He returned to the Seaton family with *Key to the Door* (1961) and *The Open Door* (1989), the latter drawing on his wartime experiences in Malaya and beginnings as a writer through the character of Arthur Seaton's brother, Brian.

He was an adept at the short story and it's often forgotten that *The Loneliness of the Long-Distance Runner* (1953) was one – again filmed memorably with a young Tom Courtney in the lead. Another collection, *The Ragman's Daughter* (1963) is one of my personal favourites. He also wrote for children and wrote poetry.

Apart from the Hawthornden award for *Saturday Night and Sunday Morning*, Alan refused to allow his books to be put forward for prizes. However he did accept an honorary doctorate from the University of Nottingham and many of his fellow-authors were at the Council House to see him receive the Freedom of the City of Nottingham in June 2008. He said it was one of the greatest days of his life.

He was a regular visitor to Nottingham, a good friend to emerging writers and a supporter of local literary endeavours – when the Arts Theatre put on an amateur production of *Saturday Night and Sunday Morning* a few years ago, he appeared at the theatre to see the show, encourage the cast and chat to the audience. He was Hon. President of Bromley House Library when he died on 25th April 2010, and his wife, the poet Ruth Fainlight, not only stepped into the breach, but generously presented the Library with Alan's own book collection which may be viewed by appointment.

Albert Finney as Arthur Seaton in *Saturday Night and Sunday Morning*

Places to visit

There are Sillitoe trails available on the web and a permanent memorial to Alan is planned.

Ilkeston Road/ Faraday Road: Arthur Seaton's local, The White Horse, is currently a take-away.

Kim Slater

"I was born at the City Hospital in Nottingham and have lived in the area all my life. After living many years in Kirkby-in-Ashfield, at the age of forty I went back to Nottingham Trent University to study an English & Creative Writing degree, followed by an MA in Creative Writing.

"Whilst at university, I discovered the vibrant and thriving writing community that exists in the area. I particularly enjoy working with young people in local schools who are always enthusiastic and bursting with ideas and creative talent.

"For the last eight years I have lived just under two miles from the city centre by the river. This view was the inspiration for the main character in *Smart* finding the body of a dead homeless man in the River Trent at the beginning of the book.

"I am delighted that my publisher is very happy for me to set my Young Adult novels in the area. Setting my stories here is something that comes naturally. I feel that knowing Nottingham so well and using that knowledge in my work, lends an authenticity to my writing.

"I continue to be inspired every day by my surroundings and some of my favourite places; the Lace Market and the Creative Quarter, Green's Windmill and Colwick Park, have all found their way into scenes in the books.

"When I am writing for young people I like to try and include some of Nottingham's history if I can, such as its past status as the centre of the world's lace industry and the legend of Robin Hood.

"Before I became a full-time writer I worked as a freelance bursar in mainly inner-city schools, where I experienced Nottingham as a diverse and welcoming place to all who live or visit here.

"I am proud to be known as a Nottingham writer."

Kim Slater's *Smart* (2014) *A Seven-Letter Word* (2016) and *928 Miles from Home* (2017) are published by Macmillan Children's Books. She is also published by Bookouture (Hachette) writing international bestselling adult psychological thrillers set in Nottinghamshire under the name K.L. Slater.

John Collis Snaith 1876–1936

John Collis Snaith was born and raised in West Bridgford, the son of a paper manufacturer. He attended High Pavement School but left at thirteen to be a clerk on the Midland Railway, picking up his education again several years later with a scholarship to University College, Nottingham. He published his first book in 1895 when he was barely nineteen: *Mistress Dorothy Marvin* is a swash-buckling tale set in the 1740s in the aftermath of the Monmouth Rebellion. For a first book, it is astonishingly well-written, with plenty of intrigue and romance.

Sadly, Snaith has been the victim of literary snobbery, but is remembered locally for *Willow the King, the Story of a Cricket Match* (1900). The author sometimes played for Nottingham Forest Amateur Cricket Club to whom he dedicated the book. The action takes place over two days, at the annual match between Little Clumpton and Hickory, for whom the narrator, Richard Dimsdale, is to play for the first time.

> ... to become a classic in one's own lifetime...
> *(Willow the King)*

> To appear at Little Clumpton v. Hickory was not the lot of common men. Only the elect could hope to do so. To take wickets or make a score at this encounter was to become a classic in one's lifetime... Therefore do not let the young think, as unhappily they do just now, that they must write a book to become immortal. Why will not a few thousands of these seekers after fame, these budding novelists and early poets, take to cricket?

The heroine, Miss Laura Mary Trentham, is known as Grace "because she keeps five portraits of that hero [W.G.] on her bedroom mantelpiece" and can "bowl like hell and hit like kicking horses." Dimsdale is bowled out l.b.w. for seven, but that enables him to sit beside Grace at the scoreboard and comment on the rest of the match. Romance, naturally, blossoms.

Snaith was apparently reclusive and revealed very little about himself, saying, "If people want to know what I am like, let them read my books." Perhaps his secret personality is to be found in the many flawed but romantic heroes he created so well in nearly forty novels, including *Fortune* (1910), a chivalric pastiche, and *Araminta* (1923), an Austen-esque comedy of manners. His heroines are invariably unconventional, spirited and funny.

He died in London, aged sixty.

frontispiece for *Willow the King*

Places to visit

Bridgford Road: The Snaiths lived here at number 68 – a stone's-throw from Trent Bridge Cricket Ground.

The Forest: Nottingham Forest Amateurs played, more humbly, here.

Michael Standen 1937–2008

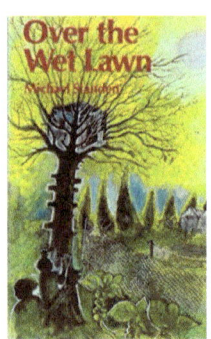

Standen was born in Epsom on 28th July 1937, but attended High Pavement School in Nottingham before doing his National Service, after which he read English at Cambridge. He taught in Manchester before his appointment as Organiser for the Northern District of the WEA.

His relatively short time in Nottingham was productive, in that his first novel, *Start Somewhere* (1965) is set firmly here. It follows a group of sixth-formers, around 1961, exploring their options, experimenting with relationships and starting to break away from their parents' aspirations and opinions.

To anyone who was at secondary school in Nottingham in that period, much of the detail and background will be very familiar. The twinned Grammar Schools – for boys and girls – must be High Pavement and the Manning School, and the coffee bar must be the El Toreador!

> **It was a museum without a roof: arboretum, aviary, shrubbery...**
> (*Start Somewhere*)

The rest is fiction, but it rings true even fifty years later. At the heart of the action is the Arboretum, where Frank Griffin, Tony Popkin and Anne Cooper trespass after lock-up one night, and set in motion a train of humorous – and painful – repercussions. This is a classic evocation of young adulthood (before the term was coined) in Nottingham in the 'sixties.

More novels followed: *A Sane and Able Man* (1966), *Stick-man* (1970) and *The Dreamland Tree* (1972) and a fine children's book, *Over the Wet Lawn* (1977), set

The Arboretum

towards the end of WW2. Standen then turned to poetry, *Time's Fly-Past* (1991) being his first collection.

Michael Standen died in Durham on 1st June 2008. He was another bird of passage flying through Nottingham, but a significant one. *Start Somewhere* was republished by Shoestring Press in 2009.

Places to visit

The Arboretum: 'The People's Park' has remained the same though the rest of Nottingham has greatly changed.

Forest Fields: In Standen's day High Pavement School was on Stanley Road and the building is still there.

Henry Septimus Sutton 1825–1901

Born on 10th February 1825, Henry was the seventh child of Richard Sutton, bookseller of Bridlesmith Gate and proprietor of the *Nottingham Review*. His elder brother John was author of the *Nottingham Date Book* and Eliza Oldham was his sister. As a young man, Sutton was apprenticed to a local druggist and later articled to a surgeon in Cambridgeshire. Being rather small of stature and of a deceptively youthful appearance, he found it difficult to be taken seriously by his clients and returned to Nottingham where he learnt shorthand and became a reporter on the family paper, the *Review*.

Henry was influenced by the works of Ralph Waldo Emerson, evident in his first prose book, *The Evangel of Love* (1847). He met Emerson when he lectured in Nottingham and they became life-long friends. Henry was appointed to the *Manchester Examiner and Times* in 1850 and began to explore the writings of Swedenborg; his *Quinquenergia: Proposals for a New Practical Theology* (1854) was the result. He joined the Swedenborgian church in Peter Street and became a lay preacher. Much of his later writing consists of theological debate. He was a vegetarian and a total abstainer – as were the Oldhams.

> "Another drop of that still-flowing tide."
> ('The Hemlock Stone')

Henry Sutton was an able poet. *Clifton Grove Garland* (1848), dedicated to Eliza, is an affectionate tribute to his literary contemporaries: Henry Kirke White, the Howitts, Thomas Miller, Spencer Hall, Philip James Bailey, and their friend Charles Pemberton – not a Nottingham writer, but an actor and philosopher who appeared on the scene from time to time. Sutton imagines them all together, walking, talking and enjoying those places along the Trent which inspired their writing. Pemberton tells the legend of 'The Fair Maid of Clifton' – and then Sutton emerges from the idyll and goes home.

For a change of scenery, this extract from 'The Hemlock Stone' is a nice meditation on an ancient Nottinghamshire landmark:

The Hemlock Stone

> Haply the Roman soldier here has stood,
> Stray'd from his camp far into the wild wood:
> The monk, at least, on palfrey ambling past,
> Shaken by the rough bridle-road, has cast
> A hot glance on thee: the knight, steel-array'd,
> A breathing moment near thy bulk has stray'd
> To bid his squire behold: gay Cavalier
> And solemn stern old Roundhead have been here:
> Lovers and maidens: lords, and squires, and pages:
> Serf, farmer, village-fool. Ages on ages
> Of human life hast thou seen onward glide.
> At last I stand upon thy wither'd side,
> Another drop of that still-flowing tide.

Sutton died on 2nd May 1901 in Yarborough Street, Moss Side, Manchester.

Places to visit

The Hemlock Stone: An ancient outcrop of sandstone at Stapleford. A free festival takes place on the site in June.

Jenny Swann 1955–

"I was born in Hampstead, London in 1955. I moved to Nottingham in 2004, where I continue to live. My poetry collections include *Flesh Tones* (2000), *Soft Landings* (2002) and *Stay* (2003) and my poems have featured in various anthologies, including *The Forward Book of Poetry*. Much of my poetry was written before I moved to Nottingham, although one pre-occupation in my last poetry collection, *Stay* (published by Nottingham's Shoestring Press) was my imminent move to the area. I have also published works on children's nutrition, including *Lunchbox Pro* (2005) and *Five-a-Day Pro* (2006).

"In 2008 I set up Candlestick Press in Beeston and ran it until 2016 when I stood down. Nottingham was the perfect place to set up the Press, as it offered – and

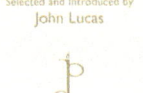

continues to offer – just the right cultural mix of North and South, modesty and determination, creativity and humour! One of our publications, *Ten Poems about Nottingham*, has always felt to me like a small 'thank you' to Nottingham for the literary infrastructure that enabled the Press to flourish.

"The literary community is alive and generous and exciting. Who could ask for more?"

Charles Bell Taylor 1829-1909

Born in Nottingham, Taylor was an ophthalmic surgeon at Nottingham Eye Infirmary from 1859 for nearly fifty years, where he is said to have had hundreds of consultations and performed up to ten operations a day. He opposed the Contagious Diseases Act, vivisection and compulsory vaccination and published a number of lectures, including *The Statistical Results of the Contagious Diseases Acts – showing their total failure in a sanitary point of view. Being a paper read before the Medical Society of London, etc.* (1872) and *For Pity's Sake*, published by the London & Provincial Anti-Vivisection Society (1908).

In an impassioned address, *Vivisection: is it Justifiable?* given to the Medico-Chirurgical Society of Nottingham in 1892, he concluded:

> The main task of civilization has ever been the vindication of the rights of the weak. Animals have rights (so much is conceded by our laws), and men have duties towards them; and for us to ignore the one, or counsel neglect of the other, is simply to proclaim ourselves enemies of the human race and its destined progress.

The dog... sat up and begged for its life.
(Vivisection)

He lived and died at Beechwood Hall in Mapperley Park, thought to be 30a, Mapperley Road, a Fothergill Watson design. He has an impressive grave in the General Cemetery which bears the inscription, "A generous benefactor of the poor, a devoted friend of animals, an opponent of every form of cruelty and oppression, and a fearless champion of liberty."

There used to be a sculpture of a little dog on his grave but it has run away.

Places to visit

General Cemetery: Take the path straight ahead from Canning Circus, go through the small car park and turn immediately left as you leave it. The Taylor monument is in a dip off the path – you can't miss it!

The Taylor monument,
General Cemetery, Nottingham

Christopher Thomson 1799–1871

Born in Kingston-upon-Hull on 25th December 1799, Thomson was the son of a Scottish shipwright, to whose trade he was also apprenticed, but learned little. What he did discover was a talent for art, a thirst for education and an obsession with the theatre. He joined a whaling ship to Greenland but was a poor sailor and decided to try the stage instead, convinced that plays were a means of elevating poor working people: "Many a time have I felt my soul light up with pure and holy fire at the altar of our Shakespeare..." The reality was harsher; Thomson joined one company of strolling players after another, accompanied by his wife and children. They were often starving, walking from one town to another with their props and scenery on their backs.

> **Brother artisans, up, then, with the banner of education!**
> (*Autobiography of an Artisan*)

Thomson contributed to Plumbe's *Sherwood Gatherer* and wrote one book, *The Autobiography of an Artisan* (1847). It is a valuable insight into an actor's life in the early nineteenth century, but more remarkable is his burning desire to make literacy and knowledge available to every working man and woman, which was truly ignited when he settled in Edwinstowe in 1832 as a house painter. He was instrumental in establishing an Artisans' Library and Mutual Improvement Society, membership a penny a week, as well as free evening classes and lectures, to help lift people out of poverty.

From this endeavour grew the idea to append a literary element to the annual village feast, and the Sherwood Forest Gatherings began. The first was in November 1841, spearheaded by Thomson, Spencer Hall and a Mr Trueman. It received enthusiastic coverage in the local press. Participants travelled miles to celebrate their literary heritage, with toasts and song to honour the Howitts, Thomas Miller, Charles Plumbe and Sidney Giles.

Hall said of Thomson:

Ye Olde Jug and Glass, Edwinstowe

... he had a wonderful power of stirring latent cords of thought and feeling, till, under his vivid mind, even the commonest topics would partake something of his own picturesqueness and novelty. Wherefore, whether in the village club-room, the 'Sherwood gathering', the more popular and urban assembly, or some circle by the private fireside, there was always a true ring of his metal, however unpolished it might be. (*Sketches*)

Thomson died in Sheffield in January 1871, followed a few days later by his wife Hannah.

Places to visit

Edwinstowe: Ye Olde Jug and Glass pub on High Street, where Thomson began the first penny library in 1838, and the Reading Rooms, opposite.

John Ronald Reul Tolkein 1892–1973

The author of *The Hobbit* and *The Lord of the Rings* used to stay with his Aunt Jane Neave at Phoenix Farm (originally Church Farm) at Gedling, where in 1914, at the age of twenty-two, he wrote 'The Voyage of Earendel the Evening Star,' a poem which was the germ of the great mythological landscape of his famous books. Tolkien's mother had died when he was twelve and her sister, "dearest Aunt Jane" took the Tolkien boys under her wing.

Jane Suffield was a science graduate and a teacher until her marriage to Edwin Neave in 1905. His work brought them to Nottingham and they lived in The Cottage, Shearing Hill. After Edwin died in 1909 Jane spent a couple of years working as Warden at University Hall, St Andrew's, returning to Gedling when she and her friend Ellen Brookes-Smith bought the farm from the Manvers Estate and embarked on an agricultural project between 1912 and 1922. After leaving Gedling, Jane continued farming at Dormston, Worcestershire. The farm was called Bag End, a name familiar to readers of *The Hobbit*.

Dearest Aunt Jane...

For more details of Phoenix Farm and the poem, see *Tolkien's Gedling* by Andrew H. Morton and John Hayes. I am indebted to them for this interesting piece of research.

Places to visit

Phoenix Farm: This stood close to All Hallows Church, on the opposite side of Arnold Lane, roughly between Wykes Avenue and Jessops Lane. Unfortunately it was demolished by the Coal Board in 1953–4, but it was very similar to Manor Farm which still exists a little further up the road, on the right, just before Avon Road. Take a look.

Manor Farm, Arnold Lane, Gedling

Geoffrey Trease 1909–1998

Robert Geoffrey Trease was born in Nottingham on 11th August 1909. His grandfather came from Loughborough to take over Weavers Wine Merchants in 1897, and Geoffrey was brought up at 142, Portland Road. He describes his childhood world as "narrow" but his imagination was boundless. In *A Whiff of Burnt Boats* (1971) he writes: "I preferred on the whole to go to school by myself, muttering stories as I trotted along, accelerating to a wild gallop as I passed shadowy gateways that threatened ambushes by Germans, highwaymen or Amazonian Indians."

He followed his two brothers to the High School and went to Oxford on a Classics scholarship, but was bored and left after a year. He worked in a settlement in the East End of London and became involved in left-wing politics, and out of these experiences came his first children's book, *Bows Against the Barons* (1934), a radical take on the Robin Hood stories which Anne Thwaite declared, "A milestone in the history of children's literature" (Obituary, *Independent*). Trease had begun his long, successful writing career, writing 113 books between 1934 and 1997.

> **The royal castle ... like a lion upon its tawny rock.**
> (*Red Towers of Granada*)

He is well-known for his historical novels for children – no mock-mediaeval language, just plain English – and several have their roots in Nottingham history, for example, *The Red Towers of Granada* (1966). In 1290, a boy called Robin, branded a leper and cast out of his village, rescues an elderly Jew from an attack in Sherwood Forest. Solomon, a doctor, is certain Robin is no leper and they head for Nottingham, to the Jewish quarter between Hounds Gate and Castle Gate, where Robin's skin complaint is soon healed. King Edward I and his entourage visit the town and Queen Eleanor asks Solomon to obtain for her the Elixir of Life. So, Solomon and Robin set off for Spain to find it. It is a brilliant story, enhanced in the original edition by Charles Keeping's illustrations. A

book for younger children, *A Flight of Angels* (1988), is set in the network of caves beneath the city.

Trease wrote non-fiction, including *Nottingham, A Biography* (1970). He also wrote plays – a programme survives for *Colony*, an unpublished play set on a sugar plantation, produced in Nottingham by the Socialist Progressive Theatre. Trease wore his politics bravely.

Geoffrey and his wife Marian moved to Colwell near Malvern where they lived for thirty-two years. Geoffrey died in Bath on 27th January 1998.

Places to visit

Nottingham: Many old streets around the Castle were 'redeveloped' in the 1960s but Trease remembered them: St Nicholas Street, behind the 'Royal Children' was known in 1255 as *Venella Judaeorum* or Jew Lane. The Trease house on Portland Road has gone, but Weavers Wine Merchants is still in the family and thrives on Castle Gate – highly recommended!

Sarah Agnes Turk 1859-1927

Vista Villas, Corporation Oaks, Nottingham

Sarah Ann Agnes Turk was born in 1859 in Manchester, the daughter of George Turk, a gunner in the Royal Artillery, and his Irish wife Sabina. By 1881, George had left the Army and become a gardener in Mapperley, where Sarah worked as a dressmaker and her younger sister Maria was a pupil teacher. In 1893 the widowed Sabina and her daughters moved to Winchester. Both were teaching in Sleaford when their mother died in 1904.

Sarah began to emerge as a published author in 1908 with *Nemesis*, a book of short stories. Then in 1909 she wrote *Joan of Arc: a Sacred Drama*: it's not a great play, but was worthy of notice from the Vatican, who awarded it a Papal Blessing.

> ... the Banshee of Carickferneagh – the doom of the McDermots!
> (*The Secret of Carickferneagh Castle*)

In 1911 followed *Walter Chisolm's Niece*, a moral tale about a fashionable London physician who has abandoned his faith, but through the saintly example of his niece is safely brought back into the Catholic Church. *The Master of Lishmaire Grange* has a similar theme, with a liberal sprinkling of tempests, long-lost husbands and mysterious portraits for good measure. Sarah continued in this style with *The Secret of Carickferneagh Castle, an Irish Romance* (1914):

> It was a wild night, the wind swept around the ancient Castle of Carickfearneagh in a terrible hurricane; it

howled and shrieked through the corridors like a demon let loose...

It is the Banshee of the McDermots which howls as the Witch of Carickfearneagh appears with a dead girl in her arms – the abandoned child-wife of the wicked Lord. Poisonings, shootings, stolen inheritances and babies swapped at birth proliferate, but gallant Detective Mara and the French maid untangle all the plots. Turk packs enough action into 200 pages to fill a triple-decker novel.

Turk grave, General Cemetery, Nottingham

Maria seems to have collaborated with at least one of Sarah's novels, *The Marriage Bond Only Death Can Sunder* (1912), writing as 'Jeannie Turk'.

The sisters returned to Nottingham. Sarah died on 6th February 1927 at Vista Villas, Corporation Oaks, and Maria at 85, Allendale Avenue, Aspley in 1932. They are buried in the same plot as their parents in the General Cemetery.

Places to visit

Vista Villas, 18, Corporation Oaks: The name is on the gate-post.
General Cemetery: Follow the centre path downhill from
 Canning Circus. The Turk grave is on a bend on the left.

Anna Mary Howitt Watts 1824–1884

sketch by Dante Gabriel Rossetti

The eldest daughter of William and Mary Howitt, Anna was born in Nottingham and received her early education with a Miss Stone, a Unitarian, alongside Eliza Sutton (who became Eliza Oldham). Anna and her sister Margaret received some further education at Ackworth School, Pontefract. Anna was a gifted artist and at the age of fifteen, illustrated her mother's *Hymns and Fireside Verses*.

The Howitts lived in Heidelberg for three years, then returned to live in Clapham, and in 1846 Anna attended Henry Sass's Art School in London, one of the few places open to women. Rossetti and Holman Hunt were students there and Anna's style placed her with the Pre-Raphaelites. Frustrated in not being able to study in the Royal Academy Schools, she and her friend Jane Benham, a book illustrator, went to Munich in 1850 for two years to study art. From this enriching experience came *An Art Student in Munich* (1854). In the book Jane is 'Clare' and their friend Barbara Leigh Smith is 'Justina'. Together these women formed a support group, 'Sisters in Art'. The last few pages of the book reflect upon women's issues and their place in a man's world.

> **Noble women who have yet to arise... enact noble deeds.**
> *(An Art Student in Munich)*

The subject matter of Anna's paintings – often a comment on the double sexual standards of the time – earned Anna only criticism. John Ruskin was hostile and derogatory about her work and wrote to her in terms which devastated her, to the extent that she destroyed all her pictures and never painted again, though she did continue to illustrate her mother's books.

Anna had a serious breakdown and retreated into spiritualism from which later came *Pioneers of the Spiritual Reformation* (1883), part of which is about her father, William. Aged thirty-five, she married Alfred Alaric Watts and together they wrote a book of poetry, *Aurora: a volume of verse* (1884). Anna died suddenly of diphtheria on 23rd July 1884 whilst visiting her mother at Dietenheim in the Tyrol and is buried in the Catholic cemetery there.

Places to visit

South Parade: (site of Wetherspoons) where Anna spent her childhood – the property is believed to be that described in Mary Howitt's *The Childhood of Mary Leeson*.

ARCHWAY OF THE VILLAGE CHURCH.

Village church at Deitenheim, where Anna Mary Watts is buried

Matthew Welton 1969–

"Just about the most f*****-up thing a childless, forty-something, unmarried man can do is to move from the city in which he's been mostly happy all his adult life and go back to the city in which he was born and brought up. At least that's what my therapist said.

"Manchester is a place people go to make things happen. The legacy of the industrial revolution is a city that doesn't do a thing without doing it with ballsiness and bustle. I'd moved there to go to university, and had stayed twenty years. And the things that I felt made my life what it was were, I thought, all Manchester things. Endless afternoons trawling galleries and bookshops; endless evenings at poetry readings and gigs, followed up with long conversations in a corner of a buzzy bar; endless mornings at my table by the window, not going out until I'd actually written something. Outside of Manchester, I wasn't sure that these things even happened.

"Another thing the therapist said was it is our needs that define who we are, and on some level I knew needed to live somewhere quirkier and quieter. And when a job came up at the University of Nottingham it was enough to bring me home.

"The thing with Manchester was that in a way it always felt that everybody was fighting for the cause, though it was never exactly clear what that cause was. Nottingham isn't the kind of place that's always in the headlines, but its stories endure because they're all mildly weird. I grew up hearing about cricketers whose graves are the length of a cricket strip apart, and being proud of workers smashing up weaving machinery. The world's most famous dispensing chemist. Evangelists with tambourines. There's a music hall still standing. The windmill hasn't gone away. Who'd want to be famous for ice dancers?

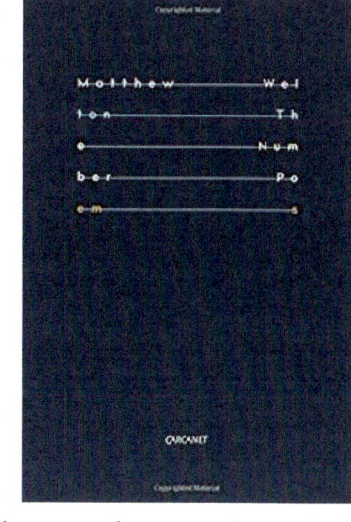

"And I would like to think that there's something of that mild weirdness in my writing. My poems are more like lists than poems. Or like skipping rhymes that go on forever and ever. And if someone asks me to write something of 400 words, for example, 400 words is exactly what they'll get.

MATTHEW WELTON *The Book of Matthew*

"So I'm still here making my weird little poems, feeling appreciated but in no danger of getting famous. 'Can any good ever come of this?' somebody once asked me. More than ever, I'm thinking it might."

Dorothy Whipple 1893–1966

Dorothy Stirrup was born in Blackburn, the daughter of an architect. In 1917 she married Henry Whipple, and in 1925 they moved to Nottingham when he was appointed Director of Education. They lived on Ebers Road, where her writing career began. In the 1930s she and her husband rented one of the lodges at Newstead Abbey as a weekend retreat. She writes in her autobiography, *The Other Day* (1950):

> The avenue of the years stands before my mind's eye... Any excuse will serve to look again at this lovely, dreaming vista. The path under the arching trees leads somewhere out of sight, and because of this, enchantment lies upon it.

She was very fond of the cottage and of the Abbey itself, which provided inspiration for Saunby, the decaying country house, in her fifth novel, *The Priory* (1939):

> So, one evening as the May dusk was falling, Christine returned. Stiff after the long drive, she clambered out of the car and stood once more on the gravel sweep before the Priory. The air passed like a cool hand over her eyelids and round the back of her neck. In her creased suit, her figure distorted, she stood, letting her eyes visit every feature of the West Front. It was always the West Front you looked at first at Saunby. The birds were nesting, as usual, she noticed, in the Virgin's crown... 'This is my home. This is what I love,' she was thinking, and her thoughts showed in her face.

... enchantment lies upon it
(*The Other Day*)

Whipple wrote sixteen novels and collections of short stories. *They Knew Mr Knight* (1934) and *They Were Sisters* (1943) were made into films. A popular novelist of the 1930s and 1940s, she had been undeservedly neglected until Persephone Books began to reprint some of her best novels, including *Someone at a Distance* (1953) and *High Wages* (1932), as well as those already mentioned.

After Henry's death in 1958, Dorothy returned to Blackburn and died there in 1966.

Places to visit

Newstead Abbey: Walk up the avenue from the gates, if you are able, and view the West Front – there may still be birds nesting in the Virgin's crown.

Ebers Road, Mapperley Park: The Whipples lived at number 35.

Henry Kirke White 1785–1806

Henry Kirke White was born 21st March 1785, the second son of a butcher, John White, and his wife Mary Neville, in Exchange Alley, Cheapside. He was something of a prodigy, articled to Coldham and Enfield, attorneys, at the age of fourteen. In spite of working twelve hours a day, he read and studied voraciously, learning several languages and experimenting with the poetic form. By 1801 he was a regular contributor to different periodicals.

In 1803 his first book of poetry, *Clifton Grove*, was published:

> Now, now, my solitary way I bend
> Where solemn groves in awful state impend,
> And cliffs, that boldly rise above the plain,
> Bespeak, best Clifton! thy sublime domain.

Beneath this yew I would be sepulchred
(*On Recovery from Sickness*)

He is forever connected to Wilford because the area inspired many of his poems. After his death, 'Kirke White's Cottage' became a tourist attraction, though he only spent a few weeks there before going to university. Benefactors, including William Wilberforce, made it possible for Henry to go to Cambridge with the intention of entering the church, but he was already in poor health and died of consumption on 19th October 1806, aged twenty-one.

Robert Southey, the Poet Laureate, edited White's poetry and the melancholy romance of the poet's untimely death caused a rash of poetic tributes at the time, including one from Byron, who observed that "even his prejudices were respectable"! He referred to the poet's Christian piety and the hymns he wrote, including 'Oft in Danger, Oft in Woe'.

White wrote 'On Recovery from Sickness' in Wilford churchyard:

> Here would I wish to sleep. – This is the spot
> Which I have long mark'd out to lay my bones in;
> Tired out and wearied with the riotous world,
> Beneath this yew I would be sepulchred.
> It is a lovely spot!

He was buried at All Saints, Cambridge, but legend has it that when the church was demolished in 1870, his remains were cremated and scattered at Wilford, as he had wished.

Wilford churchyard

Places to visit

Wilford Church: White's ashes may or may not be scattered there, but the church has two memorials to him – a portrait plaque high up on the north wall inside, and a memorial window of the Nativity based on his poem, 'The Star of Bethlehem'.

White's birthplace: Demolished when the present Council House was built, it was in the vicinity of modern Cheapside to the right of the Council House.

Nottingham Castle: A handsome memorial bust in the colonnade.

Amanda Whittington 1968–

"We all need a place to begin. A place like Nottingham Playhouse in the mid-1980s with a 50p schools ticket once a month, where I saw plays I had no knowledge of until the curtain came up: *Mother Courage and Her Children*, *The Rocky Horror Show*, *The Normal Heart*, *Blood Brothers*. Four shows that resonate still, and so many more which laid out a vision of what theatre was and could be.

"What I didn't see in the 'eighties were new plays by people like me. Playwrights were old or dead or foreign or male. I'd wanted to write since I'd learned to read, but how would I find a way in? The stage door appeared locked and bolted, but aged nineteen, with a typewriter and a £40-a-week grant from the Enterprise Allowance Scheme, I set myself up as a journalist. Like Julie Burchill, I hoped.

"My first paid job was a 2,000-word feature for not-so-cutting-edge magazine, *Office Secretary*. Yet soon after, the *Evening Post* let me loose on a music column and later, a weekly 1000-word feature. This gave me an ear for stories, which soon found expression in the plays I'd started to write. (Well, type.) Nottingham's Takeaway Theatre produced my first two plays, in the Old Vic and the Filly & Firkin pubs. I worked for ten years as a journalist but little by little, the stage door was opening.

"The local paper and pub theatre were my apprenticeship. The two aren't so different: a features writer shapes stories from interview quotes, a playwright tells stories in dialogue. I got a Mac and cut my theatrical teeth on commissions for New Perspectives: six in all, three for youth theatre and three touring shows. As I learned my craft in Nottingham, British theatre was changing. The so-called 'development culture' opened the door to a new generation of new writing. When Soho Theatre staged *Be My Baby* in 1998, I was on my way too.

"I've now written over thirty plays for theatre and radio: *Mighty Atoms*, *The Thrill of Love*, *Ladies Day*, *Amateur Girl* and *D for Dexter* among them. They've played in theatres great and small, in regional reps from Oldham to Salisbury, in village halls and schools. Three were produced by Nottingham Playhouse, which in the last twenty years has brought forth so many Nottingham playwrights, including myself. We all need a place to begin, but we don't make the journey alone. I found champions, comrades and friends here in Nottingham. I found my voice."

Sarah Johanna Williams 1806–1841

Inscription to the 'Centre Oak' on Cromwell House, Mansfield

Sarah Johanna Williams (known as Joanna) was born in Halifax, the second daughter of Rev. John Williams and his wife, Bridget Aldred. In 1811 her father was appointed minister of The Old Meeting House in Mansfield, where he also ran a Commercial Academy, offering, "An extensive and increasing Library, including Philosophical apparatus etc. etc. in order to call forth and gratify spirit of curiosity and enquiry." It appears that his children – including his daughters – also benefitted from these facilities.

> **Thou woulds't not be forgot**
> ('Sherwood Forest: a poem')

Spencer Hall mentions Joanna attending Richard Howitt's literary gatherings in the 1830s, with her "truly bright thoughts... like a star apart." In 1831, she won a prize offered by the Literary Society of Nottingham for a long poem which was published and received enthusiastic reviews. 'Sherwood Forest: a Poem' has forty-seven verses which the twenty-five year-old author was obliged to read aloud to the Literary Society – no mean feat. It is well-written, drawing upon archaeological evidence of people like Thoroton, Throsby and Rooke, and describes the forest's long history as the Romans, Saxons, Danes and Normans in turn passed through it.

One of the final verses chimes in well with the concerns of the Sherwood Forest poets:

Change is on all things round us, thine, and ours,
The silent, ceaseless flight of time is seen
In forests, even as in forest flowers;
Yet, in thine age, thou art a noble scene –
Though other things should be where thou hast been.
Should cities fill thy site, and naught remain
Of what thou art, no e'en one blade of green,
There is such power and interest in thy name,
Thou woulds't not be forgot, nor all thy ancient fame.

The forest is changing, she says, but it always has, and will survive whatever the assaults of history.

Joanna died on 28th May 1841, aged thirty-five, and joined her parents in the burial ground of the Old Meeting House, though their headstones have long disappeared. Later that year, at the first Sherwood Forest Gathering at Edwinstowe, when toasts were

The Old Meeting House, Mansfield

drunk to absent friends, Hall said, "Nor should we forget Joanna Williams, whose kindly spirit is rejoicing in the 'land o' the leal.'" Thomson (1847) records that this was accompanied by the glees, 'Strike the Lyre' and 'Sleep, Gentle Lady'. Evidently, she was considered of sufficient stature as a poet to be honoured in this way.

Places to visit

Mansfield: The Old Meeting House (Unitarian), off Stockwell Gate. The oldest dissenting chapel still in use in Nottinghamshire and a little gem. Open for Sunday services and on Saturday mornings 10–12.

Leslie Williamson 1922–2006

Born in Eastwood in 1922, Williamson worked as a laundry boy, ran errands and worked on the shop floor of a hosiery business. He joined the RAF in World War II and was posted to Malaya, then after the war to Indonesia where an explosion left him partially deaf. On his return he worked in the hosiery trade for forty years and wrote fiction, poetry and plays. He also wrote for a string of newspapers in Nottinghamshire and Derbyshire.

He was a passionate admirer of D.H. Lawrence, but his novel, *Jobey* (1953), set around the pits at Moorgreen, is not just an imitation of Lawrence, the style is his own.

> He looked towards Misk Hills and the trees which ran down to the water's edge. The setting sun made helter-skelter shadows which accentuated the steepness of the gullies. The sharp reflection of the trees undulated slowly here and there as the trout gently shook their blankets, making ready for the night.
>
> Jobey felt at home here, as if everything was thrusting down to reach his seam of coal. Sometimes when no-one was about at the coal face he put his hands on the roof to feel the weight of the trees and the water... there was no room to spare in that thin black slice of manna which fed the whole of Moorgreen.

... the weight of the trees and the water...
(Jobey)

Jobey is set at the time of the General Strike in 1926. Jobey Rainbow is a young man of prodigious strength, in love with Margaret, the pit manager's daughter. As the strike bites, he gives in to her father, becoming his security man and setting himself on the wrong side of the Union. Everyone has mixed motives and loyalties in this closely-knit community. Unlike Lawrence, Williamson salts his degradation and tragedy with humour and produces some wonderful characters like Beggarlee Bulldog, a hell-fire preacher and faith healer.

Moorgreen and its surroundings provide the above-ground backdrop to this story but below ground, Williamson evokes a kind of hell where the natural forces of the earth wait to claim the miners.

Williamson wrote a verse sequence, *D.H. Lawrence and the Country He Loved* – and murder mysteries, including the darkly humorous *The Crowded Cemetery* (1981) which is set in a fictional Bestwood. Two eccentric old brothers, Lion and Jonty, live up on the moors with their goats and killer owls, and the plot involves witchcraft, orgies, cannabis-growing and grave-robbing, which local bobbie Constable Francis 'Franny' Booth attempts to solve.

Leslie Williamson died in 2006. At his funeral it was mentioned that he appeared as a double on screen for Robert Maxwell.

Places to visit

Moorgreen: Collier's Wood, off the B600, is on the site of the old Moorgreen Colliery, closed in 1985. Byron called the Misk Hills "The Hills of Annesley." There are some pleasant walking trails in the area.

Nick Wood 1949–

"Can a place influence the way you work? Change the way you write? I've no answer except to say I'd been failing to write a play good enough to be produced until...

"1986. Move from Sheffield to teach drama at the Dukeries Community College, Ollerton.

"2001. Leave teaching to become a full-time playwright.

"In the years in between Nottingham taught me how to be a writer.

"Here I found my voice. Thirty-two kids of varying ages need a play. Two sixth-formers have an idea – can I help them make it work? I promised in my interview I'd produce a community play, the writer I hoped would do it can't, so I'd better deliver. Learning on the job.

"The more I wrote, the more it seemed to work, so I went back to writing my own stuff. This time round everything felt more real because I've learned to look outside myself. My characters started to live and breathe, were rooted in their world, because I've learned to listen. I've had to. You can't fool kids, and I stopped wishing I was a playwright and just got on with the job. Then, miracle of miracles, my work got noticed by Nottingham Playhouse and I was given a commission.

"The Playhouse. What an asset. Writers in other parts of the country can't believe the support they give us. Without trying I can think of a dozen Nottingham playwrights who've been helped to production. It's an unprecedented investment.

"Nottingham offers you opportunities and wants you to take them. It has a passion for life that buoys you up. It respects hard graft and honesty. My writing feeds off its voices, its humour, its stubbornness, its warmth. I'm nurtured and supported by its ever growing community of creatives, we've got novelists, artists, directors, musicians, poets, games makers, photographers, travel writers, film makers, you name it, you'll find them here. It's a joy to catch the bus into town and mooch around the pubs, the markets, the galleries, the parks, the cafés. I love the river. I love the Runner, the Rescue Rooms, the Maze. On Broad Street I can always find someone who'll let me have a moan when I get stuck.

"Yes, I come from London, and I'll always love London, but how lucky was I to end up in Nottingham? Very. I'm grateful and I'm staying."

Gregory Woods 1953–

"I was born in a suburb in 1953. Because that suburb was Zamalek, an island on the Nile in Cairo; and because I was expelled from Egypt when I was three; and because I went to school in Accra and Takoradi in Ghana and then Ringwood, New Milton and Canford Cliffs in Hampshire; and because I was sent away to boarding school in Berkshire; and because I went to university in Norwich; and because I eventually began my academic career at the University of Salerno – I have a shifting, deracinated sense of home.

"I was brought to Nottingham in 1990 by the forces of contingency. About to take up a post in Wroclaw, Poland, at the last minute I accepted a teaching position for a year at Nottingham Polytechnic instead. The year was renewed and renewed again before the death of a colleague gave me a long-term contract. Eventually promoted to Professor of Gay and Lesbian Studies and then wafted out to the Elysian Fields of retirement, I've lived here ever since.

"Nottinghamshire is a nondescript county, a blank space to be half-heartedly skirted by the main railway lines, sped through by the M1, neither as high as the Peaks nor as low as Lincolnshire, its glories gutted (Wollaton Hall) or gone (Lenton Priory). I'm exaggerating, of course, but not by much. Yet Nottingham is a belongable city and Nottinghamshire is the side I support when I spend a day at Trent Bridge.

"I make my suburban home in West Bridgford. Suburbs are nondescript places, neither rural nor urban, or not neither but both. The indeterminacy suits me. I go for a rural walk every day, not in the country but in a country park.

"Even my house is only semi-attached. It still, twenty years on, has much of the wallpaper and even, in some rooms, the curtains I inherited from the woman who lived here before me. It's full of books, each opening onto somewhere else. I've no reason to look at wallpaper or curtains, or out of the front windows at the houses in front, or out of the back windows at the houses behind.

"It is impossible to ignore the spectral presence of D.H. Lawrence on the land around Nottingham. I read him a lot, his prose and his verse. As either critic or poet, I've written about him and other man-loving men from the East Midlands: Osbert Sitwell (who fled to Italy), Isaac Newton (who loved an Italian), Byron (Greece) and Samuel Butler whose father was vicar of Langar and who loved a sheep farmer in New Zealand."

Gregory Woods is author of *Articulate Flesh: Male Homo-erotocism and Modern Poetry* (1987), *A History of Gay Literature* (1998) and *Homintern: How Gay Culture Liberated the Modern World* (2016), all from Yale University Press; and of five poetry collections from Carcanet Press, the latest of which are *Quidnunc* (2007) and *An Ordinary Dog* (2011). His book of essays The Myth of the Last Taboo (2016) was published by Trent Books.

The Sherwood Forest Group
Rowena Edlin-White

Whilst researching this book, one of my most exciting discoveries was the Sherwood Forest Group of writers, a self-identifying company of radical ruralists of the early-to-mid-nineteenth century which stands at the heart of Nottinghamshire's literary history. Here we have a dozen or so committed men and women – plus a handful of incidentals – who gathered regularly over Richard Howitt's pharmacy on Lower Parliament Street to read their work and encourage one another.

William and Mary Howitt, Sidney Giles, Robert Millhouse, Thomas Miller, Samuel Plumb, Joanna Williams, Jane Jerram, Matthew Henry Barker and Spencer T. Hall formed the core group. Some, like Hall who lived at Sutton-in-Ashfield, walked miles after work to attend, for most were framework knitters, shoemakers, basket-makers and shop-keepers; amateurs in the true sense, self-educated in the Artisans' Libraries and Evening Institutes; Reformist in their politics and dissenting in their religion. These poets, journalists and novelists shared a common cause: the defence of the countryside as enclosure swallowed up the birthright of the common people, the well-loved locations municipalised, the footpaths closed or diverted – and the Forest, which had once reached down as far as St Ann's Well and Lambley Dumbles, pushed further and further away.

Whilliam Howitt wrote of the effect of the enclosure system on the forests:

> The enclosure system was one of the most unexampled absurdity and injustice. It has been conducted on the principle of – 'Unto him that hath shall be given, and from him that hath not shall be taken away even that which he hath.'

> But it is not merely the poor that would lose by it. The miner, the artist, the naturalist, the poet, the antiquarian, the lover of the

country, and the frequenter of it for health or relaxation, all would suffer most seriously by it, and the country would suffer with them. (*Rural Life of England*, 1844)

So it was that the imminent loss of the ancient forest of Sherwood with its well-loved legends and arboreal mysteries became their major theme.

Much of what we know of this group and their associates – people like Charles Plumbe, Thomas Brown, Edward Hind, Charles Hooton, Henry Sutton and others – was recorded by Spencer T. Hall, who wrote up his rural ramblings as 'The Sherwood Forester', which may have been the origin of the group's name. They were all tremendous walkers from necessity and by temperament: William and Mary Howitt thought nothing of walking five hundred miles on their honeymoon, assiduously documenting the changes in rural life and the natural world along the way.

Sam Plumb of Lambley felt deeply the loss of his favourite footpaths; Robert Millhouse remembered roaming the old deer-park belonging to the Castle before it was divvied up and the toffs began to build their grand houses on it, and mourned his "beautiful Larkdale," the track that once led from the windmills on Forest Road into the town. Joanna Williams wrote of the famous 'Centre Oak' in Mansfield which, it was said, once stood within Sherwood Forest itself; and even Lucy Joynes, an urban poet, ever-enthusiastic about the coming of gas-light and the railways, noted the gradual loss of Nottingham's innermost wastelands and wild places.

Through their topographical writings, their poetry and stories, these writers plotted their personal landscapes, naming the places they loved lest they be forgotten, leaving landmarks in verse and prose. In time the town would expand greatly, eventually to be re-greened with chases and parks and beautiful municipal cemeteries. Ironically, Millhouse was one of the first people to be interred in the General Cemetery which largely runs the course of his beloved Larkdale – but these were polite, civic, controlled environments, not wild places.

Members of the group came and went, back and forth to Nottingham: the Howitts moved to Esher in Surrey in 1836 because they wished for somewhere quieter. Jane Jerram married and moved to Derbyshire; Miller went to London to seek his fortune and Hall went to York, Derby, Ireland and Cumbria, but was regularly drawn back to his roots. In 1832 Christopher Thomson, a travelling actor, house-painter and fervent educator, settled in Edwinstowe on the very fringes of the Forest and was drawn into its spell. With Spencer Hall, in 1841 he organised the first of the three great Sherwood Forest Gatherings: a literary and musical festival, bringing back together the Sherwood Forest writers and hundreds of their admirers, reaffirming their identity as a visionary group. His account of the Gatherings in his *Autobiography of an Artisan*, describes them in affectionate detail. It needed an incomer to recognise their true significance.

Many, if not most, of the Sherwood Forest Group have been forgotten. Some, like Plumb and Brown, never published a book but contributed regularly to local newspapers and journals; others like Sidney Giles, Edward Hind and Charles Hooton have now simply faded away. Most died in poverty, leaving their fellow-authors to write their epitaphs and have a whip-round to pay for their headstones: it took three years' worth of collections at the Gatherings to buy the elegant memorial on Millhouse's grave – it cost £27.18s.3d; they didn't stint on it. And Spencer Hall, who had a whole other career as a mesmerist and hydrotherapist, and who wrote several important works including *The Peak and the Plain*, *Days in Derbyshire* and the invaluable *Sketches of Remarkable People* from which we know so much about this circle of literary friends, died a poor man in Blackpool. His friend Charles Plumbe, a cousin of Sam's, who would be the last surviving member of the group, paid for his memorial.

Were they simply sentimentalists trying to hold back the tide of progress? To some extent they took up the baton of the Romantic Movement – Wordsworth, Coleridge and the other Lake Poets, who convinced their readers that the frightening mountainous ranges, the scary forests and deep waters of Cumbria were really beautiful and approachable; but the next generation, the Howitts, Halls, Millhouses and Plumbs, reached out to their own wild places only to see them shrink before their eyes as industrialisation and economic expansion moved through the fields and forests like wildfire. As mainly working-class people, they felt the loss of the only beauty they knew deeply and sorely. Maybe Joanna Williams was the only one, in her epic poem *Sherwood Forest*, able to take the longer view: that the Forest had been constantly invaded and changed over thousands of years of history, but its spirit would always, in some shape or form, endure to inspire other local writers fifty, a hundred, two hundred years on.

Recently a word has been coined for what this group were trying to express: solastalgia – the distress experienced when familiar landscape begins to change and we feel like strangers on our own home-patch. It is not a modern malady, but one frequently suffered by poets and other creative artists. As writers, readers and lovers of our literary heritage, we must name and claim this company of fellow-travellers; their vision and passion is needed once again as climate change, environmental vandalism and short-term planning threaten our Nottinghamshire landscape.

Old Nottinghamshire Libraries
Peter Hoare

During the Middle Ages there is not much evidence for any library with public access. There were monastery libraries – Lenton, Thurgarton, Beauvale, Rufford, Worksop – and a handful of books from these survive. Typically these are manuscripts, and not just theology – there's a twelfth-century Bestiary, with accounts of real and fabulous beasts, from Worksop Priory and a book on astronomy from Thurgarton. Not all manuscripts either – there's a 1495 printed book from Beauvale. Monastic libraries were swept away with the monasteries in the mid-sixteenth century, though other church collections continued.

The invention of printing around 1450 led to a huge rise in the number of books, and they were cheaper than manuscripts too. There's a nice list by the Nottinghamshire nobleman John Holles, Earl of Clare, of 'My mother's books left in the closet at Nottingham', just after the Civil War. Lady Clare had 164 books, a quite sizeable collection for those days, sixty-five in English and sixty-five in French – most of the rest in Italian. In the seventeenth and eighteenth century big libraries grew up in the Dukeries and at Wollaton Hall, which give some insight into the minds of their owners. The catalogue of Francis Willoughby's library at Wollaton is strong in scientific literature, reflecting his own works on birds and fishes. But none of these was really accessible, except by grace and favour.

A little more open, perhaps, was the library of the Jesuit mission at Holbeck near Worksop. The Jesuits were illegal at the time and the library was definitely not open to the general public though it may have been used to lend books to potential converts. The books were seized in 1679 on the King's orders during the witch-hunt connected with the Popish Plot, sent to London and sold off.

By the seventeenth century the Anglican churches were beginning to be centres of public literacy. Queen Elizabeth I ruled that copies of the Bible and other good Protestant works were to be available in every parish church for public use – there are some chained books of this sort at East Leake. Libraries were being founded in the churches, so we know about parish libraries at Elston, Retford, Costock, Worksop – and at Newark where Bishop White's Library is still to be seen in its own room above the south porch. Not a lot of popular reading there but not all theology by any means. It was designed for the general use of the town, not just for the clergy. At Southwell the Minster Library started up again after the Restoration and preserves records of borrowings from two hundred years ago. They have also preserved the old music books with rude comments written in by choirboys and choirmen about the organist or about the music they had to sing.

There was one library of this sort about which we know a little more – a mixture of church and town library – in Nottingham, founded by the Rev. William Standfast in 1744. It was for the use of "the Clergy, Lawyers, Physicians and other persons of a Learned and Liberal Education". Standfast was vicar of Clifton and had also studied medicine. About a fifth of his books were medical, the rest vary between theology, history, science, and a good deal in Latin. He set up this library in the Blue Coat School at Weekday Cross, with a published catalogue, and those who used it had to pay a subscription, from a shilling a year upwards. Sadly, the books don't seem to have attracted many readers and in 1817 it was taken over by the new Subscription Library which I'll come to later. Some of Standfast's books are still in Bromley House Subscription Library.

Commercial libraries, circulating libraries as they are known, began in the eighteenth and nineteenth centuries. The one I know most about is in Nottingham, but there were many all round the county – eight in Mansfield, eight in Newark, a couple in Worksop and one at least in Retford. Nottingham had forty-two (not all at the same time!). Not everyone approved of them – because they were 'popular' they were dangerous and stocked books that they shouldn't have, improper things like novels.

Joseph Heath's bookshop and library was 'near the Boot and Shoe in the Market Place' in Nottingham. His library books were lent out at one penny upwards, or you could have a subscription and borrow as many as you wanted. The books in his catalogue are a splendid mixture. But Joseph Heath didn't only sell and lend books. He also advertised his shop as selling medicines – Daffy's Elixir, Godfrey's Cordial and the best Scotch snuff. Circulating libraries continued in various forms almost up to the present day – twopenny libraries in the back of newsagents or tobacconists, more sophisticated ones like Harrod's, in London, which sent books all over the country, and Boot's Book-Lovers Libraries, which closed down in the 1960s.

There weren't any public libraries, in anything like the present sense, until the later nineteenth century. It wasn't legal to use public funds for anything so frivolous – until after the 1850 Public Libraries Act – and even then you had to persuade a majority of the rate-payers, many of whom were violently opposed.

But there were plenty of other libraries, besides the commercial circulating libraries, though most of them made you pay to use them. That even applies to some of the chapel libraries that grew up in towns and villages in the nineteenth century, where many Methodist chapels, for example, had libraries of improving literature lent out perhaps at a penny a time. Some served special groups, like the Nottingham Law Library or the Medical Book Society in Newark. Others were socially exclusive with high subscription rates. There were subscription libraries or literary societies – like clubs, really, usually more or less in middle-class

– in all the bigger towns of the county in the early nineteenth century.

The most prominent of these, and the only one to survive, was Nottingham Subscription Library, founded in 1816 and since 1820 housed in its own splendid Georgian house, Bromley House in Angel Row in the centre of Nottingham, where it still flourishes, with around 1,500 members. It has wide-ranging collections of books, including many old ones, such as a fine selection of Victorian novels (there was some censorship by the committee, even in the 1930s, of immoral books like *Wonder Women of History* – though *Lady Chatterley* was bought in the expurgated edition). As well as rescuing the Standfast Library in 1817 it soon became one of the intellectual centres of Nottingham life, with meetings and lectures on scientific and literary topics (as well as a fine billiard table and a newspaper room). Michael Faraday visited it as a guest of George Green (of Green's Mill) and there are still traces of its scientific past – a wind-vane with a dial behind the counter, and a brass meridian line which allows you to check that the sun is in the right place at midday. And it housed the first photographic studio in Nottingham, opened in 1841. The attic continued to be used in this way until about fifty years ago. Bromley House Library, as it is usually known, has always been an oasis from the hustle and bustle of the city, with its garden, its handsome rooms and elegant staircase – but it has had its ups and downs. Its earlier librarians included characters like the assistant librarian William Richardson who was allowed to join the Rifle Corps in 1859 but was sacked two years later on becoming insane. John Banwell was also sacked as Librarian in 1893 – he has shown 'a good deal of laxity in keeping records', then William Moore in 1899 and Arthur Lineker in 1926 were both dismissed for embezzling library funds. One of the most unexpected figures to be librarian of Bromley House was Count Ubaldo Marioni, an

Italian refugee who had been a member of the government of the short-lived Roman Republic under Mazzini and fled to England in 1849.

Bromley House was, and I suppose is, a largely middle-class place, though it has opened its doors more widely especially since becoming a charity a few years ago – but many of the other libraries in Nottingham and elsewhere in the nineteenth century were also designed for particular social groups. The Artizans' Library is an example – founded in 1824 and notable for allowing apprentices to join as well as tradesmen. It was soon followed by the Mechanics' Institute, which still exists although its library is almost entirely lost, and the People's Hall, which is now a snooker hall. All these were set up as charitable enterprises with middle-class committees and set out to improve the lot of the working classes 'from above'. I suspect that the Mechanics' Institutes in Edwinstowe, Mansfield and Newark had similar constitutions. As such, they certainly had a beneficial effect on the working classes – D.H. Lawrence's and Jessie Chambers' use of the Eastwood Mechanics is well recorded. But given the radical nature of Nottingham workers, particularly in the Luddite years and the Chartist period, this patronising attitude did not always go down well.

That leads onto one of Nottingham's more remarkable library features – the Operatives' Libraries, which don't have a close parallel anywhere else in Britain. These began in 1835, when the Artizans' Library refused to buy William Howitt's *History of Priestcraft* – seen by the library committee as a dangerous and inflammatory book. A small group of 'operatives' (probably framework knitters) resigned from the Artizans' and contributed to buy a copy for their own use; they were soon joined by others, bought more books and set up the first Operatives' Library in a room in a pub, the Rancliffe Arms in Sussex Street. Other groups followed suit, until there were around twelve operatives' libraries in pubs all round the city – always in working-class areas. One at least seems to have lasted until around 1900, though most of the others disappear from sight quite early on. They were radical in their politics: these were libraries for the workers, financed and run by the workers. Regular meetings of all the members agreed on what was to be bought and reproved misbehaviour, and annual dinners celebrated the success of the movement. What is more, some of them at least had sections for children and positively welcomed women readers. In the words of Library No. 3 in 1850:

> We should open the doors of our institution as wide as possible. The female and juvenile classes claim our special care; the latter will be the people of the future. Many of the wise have said that the forming of the youthful mind depends on the female; if she be well informed, her children will be wise and virtuous.

There are some quite splendid speeches reported from the annual meetings, like this comparison between 1835 and 1845:

> Then, the works of our greatest writers were, by their price, sealed books to those who most stood in need of their ennobling influence. Then, the majority of operatives desirous of spending their leisure in reading, could only have that wish gratified, by obtaining at a high charge the loan from some circulating libraries or other, tales, whose mawkish sentimentality or gloomy horror can only result in a morbid state of feeling, and tend to close the avenues of the mind to that knowledge which can have a refining and beneficial influence upon society. Now, we have thousands of volumes of the choicest works in the language placed at the disposal of the sons of toil, and the town swarming as it were with institutions claiming support from the working man, and resting those claims on the liberality of their laws, and the valuable nature of their ultimate objects in a moral and social point of view.

These are matched by complaints from the Mechanics at their annual meetings that they can't attract the 'lower' working classes.

Most of these libraries were really wiped out by the growth of public libraries. The first in the county was Nottingham, in 1867. It took over the stock and premises of the Artizans' Library which had gone bust. The Free Public Library was run for forty-seven years by the energetic John Potter Briscoe, then for another eighteen years by his son – sixty-five years in one family, with the result that it was one of the best municipal libraries in the country. Briscoe set up the first public lending library for children in Britain (but he had been beaten by the Operatives!). From 1881 the Public Library shared a building with the University College on Shakespeare Street in Nottingham, and provided the college library as part of its services to the town, until the move to Highfields in 1928. You'll find references to the old set-up in D.H. Lawrence's *The Rainbow*.

Elsewhere in the county, Newark started in 1883 – the Gilstrap Library is now the local tourist information office. Hucknall started in 1887 boasting a games room as well as offering half-hour lectures, Carlton a year later, then Sutton-in-Ashfield and Mansfield in the 1890s. Worksop was the centre for a trial library service for rural areas. Nottinghamshire County Library didn't start until 1924, but through the Worksop scheme Nottinghamshire was in some ways a pioneer of what is now a nationwide service with branches or mobile libraries serving the whole country.

Charles Dickens in Nottingham
Derrick Buttress

Charles Dickens came to Nottingham four times. Each visit was strictly business, theatrical business that is. The record shows that he performed at the Mechanics Hall on Milton Street, and that he stayed at the George the Fourth, now the Mercure, Hotel. But there's little evidence that he had friends here, walked the streets, or visited the homes of the locals who came to applaud at his performances.

Dickens, as well as being an immensely productive novelist, was also a conscientious magazine editor, an amateur actor, producer and director and, in his spare time, a man who would take a five to ten mile walk daily. One of his friends called these walks Dickens' 'brain spinning' time when he would become preoccupied with working out his writing problems.

It was Dickens' love of theatrical performance which brought him to Nottingham in August 1852. The previous year his friend Bulwer Lytton had written a short play especially for him. A group of well-known artists and writer friends, which included Wilkie Collins and John Tenniel, first performed the play in front of Queen Victoria and Prince Albert before taking it on a nationwide tour, with Nottingham on their itinerary.

It was an expensive night for the Nottingham crowd, all 600 of them, who were packed into the Mechanics at seven shillings and sixpence a seat. Amateur writers the group may have been but their star billing in the literary and art world meant that they were able to squeeze a large fee out of the Mechanics management. Dickens' share of it amounted to £190. After a successful performance Dickens retired to the George with his wife and one of his daughters. He must have had a good time there judging by his bill of £37 and 17 pence – enough to pay the wages of a housemaid for a year. The next day he walked the fifteen miles to Derby, writing to another of his daughters that he felt 'fresh as a daisy', an indication of his prodigious energy.

Dickens paid subsequent visits to Nottingham in October 1858, October 1859 and February 1869. On these occasions he read his own work as a solo performer on the stage at the Mechanics. Contemporary reports reveal that he was a very effective actor with a voice capable of convincing characterisation in a variety of roles from his novels. Not only was he able to bring tears to the eyes of his audience through his readings from *Christmas Carol* and *Dombey and Son*, he could also make his listeners ache with laughter when he performed the trial scene from *Pickwick Papers*. He amazed his devotees by reciting enormously long passages from the novels from memory, never once glancing at the text open before him.

In 1859 Dickens' trip to Nottingham was less successful. The Mechanics management failed to advertise the event sufficiently. As a result, Dickens cancelled his second performance of his visit, returning to London, reluctant to give his all to a 'thin' house. The two-hour readings had become emotionally and physically draining for Dickens, even although the adulation of an enthusiastic audience lifted him like a drug. To him, a sparse audience wasn't worth the trouble of turning up at the venue. He was so rich, and so popular, that he could afford to turn his back on an indifferent Nottingham. It was ten years before he returned.

By 1869 Charles Dickens was a sick man, worn out by his insatiable need to travel, perform and write. Work was a demon he couldn't deny. He arranged yet another tour, this time of one hundred 'farewell' readings, which brought him to Nottingham for the last time on 4th February 1869. He suffered a minor stroke later that year, then succumbed at the age of fifty-eight to a paralytic stroke in June of 1870. The only direct evidence left of

Charles Dickens' four visits to Nottingham is the cheque he wrote for that first stay at the George the Fourth Hotel, signed with the underlined flourish of a man who knows he's a genius.

Graham Greene in Nottingham
David Belbin

When Graham Greene arrived in Nottingham in November 1925, he was a new Oxford graduate, just turned twenty-one, who wanted to get into journalism. He hoped that a brief spell as an unpaid trainee sub-editor on the *Nottingham Journal* would stand him in good stead for a post in London. On 1st November 1925, he moved into lodgings on Hamilton Road in Forest Fields. The exact house number is unknown and the building itself is long gone.

In his 1971 autobiography, *A Sort of Life*, he wrote:

> When I read Dickens on Victorian London, I think of Nottingham in the twenties. There was an elderly 'boots' still employed at the Black Dog Inn, there were girls suffering from unemployment in the lace trade, who would, so it was said, sleep with you in return for a high tea with muffins, and a haggard blue-haired prostitute, ruined by amateur competition, haunted the corner by W.H. Smith's bookshop. Trams rattled downhill through the goose-market and on to the blackened castle. Against the rockface leant the oldest pub in England with all the grades of a social guide: the private bar, the saloon, the ladies', the snug, the public… I had found a town as haunting as Berkhamstead, (one) where years later I would lay the scene of a novel and of a play… it was the focal point of failure, a place undisturbed by ambition, a place to be resigned to, a home from home.

Greene visited many of the town's cinemas, where matinee seats in the stalls cost fourpence. He would watch movies back to back, deepening the relationship with the cinema that was to feed the film criticism and scripts he was to write in the next three decades. He spent so much time at the city's numerous cinemas because of the hours he worked at the *Nottingham Journal*: 5.30 to midnight, allowing him plenty of time for cheap matinees.

He didn't stay long in Hamilton Road, where the boarding

house's other residents were two old ladies, with whom he played cards on his first night, and 'an awful man… whose mind is the lowest cesspool of dirt I've ever come across.' But he had trouble escaping. He told his landlady that he needed a room to himself. She promptly put her sitting room at his disposal, at no extra cost. He then told her that he wanted to bring over his dog, Paddy, from Berkhamstead. She said she loved dogs. He wrote to his fiancée: "I can't very well explain that I don't like having meals at a table with other people, & that I intensely dislike some of her guests."

His negative feelings about the city were probably affected by how much he missed his fiancée, Vivien. But he did find things to like.

> There's a most marvellous fog here today, my love. It makes walking a thrilling adventure. I've never been in such a fog before in my life. If I stretch out my walking stick in front of me, the ferrule is half lost in obscurity. Coming back, I twice lost my way, & ran into a cyclist, to our mutual surprise. Stepping off a pavement to cross to the other side becomes a wild and fantastic adventure… if you never hear from me again, you will know that I am moving round in little plaintive circles, looking for a pavement.

Not long after writing this, in mid-November, he moved to new digs near the Arboretum, ten minutes walk from work, where he had his own room. In his autobiography he described it as "a grim grey row with a grim grey name, Ivy House, All Saints Terrace." Full board was thirty-five shillings a week and he had his own living room.

> My landlady was a thin complaining widow with a teenaged daughter, and when my future wife, Vivien, visited me for a holiday weekend, the girl let down a cotton-reel from upstairs and banged it on my ground-floor window to disturb our loving quiet… On overcast mornings, before going on with my hopeless novel, I would take (Paddy) for a walk in the nearby park where, when you touched

the leaves, they left soot on the fingers. Once I took a lace worker to high tea, but she didn't sleep with me for all that. Oxford seemed more than six months away and London very far. I had fallen into a pocket out of life and out of time, but I was not unhappy.

The landlady, Mrs Loney, was evidently lazy. Her 'gentlemen clean their own shoes,' she told Greene. And she was nosy. She lived in the basement of the house which meant that she could not see across the street. One day she asked Greene whether she could use his ground floor window to observe a man down the way being taken to hospital. Another time Greene came home to find her in his room, writing a letter. She had a penchant for tinned salmon and gave it Greene for tea most nights. He often shared it with his dog, even though it meant that Paddy would be sick on the floor.

All of the time that he was in Nottingham, Greene kept returning to Vivien in London, where he chased up contacts who might give him a job on a London paper. He also wrote to the *Yorkshire Post*, *Glasgow Herald* and *Manchester Guardian* in search of paid work.

He wrote:

> The *Journal* prided itself on its literary tradition. The paper might be considered vulgar but at least it was bohemian. Sir James Barrie (author of *Peter Pan*) had once been a member of staff, and there was even a living novelist who had graduated on the *Journal* and had a house in the town.

This was Cecil Roberts, now best known for the room named after him in Nottingham's City Library but, in his day, a prolific and popular novelist. Roberts invited Greene to tea where

> he told me that in the seven years since he had become independent of journalism he had saved enough to give him a settled income of four hundred pounds a year… Perhaps I looked at him with too great an envy – I could have married on four hundred a year – for he hastened to tell me how perilous the future was. (He really was

Mr Micawber in reverse.)

Greene gave him a copy of his slim pamphlet of verse, *Babbling April*, and they talked for an hour, after which Greene wrote to Vivien "an educated person in Nottingham is as precious & rare a find as jam in a wartime doughnut!"

Greene did meet one other educated person in Nottingham, one who had a huge effect on him. In order to marry Vivien, it was necessary for Greene, an atheist, to convert to Roman Catholicism. Soon after his arrival, he 'took Paddy for a walk to the sooty neo-Gothic Cathedral – it possessed for me a certain gloomy power because it represented the inconceivable and the incredible. There was a wooden box for enquiries and I dropped into it a note asking for instruction. I had no intention of being received into the church. For such a thing to happen I would need to be convinced of its truth and that was not even a remote possibility.'

He was given a tutor, Father Trollope, once a West End actor and himself a late convert. Greene didn't at first tell him that he wanted to marry a Catholic girl. Once or twice a week, he took instruction for an hour. In his autobiography he says he became convinced by Catholicism but has long since forgotten why he was convinced. Nevertheless, in his last month in the city, February, he was received into the church. In *A Sort Of Life* he writes that his first confession was

> a humiliating ordeal. Later we may become hardened to the formulas of confession and sceptical about ourselves… But in the first Confession a convert really believes in his promises. I carried mine down with me like heavy stones into an empty corner of the Cathedral, dark already in the early afternoon, and the only witness of my baptism was a woman who had been dusting the chairs. I took the name Thomas – after St Thomas the doubter and not Thomas Aquinas – and then I went on to the *Nottingham Journal* office and the football results and the evening of potato chips.

The Catholic novelist was born.

Greene lived in Nottingham for only four months, a period he shortens by a month in his autobiography. He left without a job to go to, and wrote to Vivien from London: "Thank God, Nottingham is over. It's like coming back into real life again, being here." Ten days later, he got a job on *The Times*, a job he wouldn't have got without his experience on the *Nottingham Journal*.

"Four months is quite a large slice of existence," he wrote to Vivien. And for him, this turned out to be true. Greene set one of his best early novels, *A Gun For Sale*, in Nottingham, lightly fictionalised as Nottwich, as well as his play *The Potting Shed*. Nottwich is also referred to in his fine 1958 novel *Our Man in Havana*. Versions of Ivy House and Mrs Loney appear in several novels. Although he later talked about the city affectionately, this was rarely his attitude in the letters to Vivien. "This town makes one want a mental and physical bath every quarter of an hour," he wrote. "There's absolutely nothing worth doing in this place. No excitement, no interest, nothing worth a halfpenny curse." Yet the city was important – many argue, crucially important – to his fiction, presenting him with a first-hand experience of the working class that may have prevented him from becoming just another chronicler of upper-middle-class life in London.

A fuller account of Greene's period in Nottingham can be found in chapters 17–18 of the first volume of Norman Sherry's three-volume official biography, to which I am indebted. Sherry is inaccurate in just one regard. He includes a photo of the second boarding house where Greene stayed, but it does not show the building he refers to in the text, one that most Greene scholars consider to be 'Ivy House'. Number 2, All Saints Terrace, is a multi-occupation house on a slightly tricky to find corner equidistant from Forest Road West and Waverley Street. It is near the Arboretum, a short walk from the city centre.

A few years ago I showed number 2 to David Lodge, a Catholic novelist and great admirer of Greene, when he came to give a Graham Greene memorial lecture. David wrote about his visit in a diary piece for the *New Statesman*. 'There is no plaque,' he concluded. The absence of a plaque is probably to the good. I have since discovered that I didn't just take him to the wrong house. I took him to the wrong street.

When I was asked to write an earlier version of this essay by Nottingham Playhouse, I came across a blog piece by Andrew Schlich and Jim Thornton. These Nottingham Greene fans had a new theory about where the author lived during his brief spell in the city. It couldn't be 2, All Saints Terrace, they argued, because number 2 has no room for a basement flat, which doesn't fit with Greene's account of his landlady living in one. Furthermore, they argued that the current All Saints Terrace wasn't so named in the 1920s and that what Greene referred to as All Saints Terrace was the back of All Saints Road. This road used not to have a name, but is now called Goodwin Street. The two lines of houses that back on to Goodwin Street fit Greene's description in his one Nottingham novel, *A Gun for Sale*, where he writes of "two rows of small neo-Gothic houses lined up as carefully as a company on parade".

In 2010 I went for a walk along Goodwin Street and its environs with Andrew Schlich, who works in the area, and screenwriter Michael Eaton, an avid Greene fan, who lives nearby. The big, multi-occupied houses that back onto Goodwin Street have the requisite basement rooms where the landlady might have lived. Also, Greene would have needed to climb some stairs to get to his ground-floor bedsit, as his letters suggest, and that fits too. We were convinced.

Short of getting hold of all the property deeds for the houses on All Saints Road and Goodwin Street and happening upon the names of Mrs Loney or 'Ivy House', there seems little chance of establishing which particular building used to be Greene's lodgings. Andrew would like to see a blue plaque on the end of the street anyway. Good luck to that. Some would argue that Greene was in Nottingham for such a short time, and was so rude about it, he's lucky to have even one memorial in the city. For there is already a plaque recalling Greene the journalist in the Watson Fothergill building that used to house the *Nottingham Journal and News* offices on Upper Parliament Street. Given that he wrote about how little he learnt there (and complained that he was forced to draw an allowance from his headmaster father 'who could ill-afford it') even this plaque might seem rather generous.

In London, Greene ditched the dog and moved to Battersea. He worked from four to eleven at *The Times* for five pounds a week. The novel he was writing in Nottingham was never published. Nor was the one after. It would be 1928 before Heinemann accepted his third attempt, *The Man Within*, which appeared the following year. But his recollections of and relationship with Nottingham never left him. In time, they would be transmogrified into one of the seedier sections in a new territory, one that would come to be known as Greeneland.

Comics Creators of Nottingham, Arise!
John Stuart Clark

Several millennia before the tyranny of prose colonised storytelling and drove out the non-linear thinkers, narratives were told in pictures, and, much later, in a marriage of pictures and words that looked like pictures. It would be wonderful to report that Cresswell Crags is decorated with a smörgasbord of Mesolithic social dramas, except only a solitary bone bearing the engraving of a horse's head has been found. Equally, but 13,000 years later, the twelfth-century Cluniacs at Lenton Priory were not (to our knowledge) engaged in writing and illustrating manuscripts in the manner of the beautiful medieval sequential stories (aka comics) finally exciting art historians.

Little digging has been done, but the earliest we can nail a local comics creative into the history of literature is the end of the nineteenth century. His name was Tom Browne and he was a powerhouse.

Back in the days when Nottingham and its environs boasted a strong industrial base, we were rich in graphic communicators. Every manufacturer and print shop had its own art and design studios, and learning the skill of visual communication was an important plank of the nation's education system. After a five-year apprenticeship at a Lace Market print house, Tom Browne turned freelance, moved to 'The Smoke', and instantly made his name as a prolific contributor to Alfred Harmsworth's seminal *Comic Cuts*. A year on and he was writing and drawing page blocks for all the major street comics, as well as for *Punch* and *The Tatler*. Walworth lad, Charles Spencer Chaplin, credits Tom's brilliantly cutting 'Weary Willie and Tired Tim' for *Illustrated Chips* as the inspiration for his Tramp. Tom's inspiration for 'Weary Willie' was Miguel Cervantes' *Don Quixote*.

Between the wars, and during and after WWII, it is difficult to identify local talent working in the graphic narrative medium, largely because nobody has done the research. Big publishers like DC Thomson never credited their creators and, to this day, they ferociously (and illegally) retain possession of creator copyrights. The exception might be the two blocks written in 'Modern Scots' and illustrated by local lad, Dudley D. Watkins. 'Oor Wulley' and 'The Broons' are exceptional works of dour humour that have stood the test of time. They were originally published in Thomson's newspapers, but how much the factory system allowed Dudley to stick his ha'penn'orth into the scripting is anybody's guess.

In the Thirties and Forties, comics for grown-ups were sadly and badly undercut by the speed, cheapness and comparative ease of creating and publishing paperback prose. When graphic literature did return, homegrown products were swamped by American 'trash mags' imported as space fillers for crates of pornography. Primarily superhero and horror stories, they were thinly disguised responses to the renascent fascism disguised in the States as the threat of Communism, and mostly produced by European immigrants.

The modern era, however, finds this city home (or once home) to a sizable crop of comics creators, most of them emerging from the indie world, where self-published comics are considered the R&D department of the mainstream. Among the notables are Jamie Hewlett (*Tank Girl*, *Gorillaz*), D'Israeli (*Ordinary*) and I.N.J. Culbard (*Celeste*), all of them illustrators with more than a passing acquaintanceship with scripting. Comics are a collective effort, even outside the mainstream, and it can be difficult to isolate roles in a medium where text and image are interlocked like the fingers of two hands clasped in prayer. D'Israeli and Culbard have bountiful credits to their names, and one wouldn't want to speculate on how much they contributed to their writers' material. At the very least, an illustrator will be a harsh editor of text. If a comic doesn't work visually, it doesn't work, period, no matter how brilliant the writing.

Luke Pearson (*Hilda*) and Brick (*Depresso*) are published by established independent houses like Nobrow and Knockabout and are very much auteurs. While Brick also writes for others to illustrate (see page 46), Luke's focus has been on the continuing sagas of his blue-haired girl adventurer, the animated series of which is slated for release in 2018 by Netflix. Hilda looks poised to challenge Matilda for the affections of young people.

Right now, the richest area of comics creation by Nottinghamians is in the fringe world of indie publishing, self-publishing, web comics and zines. Though both have recently left the city, Lizz Lunney (*Depressed Cat*) and Philippa Rice (*My Cardboard Life*) have attained near-legend status for their extraordinary soul-searching stories and painstaking means of production. Latvian artist Mary Safro (aka Cryoclaire) is carving out an eminent position in the online comics world with her *Drug & Wires* future-present steampunk series, and award-winner Carol Adlam (*The New Wipers Times*) is now one of the most highly rated creators in the U.K. working in the sub-genre of 'applied comics'.

Zines lie somewhere between comics and fanzines, and are strictly DIY. Handcrafted by fiercely independent creators, their work goes international through a huge zine network that travels strictly snail-mail but reaches the four corners. Our city is best known in those circles for Steve Larder's *Rum Lad* series, now in its tenth issue, featuring a gloriously anarchic mash-up of witty travel writing, superb pen and ink art, and the simplest of cartoon caricatures of his fellow travellers and those he meets.

All those named are just examples of Nottingham creators being published at different levels in and beyond this country. Comics culture is growing in the city, helped by the best comic book shop in the land, a perennially maturing Comics Convention, a bi-monthly talking shop run out of the Nottingham Writers Studio, and two universities slowly waking up to what they've been missing. There are presently researchers in each institution writing up the result of their investigations into digital textiles and micro matter as graphic novels.

A Working-Class Hero is Something to Be
Ross Bradshaw

Class is that big thing we don't talk about in relation to fiction. Mostly we don't talk about it at all.

At the start of D.H. Lawrence's *The Rainbow*, he describes the pastoral scene of men working the fields, in the shadow of the church-tower, working good land in the way they had for generations. The men were stolid – "inert" writes Lawrence – the women of the farms being more the go-getters. Creeping in were the railways and the mines, ugly industries for ugly people. People whose children the girl schoolteacher Ursula would beat to show them their place on her way out of her class – and, ironically, towards feminism, socialism, lesbianism, and education.

Once, at the D.H. Lawrence Birthplace Museum, I heard a former miner berating Lawrence because of his class. Not because Lawrence's mother was a bit above the position of a miner but because Lawrence's father was an "ovverman", the man who directed the work in the pit, the one who drove the pace. Such were the gradations within the class that a barely literate miner working in filth was seen as different by the men whose work he controlled.

It was Stanley Middleton – mentioned later – who taught me something else about class, and that was to do with religious observance. The working class went to chapel, the middle class to church. You can notice it if you look. In Lowdham there is one remaining Methodist chapel of the three that once operated in a village where textiles and railways were once important. They are *in* the village, the church is on the outskirts, the nearest house being what is still called Manor House, just across the road. D.H. Lawrence's early companion, Jessie Chambers, also remarks on this about her time with Lawrence when local aspirational families moved from chapel to church.

It is often assumed that when Arthur Seaton opens Alan Sillitoe's *Saturday Night and Sunday Morning* by falling drunk down stairs this was the start of the regional working class novel. Seaton was different. Someone recently reminded me of the opening scene of the Karel Reisz film where Seaton swaggers, runs for a bus. This was his city. Nobody could hold him back, not the bosses, not the unions and not the women. He was in control (though another reading of the book (and the film) would put Seaton's Doreen winning the gender wars).

There is a progenitor to Arthur Seaton. *Penny Lace* by Hilda Lewis, published in 1946, has the Mr Penny of the title swaggering. Nothing could hold him back, not the bosses, not the unions and not the women. And he took control by learning his trade – the trade of lace – and opening a mill in Long Eaton, out of reach of the lace trade unions so he could undercut the Nottingham firms and put his own former master out of business. I've often wondered if Sillitoe had read this book. Read the two books side by side so you can compare and contrast.

But it is coal that runs through the Nottingham working-class novel. Leslie Williamson, from Lawrence's Eastwood, in *Jobey* gave the rougher side of miners' lives – describing two miners solving their disagreement by kicking each other's shins with their pit boots on until one fell. On the other hand Stanley Middleton, in his best book, *Harris's Requiem*, described the packed-out concert of the Blidworth Band: "The band all wore their military caps; we've paid for 'em, you shall see 'em. … There was none of that demanding concert-hall cough, no last minute titter. The music was starting and there was a money's worth to be got." The Band played a concert of Beethoven, *Finlandia*, and "finally a mighty tone poem, specially composed with solos galore." This was the cultured side of the mining community. Middleton mostly wrote about lower middle-class life, but he understood the class from which he came.

Mining. It is hard not to be moved by Lawrence's 'The Collier's Wife', a poem about a pit accident. Or the opening scene of the children's book *The Secret World of Polly Flint* by Helen Cresswell which starts with Polly's father being brought up injured from the pit. Or the modern writer Deborah Tyler-Bennett describing the four lines devoted to her great-grandfather in the local paper, killed in a mining accident on Valentine's Day, 1914, while "Fifty lines on how King George may visit/the Duke of Portland and attend the hunt/and thirty on a bride-to-be named Blisset/whose name on marriage will be Lady Blunt." There were once 40,000 miners in Nottinghamshire, so it is hardly surprising there are so many literary references. But the Nottingham history of textiles – once employing 25,000 workers – is less represented, perhaps because most of those workers were women.

Tony Hill brings us almost to the end of the mining era with his autobiographical novel, *If the Kids are United*, writing about Jacksdale. The title comes from the Sham 69 song (but you knew that). His book is a roughly affectionate story of that former mining town, then in terminal decline thanks to Thatcherism. In his *The Palace and the Punks* Tony also described the life and times of The Grey Topper, an unlikely successful punk venue in his home town.

I'll move on from mining, and see what the women were saying, but in Nottinghamshire and other former mining areas it's hard to leave behind. I remember going to an NUM rally at the Usher Hall in Edinburgh, in the early seventies. Hearing the mining leaders Lawrence Daly quoting Shelley long before Jeremy Corbyn did ("Ye are many, they are few...") and Mick McGahey replying with Shakespeare ("The fault, dear Brutus, is not in our stars, But in ourselves, that we are underlings.") did more to tell me of the importance of literature in working-class life than did my six years of secondary school.

Daly and McGahey were autodidacts. Older Nottingham readers will remember The Cosmo – the Cosmopolitan Debating Society. Its last years were painful, but it was once the arena for the sort of autodidacts, mostly men, who appeared in Sillitoe's novel *The Open Door* and Philip Callow's *The Hosanna Man*. One striking thing about Sillitoe's Nottingham novels is that, save for the occasional bohemian, the world outside the working class barely existed.

All I knew of Nottinghamshire writing before I came here was reading the dirty bits in D.H. Lawrence, which had no impact on me, when I was an immature teenager. Thankfully I was a bit more mature when I arrived in Nottingham in 1978 to live in the building where the magazine *Peace News* was then produced. Over the road was a large semi-permanent graffito saying "Socialism will come, riding on a bicycle". My kind of town.

Another graffito, elsewhere, was also attractive in its own way – big letters on the Forest "mmm… marijuana". Surprisingly that was either a hangover or a reprise of the same graffito mentioned in Ray Gosling's *Personal Copy: a memoir of the Sixties*: the first book that gave me a sense of place in Nottingham. *Peace News* sat on the fringe of St Anns, where Gosling had lived and campaigned against the destruction of the suburb made famous by Ken Coates and Bill Silburn's *Poverty: the Forgotten Englishman* (still available from Spokesman Books). But rereading Gosling now, it is his cameos of the City that strike me. Saturday afternoons at the Kardomah looking out over the City "'Just waiting for a friend,' you'd say to the nippie." Sundays down the Market Square, the Sally Bash at one end and the Communist John Peck on his stand at the other. Gosling describes how Arnold Wesker's *Centre 42*, a national touring project to bring culture to the trade unions, bit the dust in Nottingham with local promoters putting on competing events at the same time. There are lots of literary nuggets, Colin MacInnes, Philip Callow... and a visiting Adrian Henri, delighted to see a bus going to – or possibly called – Arnold.

The '60s was a decade of change for working-class people. Alan Fletcher, in his three self-published novels of Mod life, described himself and his colleagues as the first generation of working-class youth which had money in its pockets. Wanting to spend it on looking good. To get away from the dreariness of the demob suit and the flat cap.

Michael Standen, in *Start Somewhere* (republished by Shoestring Press) catches a moment when the previously sharp divisions in class are starting to fall apart. His novel describes a teenage romance. Mr Griffin – a grocer – warns his son: "You be careful. Their station isn't ours. They have a different road of going on. Her father's someone in the Town Hall; I've seen his name in the *Post*... If you think I'm complaining because you're mixing with a good class of person, I'm not. Miss Cooper's got real breeding... So don't start treating her like the girls round here."

Next thing, people will not be standing up when the Queen comes on at the cinema...

I mentioned women's voices. From the working class of that period, in Nottinghamshire, there aren't many that have come my way. That is not to say there are no books. The publisher Persephone has been busy rescuing Dorothy Whipple. Worth reading, but her books are those of the well-off, the people who had servants. What the servants had to say is not recorded.

A more dated writer yet is Rose Fyleman. I'll summarise one of her stories. A group of children (think *Famous Five*) come across a caravan, nearby was a baby in its cot, nobody else in sight. The obvious solution was that the baby had been stolen by Gypsies, "because they do, you know", such an assumption being confirmed by the baby being blue-eyed and blond. So, some of the children rescue the baby while others head off to the road to stop any car with "decent looking people" to get the police. Of course the baby turns out not to be a stolen baby at all, but the nurse of a nice respectable couple, holidaying in their caravan, had left it out in the open (then to be stolen by those hideous racist middle-class white children) while she went spooning with the boy in the farm next door.

A restorative read after that is Carol Lake – not Nottingham, but Derby. Lake has been overlooked of late, which is a shame, for she won the *Guardian* fiction award with *Rosehill*, set in our rival city. Her other book, *Switchboard Operators*, describes with gentle humour that now-vanished but once-important job from a woman's point of view.

Nicola Monaghan's first novel, *The Killing Jar*, was set among criminals on the Bestwood estate she was brought up on, as was Derrick Buttress in an earlier generation, while Kim Slater's novel for older children, *Smart*, paints a sad picture of life for an autistic boy in the Meadows. Nicola remarked that her novel did not reflect the positive community spirit of her estate, but that it was easier to write a novel with crime at the heart rather than a feel-good novel about people being nice to one another.

But the face of our city, our county has changed over the last few years. On the Market Square you are likely to hear Polish, Romany, one of the Kurdish languages... Working-class Nottingham has changed again. So far Kevin Fegan has been the main writer to pick up on this. In *Let the Left Hand Sing* he walks down an imaginery street, knocking on doors, asking people to tell him their stories. There you will find, beside the Jamaican woman who remembers the Anansi stories of her childhood and the Ukranian man who has lived in exile for fifty years, a woman from the Sudan "who was eight when the soldiers came". Kevin himself is a migrant, from an Irish family who came to the Midlands for want of work.

We do forget some of our past. If you've read it, can you remember the title of the first chapter of the book at the head of this article, *The Rainbow*? It's "How Tom Brangwen Married a Polish Lady", the lady in question coming from a refugee family. We go in circles. But Nottingham does remember its working-class past – Christy Fearn writes about the Luddites, as does A.R. Dance with *Narrow Marsh*, which opens with a hanging.

Thus far there is no great Nottinghamshire call-centre novel, but the working class has not yet said its last word even if, in novels like Phil Whitaker's *The Face* and in so much of John Harvey's work, it is the streets of the city that give the books their Nottingham feel as much, perhaps more than, the people who walk them. Not that there's anything wrong with writing about the streets of Nottingham. Read B.S. Johnson's *The Unfortunates* – that famous (or forgotten, as you will) book in a box with unbound chapters, to be read in any order save for the first and last, for a view of the city in the late '60s. Nottingham is never named, but it is this place and you can, just, follow the geography. The book's first words... "But I know this city!" Johnson will help you know it too.

Publisher's Note

Any book like this can only be representative. There are many writers we discussed including, and some of those perhaps should have been... but the book would have become unmanageable. One or two living authors chose not to be included. Others might be important within their genres but are pretty much unknown outside of a small circle. We were simply unable to contact a few people even though they live and walk among us.

There's an issue that we could not resolve about how Nottinghamshire you have to be to get in here. Malcolm Bradbury and Robert Harris went to school locally but are not generally known as "Nottinghamshire Writers". Indeed, Bradbury is much identified with Norwich through his time at UEA, but he did teach evening class at the University of Nottingham and worked at Nottinghamshire Libraries. In his *Liar's Landscape* he also wrote about Nottinghamians' delight in Skegness and Mablethorpe which confirms, if there was any doubt, he's one of ours!

And there are many other birds of passage who have spent part of their writing career here before moving on. We live in more transient times than the past. Should we have also included people who have never properly lived here but whose significant books are set locally? People like Mick Jackson with his *The Underground Man*, set in Welbeck, or Kathy Page, who drew on her year as writer-in-residence at Nottingham Prison to inform her novel *Alphabet*? Rod Madocks, no bird of passage, by the way, draws on Rampton secure hospital for his first novel, *No Way to Say Goodbye*, adding to the local sub-genre of writing about the criminal justice system.

Nottingham is a place that prides itself on being multicultural, but this is, surprisingly, not the case among local writers, or at least among those who write for the page. Songwriters and performance poets, sure, but primarily this book is about writers whose works you can access through bookshops and libraries, through playscripts, novels and poetry collections. Having said that, a number of the writers included are of an Irish background, and some from a Traveller background, though that is not apparent from their texts. Hilda Lewis and Rose Fyleman were Jewish, as is the academic writer Michael Billig. Eve Makis is a rare local contemporary writer directly drawing on her family background from elsewhere, in her case Greek Cypriot.

Jenny McLeod, for a period a successful playwright, drew on her family background for her one novel, *Stuck Up a Tree*, published in 1998, which was set in the Black community in St Ann's. Mufaro Makubika, another playwright, reaches back further in St Ann's history with *Shebeen*, set in 1958, premièred at Nottingham Playhouse in 2018. The poet Mahendra Solanki's work often refers to his African-Asian heritage. At least one significant local writer, the Romanian-born Ursula Ackrill, writes in another language, in her case German, while Mariano Doronzo is published in Italy and Shreya Sen-Handley is published in India.

But these are exceptions. We hope that in any future edition of the book this will change.

Ah yes, future editions. We do want people to explore Nottinghamshire writers. This book's strength is in the past, with a leavening of contemporary writers. There are so many more contemporary or near-contemporary writers to explore too. This is only a partial list…. Joanne Limburg wrote her first poetry collection, *Feminismo*, here while active around Nottingham Poetry Society, the Irish writer Catherine Byron is another poet who was very active in the local poetry scene, while Peter Sansom and Jacqueline Gabbitas have both written in local dialect. These last two are also publishers, as is Alan Baker, another important poet in his own right. Vicki Feaver came from here too, as she put it, growing up in Nottingham "in a house of quarrelling women". Elizabeth Chadwick is one of Britain's best-selling writers of historical fiction, and Jon McGregor is one of our best-selling writers of literary fiction, twice having been long-listed for the Booker Prize. Matt Haig is rarely out of the bestseller list for his fiction, and also writes on mental health. He grew up in Newark, the setting of his second novel, *The Dead Fathers Club*. Other literary figures include Catharine Arnold, now a City Councillor, Clare Brown, and Sam Taylor, now best known as a translator. Frances Nugent also had a day in the sun with her fiction. There's a recently-passed generation of crime writers - Julia Burrows, Ray(mond) Flynn, the journalist-turned-crime-writer Frank Palmer, and Keith Wright, who split his time between serving as a police officer and writing crime. Then there's Clare Littleford, whose first two crime novels, *Beholden* and *Death Duties*, are set locally. Stella Rimington, like Julie Myerson, went to the Nottingham Girls' High School before becoming a spy and then a crime writer. That's Stella R. who became a spy, not Julie M. And a new generation of popular fiction is represented by the former journalist Mhairi McFarlane and Cathy Bramley.

What about the specialists? People like the late Angus Wells (westerns and fantasy); Liz Babbs (Christian); David McVay (football); Paul Adam (a bird of passage who wrote some great thrillers when he lived here); Neil Fulwood (film, and now poetry); Michael Wilson (football books for reluctant readers); children's writers Tom Barber, Elizabeth Baguley and Michael Cox (whose son Tom Cox writes humour); jack-of-all-trades Roy Bainton; Alison L.R. Davies (storytelling); George Mann (steampunk fiction); Judith Jesch (Vikings); Mark Patterson (Romans); Rob Jovanovic (popular music); Robert Macfarlane (nature writing); Ken Coates (politics); David Matless (landscape); Moira Stirland (paganism)... and our own Jones the Planner (um, planning). There are many, many more poets – Andrew Graves, Andrew Taylor, and some not called Andrew, like Panya Banjoko and Georgina Wilding (the new Nottingham Young Poet Laureate). We could go on... apologies if your favourite writer is missing or if *you* are missing.

There's a world of reading out there, written on our doorstep.

Ross Bradshaw
Five Leaves Publications/Five Leaves Bookshop

Bibliography and References

Entries are listed in order of the Nottinghamshire author they are relevant to, with that author's surname in capitals. Entries relevant to more than one author are listed at the end of this section.

BAILEY, T. *Annals of Nottinghamshire, 4 Vols*. London: Simkin, Marshall & Co., 1853.

(BARKER) 'A Wanderer'. *Walks Round Nottingham*. London: Effingham Wilson, 1835.

(BRYAN) Spur, F.C. *The Field of Boaz, Gleanings by Ruth Bryan + Biographical Note by T.A. Lacey*. London: Society of SS. Peter & Paul, 1917.

(BUTLER) Garnett, Mrs R.S. *Samuel Butler and His Family Relations*. London: J.M. Dent & Sons, 1926.

(BUTLER) Howard, D.F. (ed). *The Correspondence of Samuel Butler With His Sister Mary*. California: University of California Press, 1962.

(BYRON) Drinkwater, J. *The Pilgrim of Eternity: Byron – a Conflict*. London: Hodder & Stoughton Ltd, 1925.

CALLOW, P. *In My Own Land*. Isle of Man: Times Press, 1965.

(CURSHAM) Boyes, M. *Queen of a Fantastic Realm, a Biography of Mary Chaworth*. Derby, 1986.

DAY LEWIS, C. *The Buried Day*. London: Chatto & Windus, 1960.

(DEXTER) Morgan, P. *Folie a Deux, William and Caroline Dexter in Colonial Australia*. New South Wales: Quakers Hill Press, 1999.

DRINKWATER, J. *Discovery, Being the Second Book of an Autobiography 1897–1913*. Boston & New York: Houghton Mifflin Co., 1933

(EASDALE) Robertson, C. *Who Was Sophie?* Great Britain: Virago Press, 2008.

(GAWTHERN) Hemstock, A. (ed). *The Diary of Abigail Gawthern of Nottingham 1751–1810*. Nottingham: Derry & Sons Ltd. for The Thoroton Society, 1980.

GILBERT, Mrs A. *Recollections of Old Nottingham*. Nottingham: H. B. Saxton, 1904.

(GILBERT, Ann) Gilbert, J. *Autobiography and Other Memorials of Mrs Gilbert (Formerly Ann Taylor), 2 Vols*. London: Henry S. King & Co., 1874.

(GILBERT, Ann) Armitage, D.M. *The Taylors of Ongar*. Cambridge: W. Heffer & Sons Ltd, 1939.

(GOOCH) Murden, S. & Major, J. *Elizabeth Sarah Villa-Real – Mrs Gooch*. Article online at: https://georgianera.wordpress.com.

GOSLING, R. *Personal Copy, A Memoir of the Sixties*. Nottingham: Five Leaves Publications, 2010.

GOSLING, R. *Sum Total*. London: Faber & Faber, 1962.

HALL, S.T. *Days in Derbyshire*. Derby: Richard Keane, 1863.

HALL, S.T. *Biographical Sketches of Remarkable People*. London: Simkin, Marshall & Co., 1873.

HALL, S.T. *The Peak and the Plain*. London: Houlston & Stoneman, 1853.

HIND, E. *My Magazine*. Nottingham: J. & H. Clarke, 1860.

(HOWITT) Howitt, Margaret (ed). *Mary Howitt, An Autobiography, 2 Vols*. London: Wm. Ibister Ltd, 1889.

(JOYNES) Edlin-White, R. *Lucy Joynes, Urban Poet & Educator*. Nottingham: Smallprint, 2013.

(LAWRENCE) Callow, P. *Son and Lover, The Young Lawrence*. London: The Bodley Head, 1975.

(LAWRENCE) Hilton, E. *More Than One Life, a Nottinghamshire Childhood with D.H. Lawrence*. UK: Alan Sutton Publishing, 1993.

LOVE, D. *The Life, Adventures and Experience of David Love, Written by Himself*. Nottingham: Sutton & Son, c.1823.

MATHESON, A. *Leaves of Prose*. London: Swift, 1912.

(MATHESON) Boos, F. 'Annie Matheson (1853-1924)' in ed. Thesing, W. *Dictionary of Literary Biography (Edwardian Women Poets 1880–1920)*. Detroit: Clark, Layman, 2001.

(MATHESON) Edlin-White, R. *Annie Matheson, Poet, Essayist & Feminist*. Nottingham: Smallprint, 2015.

(MEE) Hammerton, Sir J. *Child of Wonder, An Intimate Biography of Arthur Mee*. London: Hodder & Stoughton, 1946.

(MIDDLETON) Belbin, D. & Lucas, J. (eds) *Stanley Middleton at Eighty*. Nottingham: Five Leaves Publications, 1999.

(MILLER) Cooper, T. *The Life of Thomas Cooper Written by Himself*. London: Hodder & Stoughton, 1879.

MONTAGU, M.W. *Letters + Introduction by Clare Brant*. London: David Campbell Publishers, 1992.

MORDAUNT, E. *Sinabada*. USA: The Greystone Press, 1938.

(OLDHAM) Bell, R. (ed). *The Poems of John Oldham with a Memoir by Robert Bell*. London: Charles Griffin & Co. 1870.

(PLUMBE) Lindley, L. *History of Sutton-in-Ashfield*. Sutton-in-Ashfield: Lindley, 1907.

(RIDDING) Baud, H. *Lady Laura Ridding (1849–1939): The Life and Service of a Bishop's Wife*. Doctoral Thesis, University of Gloucestershire, July 2003.

ROBERTS, C. *The Growing Boy, Being the first book of an Autobiography*. Great Britain: Hodder & Stoughton, 1967.

ROBERTS, C. *The Years of Promise, Being the second book of an Autobiography*. Great Britain: Hodder & Stoughton, 1968.

(SAVILE) Saville, A. & Penn, M. (eds) *Secret Comment: The Diaries of Gertrude Savile 1721–1757*. Kingsbridge History Society, Devon & Nottingham: The Thoroton Society, 1997.

(SNAITH) Tennyson, C. 'John Collis Snaith' in *Life's all a Fragment*. London: Cassell & Co. Ltd, 1953.

(TAYLOR) Nottingham Medico-Chirurgical. 'Charles Bell Taylor' in: *Centenary of the Nottingham Medico-Chirurgical Society*. Nottingham: Cooke & Vowles, 1928.

THOMSON, C. *The Autobiography of an Artisan*. Nottingham: J. Shaw & Sons, 1847.

(TOLKIEN) Morton, A.H. & Hayes, J. *Tolkien's Gedling*. Warwickshire: Brewin Books, 2008.

TREASE, G. *A Whiff of Burnt Boats, An Early Autobiography*. London: Macmillan & Co. Ltd, 1971.

WATTS, A. M. H. *An Art Student in Munich*. Boston: Ticknor Reed & Fields, 1854.

(WATTS) Hirsch, P. *Barbara Leigh Smith, Feminist, Artist and Rebel*. London: Random House, 1998.

WHIPPLE, D. *The Other Day: an autobiography*. London: Michael Joseph, 1936.

WHIPPLE, D. *Random Commentary*. London: Michael Joseph, 1966.

(WILLIAMS) Edlin-White, R. *Sarah Johanna Williams, Mansfield Poet*. Nottingham: Smallprint, 2014.

General References

Mellors, R. *In and Around Nottinghamshire*. Nottingham: J. & H. Bell Ltd, 1908.

Mellors, R. *Men of Nottingham and Nottinghamshire*. Nottingham: J. & H. Bell Ltd, 1924.

Mellors, R. *The Gardens, Parks and Walks of Nottingham and District*. Nottingham: J. & H. Bell Ltd, 1926.

Wylie, W.H. *Old and New Nottingham*. London: Longman, Brown, Green & Longmans, 1853.

Acknowledgements

Gillian Elias for cover image and line drawings throughout.
Houghton Library, Harvard University, USA for portrait of Mrs Gooch.
Barbara Cast for portrait of Katharine Morris.
Nottingham Local Studies Library for portraits of Muriel Hine .and David Love and title page of *Poems, Humourous and Sentimental* (1826) by Mary Bailey.
Bromley House Library for images from early editions of works by Matthew Barker and the Howitts.
Peter Hoare for permission to use his invaluable essay on Old Nottingham Libraries.
Journal of Pre-Raphaelite and Aesthetic Studies for the sketch of Anna Mary Howitt Watts, from "A Rossetti Cabinet: A Portfolio of Drawings by Dante Gabriel Rossetti" in *JPAS* 2 (Fall 1989).
Nottinghamshire Archives for image of Mary Cursham's manuscript.
Persephone Books for portraits of Ruth Adam and Dorothy Whipple.
John Wilson for photograph of the Lambley mass dial.
Celia Robertson for portrait of Joan Adeney Easdale.

All other modern photographic images by Rowena and Rob Edlin-White.

Author's Note: We have gone to all possible lengths to identify the source of vintage images used. If anyone recognises any which have not been credited, please notify the publisher so that this may be rectified in a future edition.

Two of the essays – 'Old Nottinghamshire Libraries' by Peter Hoare and 'Charles Dickens in Nottingham' by Derrick Buttress – appeared in *County Lit*, the literary magazine once published by Nottinghamshire County Council.

Earlier versions of David Belbin's article on 'Graham Greene in Nottingham' were published in *Maps*, (Five Leaves, 2011), and by Nottingham Playhouse.

My heartfelt thanks to:

Gill Elias for her beautiful illustrations; Rob for his photos; Dee Duke, whose skill in digging out obscure information is second to none; Dr Tony Shaw, ditto, and for his interest and support; Stephen Best; Barbara Cast; Ralph Lloyd-Jones; Robin Turner Gilbert; Dawn Whatman; Penny Young; the staff at the Local Studies Library, who are always eager to rummage in the basement for hidden treasures; Bromley House Library for saving so much stuff for 200 years; Nottinghamshire Archives for all their help and advice; my kind, patient editor, Pippa Hennessy, and publisher Ross Bradshaw for suggesting this mad, seemingly-endless project in the first place. And, finally, our postie Gavin and his colleagues for delivering dozens of parcels of old books over the past seven years.

Rowena Edlin-White

Subscribers

Andy Barrett
Stephen Booth
Ross Bradshaw
Bromley House Library
Andrew Cooper
Rob Edlin-White
John Goodridge
Nicola Grange
Gwen Grant
Peter and Eve Gurd
Pippa Hennessy
Derrica J. Hodgson
William Ivory
Janet Kitson
Stephen Lowe
John Lucas
Sheila Marriott
Helena Pielichaty
Victor Semmens
Kim Slater
Susanna Zabulis

Index

Main entries for writers are in bold.

A

Ackrill, Ursula: 291
Adam, Paul: 292
Adam, Ruth: **4**
Adlam, Carol: 280
Andrewes, Launcelot: **6**, 52
Annesley: 1, 40, 58, 59, 134, 249
Arboretum, the: 23, 69, 79, 104, 220, 221, 272, 275
Arnold: 4
Arnold, Catharine: 292
Aslockton: 52, 53
Aspley: 174, 235
Attenborough: 66, 67

B

Babbs, Liz: 290
Baguley, Elizabeth: 292
Bailey, Mary: **8**, 298
Bailey, Philip James: **10**, 222
Bailey, Thomas: 10, **12**, 134, 294
Bainton, Roy: 292
Baker, Alan: 286
Barber, Tom: 292
Barker, Matthew Henry: **14**, 257, 294, 298
Barrett, Andy: **16**
Barrie, James M.: **18**, 104

Basford: 10, 13, 199
Bearwardcote: 144, 145
Beauvale: 261
Beckett, John: **20**
Beeston: 39, 112, 113, 224
Belbin, David: **22**, 69, 105, 271
Bilborough: 174, 188
Billig, Michael: 291
Bingham: 203
Bleasby: 180, 181
Blidworth: 202, 203
Booth, Stephen: **24**
Booth, William: **26**
Bottesford: 56, 57
Bradbury, Malcolm: 290
Bramley, Cathy: 292
Brewer, Ebenezer Cobham: **28**
Brick: 46, 280
Bromley House Library: 11, 86, 99, 142, 147, 155, 215, 262, 264
Brown, Clare: 292
Brown, Thomas: **30**, 258, 259
Browne, Tom: 278
Broxtowe Estate: 38, 174
Bryan, Ruth: **32**, 294
Bulwell: 168, 169
Burrows, Julia: 292

301

Burrows, Wayne: 34
Butler, Mary: **37**
Butler, Samuel: **36**, 253, 294
Buttress, Derrick: **38**, 268, 287
Byron, Catherine: 291
Byron, Lord George: 1, 9, 25, **40**, 58, 59, 66, 67, 82, 84, 132, 171, 189, 212, 242, 249, 253, 294

C

Callow, Philip: **42**, 100, 285, 286, 294
Calverton: 39
Carlton: 267
Carlton-in-the-Willows: 198
Caveney, Graham: **44**
Caythorpe: 186
Chadwick, Elizabeth: 292
Chilwell: 112, 113
Church Cemetery: 11
Clark, John Stuart: **46**
Clarke, Susanna: 2
Clifton: 14, 144, 208, 222, 223, 242, 262
Clifton Pastures: 213
Coates, Ken: 286
Collishaw, Stephan: **48**
Colwick: 122, 123
Colwick Hall: 59
Corporation Oaks: 235
Costock: 262
Cotgrave: 118, 119, 178, 179
Cox, Michael: 292
Cox, Samuel: 50

Cox, Tom: 292
Cranmer, Thomas: **52**
Cresswell, Helen: **54**, 197, 284
Culbard, I.N.J.: 279
Cullen, John: **56**
Cursham, Mary Ann: **58**, 294, 298

D

D'Israeli: 279
Dalestorth House: 190, 191
Dance, A.R.: 289
Davies, Alison L.R.: 292
Day Lewis, Cecil: **60**, 294
Dexter, Caroline: **62**, 137, 294
Dickens, Charles: 73, 161, 268
Dodsley, Robert: **64**
Doronzo, Mariano: 291
Drinkwater, John: **66**, 294
Dymoke, Sue: 22, **68**

E

Eakring: 54
Easdale, Joan Adeney: **70**, 294
East Leake: 262
Eastwood: 1, 150, 151, 248, 265, 283
Eaton, Michael: **72**, 105, 276
Edingley: 135, 198, 200
Edlin-White, Rowena: **74**, 257
Edwalton: 152
Edwinstowe: 28, 29, 60, 61, 96, 97, 107, 148, 194, 195, 228, 229, 247
Elston: 262
Emmett, Jonathan: **76**

Epperstone: 186

F

Farnsfield: 210, 211
Fearn, Christy: 288
Feaver, Vicki: 291
Fegan, Kevin: 287
Fletcher, Alan: 286
Flynn, Raymond: 292
Forest Fields: 169, 221, 271
Fulwood, Neil: 292
Fyleman, Rose: **78**, 286, 291

G

Gabbitas, Jacqueline: 291
Gales, Winifred Marshall: **80**
Garner, Rosie: **82**
Gawthern, Abigail: **84**, 295
Gedling: 199, 230
General Cemetery: 33, 51, 87, 89, 90, 117, 127, 129, 163, 173, 227, 235, 259
Gilbert, Ann: **86**, 88, 90, 295
Gilbert, Anne: **88**
Gilbert, Josiah: 89, **90**, 163
Giles, Sidney: **92**, 134, 229, 257, 259
Glaister, Elizabeth: **94**
Gooch, Elizabeth: **96**, 295, 298
Gore, Catherine Grace Frances: **98**
Gosling, Ray: 42, **100**, 285, 295
Grant, Gwen: 55, **102**, 197
Greene, Graham: **104**, 209, 271

H

Haig, Matt: 292
Hall, Spencer Timothy: 30, 92, **106**, 122, 144, 173, 200, 201, 222, 229, 246, 247, 257, 258, 259, 295
Hallam, William: **108**
Harris, Robert: 290
Harvey, John: 24, **110**, 288
Harwood, Elain: **112**
Heanor: 137
Herring, Paul Augustus: **114**
Hervey, Anthony: 33, **116**
Hewlett, Jamie: 279
Hickling, George: **118**
Highfields Park: 76
Hill, Tony: 284
Hilton, Walter: 1, **120**
Hind, Edward: 108, **122**, 258, 259, 295
Hine, Muriel: 1, **124**, 298
Hodsock Priory: 97
Hogg, Henry: 108, **126**
Holme Pierrepont: 192, 193
Holme Pierrepont Hall: 176, 177
Hooton, Charles: **128**, 258, 259
Hoveringham: 142
Howitt, Margaret Anastasia: **130**, 236
Howitt, Mary: 1, 41, 130, 131, **132**, 135, 136, 144, 170, 190, 222, 229, 236, 237, 257, 258, 259, 295
Howitt, Richard: 14, 92, 106, **134**, 136, 144, 246, 257

Howitt, William: 1, 130, 131, 132, 133, 134, **136**, 170, 190, 222, 229, 236, 258, 259, 265
Hucknall: 41, 58, 267
Hutchinson, Lucy: **138**
Hyson Green: 20, 68

I
Ivory, William: **140**

J
Jackson, Mick: 290
Jackson, Sarah: **142**
Jerram, Jane: **144**, 257, 259
Jesch, Judith: 292
Johnson, B.S.: 288
Jones, Adrian: 293
Jovanovic, Rob: 292
Joynes, Lucy: 33, **146**, 258, 295

K
Kirkby-in-Ashfield: 216
Kitchen, Fred: **148**

L
Lake, Carol: 287
Lambley: 115, 198, 257, 258
Langar: 36, 37, 253
Larder, Steve: 280
Larkdale: 258, 259
Lawrence, David Herbert: 1, 38, 43, 83, 103, 110, 143, **150**, 158, 160, 169, 174, 202, 248, 253, 265, 267, 282, 284, 285, 295
Laxton: 25

Lee, William: **152**
Lenton: 180, 261
Lenton Priory: 252
Lewis, Hilda (Winifred): **154**, 283, 291
Limburg, Joanne: 291
Littleford, Clare: 292
Love, David: **156**, 295, 298
Lowdham: 282
Lowe, Stephen: **158**, 184
Lucas, John: 39, **160**
Lunney, Lizz: 280

M
Macfarlane, Robert: 292
Madocks, Rod: 290
Makis, Eve: 291
Mann, George: 292
Mansfield: 60, 64, 65, 96, 108, 135, 136, 171, 190, 200, 201, 246, 247, 258, 263, 267
Mapperley: 43, 115, 116, 117, 186
Mapperley Park: 23, 186, 226, 241
Matheson, Annie: 50, 90, **162**, 296
Matless, David: 292
McFarlane, Mhairi: 292
McGrath, Pat: 2, **164**
McGregor, Jon: 110, 142, 174, 292
McLeod, Jenny: 2, 291
McVay, David: 292
Meadows, the: 86
Mee, Arthur: **166**, 296
Middleton, Stanley: 22, **168**, 282, 283, 296

Miller, Thomas: 134, **170**, 222, 229, 257, 259, 296

Millhouse, Robert: 127, 134, 170, **172**, 257, 258, 259

Monaghan, Nicola: **174**, 285

Montagu, Lady Mary Wortley: **176**, 296

Moorgreen: 249

Mordaunt, Elinor: **178**, 296

Morris, Katharine: 1, **180**, 298

Mortimer, Peter: **182**

Myers, Tanya: 159, **184**

Myerson, Julie: **186**, 292

N

New Basford: 38

Newark: 80, 81, 84, 85, 181, 196, 197, 262, 263, 267, 292

Newstead Abbey: 1, 12, 25, 40, 41, 58, 171, 240, 241

Normal, Henry: **188**

Norwood Hall: 201

Norwood Park: 200

Nottingham Castle: 12, 68, 79, 82, 137, 138, 139, 146, 171, 173, 208, 233, 258

Nottingham Road Cemetery: 145

Nugent, Frances: 292

O

Old Lenton: 88

Oldham, Eliza Sarah: **190**, 222, 236

Oldham, John: **192**, 296

Ollerton: 94, 177, 250

Ollerton Hall: 95

Owthorpe: 138, 139

P

Page, Kathy: 290

Palmer, Frank: 292

Palmer, Geoffrey: **194**

Park, The: 23, 79, 125, 173

Patterson, Mark: 292

Pearson, Luke: 280

Phil Whitaker: 288

Pielichaty, Helena: **196**

Pleasley Vale: 108, 109

Plumb, Samuel: 134, **198**, 200, 257, 258, 259, 260

Plumbe, Charles: 107, **200**, 228, 229, 258, 260, 296

Plumtree: 77

Prior, James: **202**

R

Radcliffe-on-Trent: 56

Radford: 23, 164, 165, 174, 198

Rainworth: 203

Ravenshead: 203

Rawsthorne, Paula: **204**

Retford: 98, 99, 170, 262, 263

Rice, Philippa: 280

Ridding, Laura: **206**, 296

Rimington, Stella: 290

Roberts, Cecil: 105, **208**, 273, 296

Ruddington: 8, 142

Rufford: 261

Rufford Abbey: 54, 55, 210, 211

305

S

Safro, Mary: 280

Sansom, Peter: 291

Savile, Gertrude: **210**, 296

Sen-Handley, Shreya: 291

Seymour, Miranda: **212**

Shearing Hill: 230

Sherwood: 22, 69, 72, 169, 182, 186

Sherwood Forest: 60, 64, 97, 116, 136, 149, 194, 195, 233, 246, 258, 259, 260

Sherwood Forest Group, the: 1, 58, 92, 106, 134, 144, 146, 152, 173, 198, 200, 246, 257

Silburn, Bill: 285

Sillitoe, Alan: 1, 38, 48, 110, 142, 158, 164, 174, 188, 213, **214**, 283, 285

Slater, Kim: **216**, 287

Snaith, John Collis: 1, **218**, 297

Sneinton: 8, 9, 26, 27, 34, 35, 92, 158, 172

Solanki, Mahendra: 290

South Normanton: 30

Southwell: 6, 40, 41, 94, 140, 196, 198, 262

Southwell Minster: 7, 95, 200, 207

St Ann's: 22, 35, 100, 101, 165, 185, 188

St Ann's Well: 12, 14, 15, 88, 172, 257

Standen, Michael: **220**, 286

Stapleford: 166, 167, 223

Stirland, Moira: 293

Sutton-in-Ashfield: 58, 59, 106, 200, 201, 257, 267

Sutton, Henry Septimus: **222**, 258

Swann, Jenny: **224**

T

Taylor, Charles Bell: **226**, 297

Taylor, Sam: 292

Thomson, Christopher: 107, **228**, 247, 259, 297

Thoresby Hall: 176, 177

Thrumpton Hall: 212

Thurgarton: 1, 121, 261

Thurgarton Priory: 120, 121

Tolkein, J.R.R.: **230**, 297

Tollerton: 77

Top Valley: 174

Trease, Geoffrey: **232**, 297

Trent Bridge: 79, 152, 153

Trent Lock: 186

Turk, Sarah Agnes: **234**

Tuxford: 196

Tyler-Bennett, Deborah: 284

U

Upton: 16

V

Valentine, Niki: 175

Victoria Cemetery: 101

Victoria Centre: 208

W

Warsop: 31, 171

Watts, Anna Mary Howitt: 131, **236**, 297, 298

Welbeck: 290

Wellow: 54, 55

Wells, Angus: 292

Welton, Matthew: 142, **238**

West Bridgford: 144, 218, 252

Whipple, Dorothy: **240**, 286, 297, 298

White, Henry Kirke: 9, 66, 208, 222, **242**

Whittington, Amanda: **244**

Wilford: 25, 84, 144, 190, 191, 242, 243

Wilford Grove: 208

Wilford Hill Cemetery: 71

Williams, Sarah Johanna: 134, **246**, 257, 258, 260, 297

Williamson, Leslie: **248**, 283

Wilson, Michael: 292

Wollaton: 124, 155

Wollaton Hall: 252

Wood, Nick: **250**

Woodborough: 198

Woods, Gregory: 142, **252**

Worksop: 102, 148, 170, 261, 262, 263, 267

Wright, Keith: 292